THE COLUMBIA GUIDE TO SOCIAL WORK WRITING

THE COLUMBIA GUIDE TO SOCIAL WORK WRITING

Edited by Warren Green and Barbara Levy Simon

COLUMBIA UNIVERSITY PRESS   NEW YORK

COLUMBIA UNIVERSITY PRESS
Publishers Since 1893
New York   Chichester, West Sussex

cup.columbia.edu
Copyright © 2012 Columbia University Press
All rights reserved

Library of Congress Cataloging-in-Publication Data

The Columbia guide to social work writing / edited by Warren Green and Barbara
Levy Simon.
  p. cm.
Includes bibliographical references and index.
  ISBN 978-0-231-14294-6 (cloth : alk. paper) — ISBN 978-0-231-14295-3 (pbk. : alk. paper) —
ISBN 978-0-231-53033-0 (ebook)
  1. Communication in social work.   2. Social case work reporting.   3. Social service—
Records and correspondence.   I. Green, Warren (Warren J.)   II. Simon, Barbara Levy, 1949–
III. Title: Guide to social work writing.

HV29.7.C65 2012
808.06'6361–dc23

2011047818

References to Internet Web sites (URLs) were accurate at the time of writing. Neither the author
  nor Columbia University Press is responsible for URLs that may have expired or changed
  since the manuscript was prepared.

To Anne and Paula

CONTENTS

A SOCIAL WORK LEADER ON WRITING

Linda Hoffman

"I SURE HOPE THAT ONE of your staff will make an urgently needed home visit to Mrs. M's apartment, at some time tomorrow, to help our staff evaluate and ensure that she is protected. Contrary to the attached letter from Mr. S, neither he nor Mrs. M has been allowing our Enriched Housing Program staff into her apartment to check on or provide services for her. In view of Mr. S's letter, we are also reaching out to the person whom Mrs. M claims to be her doctor. In addition, we have been in touch with her home attendant vendor agency during each of the last two days to apprise them of the situation as it has evolved. We will call them again tomorrow morning to urgently request that they send their RN to visit, medically evaluate Mrs. M, and help us to ensure that her health needs are identified and met before this upcoming long weekend. I deeply appreciate your ongoing support of our agency in providing the highest quality services. I am also terribly sorry to involve you in this case, but I am deeply concerned about its seriousness and, therefore, trying to ensure that our respective agencies urgently make every possible effort to visit, evaluate, and, in accordance with the law, protect Mrs. M."

A few minutes after sending that e-mail, I received the following reply: "Will forward immediately."

Before writing the above e-mail, I utilized the critical-thinking process taught by my second-year Columbia University School of Social Work field instructor. In so doing, I made sure that the beginning and end of the first and last sentences of my e-mail corresponded so that the beginning told that which I wanted to tell the recipient and the end repeated that which I had already told the recipient. As a result, my e-mail quickly got its extremely busy recipient to "get to yes" (Fisher & Ury, 1983).

Writing powerful and succinct e-mail messages is only one of the many kinds of writing that my job requires of me as president and chief executive officer of a major not-for-profit organization that serves the New York City region by providing social service programs and housing for the elderly. Part of my work is to continuously search for professional social workers who possess strong writing skills, especially those able to write government grant proposals and administrative documents. My job requires that I assume overall and ongoing responsibility for writing innumerable administrative documents, including government grant proposals, letters (especially to government officials), responses to evaluation reports, budget narratives, board meeting agendas, reports and minutes, procedures, policy statements, mission statements, case notes, brochures, fact sheets, vignettes, press releases, public service announcements, and speeches. In writing such administrative material, one must also understand, be sensitive to, and creatively think through its respective legal implications, political innuendos, and other possible ramifications to ensure that it is protective of the organization and its clients.

Over the years, I have learned that key to a successful social work career is the possession of excellent writing skills in the production of comprehensively thought-out, clear, and well-written professional documents. I have also learned that receiving A's on academic writing assignments in social work school does not mean that upon graduation MSWs possess all of the writing skills required for a successful career in a not-for-profit organization. Writing, for MSWs and most other professionals, is time-consuming and often described as "painful" and "a struggle." However, to achieve a successful career in social work, MSWs must continuously work toward enhancing their writing skills—making the resulting documents ever more compact, clear, and convincing. I have learned through hiring, training, and supervising staff that those with a positive attitude, patience, and fortitude, along with excellent analytic and creative-thinking skills and a determination to develop and strengthen those skills, can progress to higher levels.

To quote one Columbia social work professor, "If you can't think, you can't write." However, the guiding principle that my second-year field instructor taught me has proven most helpful to my staff and to me: "Know what to say, what not to say, when to say it, when not to say it, who to say what to, and how to muster your troops." The "troops" metaphor may sound a bit too militaristic for social work, but in my experience, the struggle to marshal resources for those organizations and issues that one cares about is often a battle of wits, grant applications, and well-phrased letters or e-mails.

My agency's top priority is to write and submit critically thought-through and well-presented government grant proposals and administrative documents. They are the lifeblood of our not-for-profit organization and essential to its survival during both good and bad economic times. Over the years, my staff and I have recognized that, along with writing exceptional proposals and administrative documents, it is important for a not-for-profit organization to attain an outstanding track record and reputation for providing the highest-quality services, and for its staff to develop positive working relationships with both government and community-based organizations and representatives. Basic to sustaining such relations with public and community allies is maintaining frequent contact with them, whether in person or via e-mail or phone.

Producing winning proposals, especially government grants, which provide my agency with its lifeblood, is a complex process. Along with excellent writings skills, it requires critical thinking that is "outside the box" and that demonstrates, beyond any reasonable doubt, that our agency, its board, and its staff possess the qualifications and ability to perform the social service and housing program contracts for which we seek approval.

Since requests for government grant proposals are voluminous as well as time-sensitive (usually with deadlines of six weeks or less), to meet such tight time frames and ensure that our proposals are complete, comprehensive, accurate, and justifiable, it is necessary to work on them days, nights, and weekends. Therefore, *before* the issuance of government requests for proposals we try to anticipate the questions that will be asked, and we begin researching and pulling together information from earlier proposals and administrative documents, so we can "hit the ground running" as soon as the actual request for proposals is issued. For example, prior to and in anticipation of the issuance of the "request for proposals" to renew our agency's largest social service program for an additional three years, I proactively wrote at least eight drafts of a grant application.

Upon receipt of that actual request for proposals, my staff and I noted its six-week submission deadline and immediately read the questions, together, two or three times. As we did so, we analyzed each question so that we understood it as fully as possible, letting our minds go free to think comprehensively and creatively—outside the box. While writing our first-draft response to the questions, we incorporated the information we had already gathered. Always keeping the competition factor in mind, we also incorporated our present thinking while simultaneously continuing to research and gather additional information from prior proposals and other documents relating to our current analysis so as to respond to each question as comprehensively as possible. We focused on proving beyond any reasonable doubt that our agency, board, and staff were the best qualified and had the experience and the know-how to perform the work better than any other proposal applicant. As soon as the material was typed in draft form, we reorganized the information according to our updated analysis of how to structure the answers and ensure that they clearly, comprehensively, and justifiably addressed each of the questions. We continued to update them and, again, thinking outside the box, added new ideas, clearly presenting and completing our responses to the questions in a professional, analytic, organized, and convincing manner. If two or more questions asked for the same type of, or similar, information, as appropriate, we referenced such information back and forth among our responses.

Throughout the proposal-writing process, the program narrative and budget were developed in sync. After the budget was finalized, staff utilized a template that our agency developed to write a comprehensive and justifiable budget narrative. We submitted a carefully proofed proposal that included a program narrative, a budget, a budget narrative, and numerous supporting documents. That two-inch-thick winning proposal was clearly and concisely written, so, as I explained to my staff, "if we were no longer administering the agency's programs and Martians came down and read our clearly written proposals, they could understand how to successfully implement and administer our agency's social service and building programs."

There are many program planning and political innuendos that we must continuously and critically keep in mind when writing a proposal. For example, with the thought that there might be cat lovers on the proposal review team, we decided to remove a vignette from a draft of the proposal that explained the need to approve the extermination of 30 physically ill cats that were living in a guardian client's home. In another situation, while creatively thinking about and planning to write another winning proposal to construct a 150-unit senior-citizen apartment building on a hilly site, we recognized the need for its main entrance to be located at the top of a hill so that it would be level and wheelchair accessible. A competing proposal for the same site located the entrance at the bottom of the hill, thereby requiring both steps and a wheelchair ramp. While working late one Saturday on another proposal that was due the following Monday and that required a program name to obtain funds to purchase a van for the development of a new transportation program, I began to force myself to creatively think of a relevant name. Suddenly the word *cart* came to mind as a cute acronym for a transportation program. I immediately decided to name the proposed program Project CART and miraculously backed into creating the now full name for its acronym, which is "Community Arranged Resident Transportation."

Another important public document that must be written by a not-for-profit organization is the minutes of its board of directors meetings, which are quite detailed as well as legally and politically sensitive. In writing our agency's board minutes, I ensure that such public documents accurately demonstrate that the board is legally fulfilling all of its corporate governance responsibilities. I also assume the responsibility of thinking through and writing all board meeting invitations, agendas, my president's report, and, as requested, drafts of the board chairman's remarks and the nominating committee chairman's report for their respective reviews, modifications, and/or approvals, prior to each meeting. I ensure that all of the board meeting information regarding each of the programs administered by the agency is reported in a clear and concise manner at the meetings and in the board minutes. Paying attention to detail and taking the time to think through and write each board report, ensuring that the grammar, syntax, and spelling are correct, afford me the ability to quickly and easily write board minutes immediately after each meeting. In addition to writing my agency's board minutes, I write the board minutes of the 13 legally separate corporate entities under its sponsorship.

I have worked on both the not-for-profit organization "begging side" and the government agency "giving side," and I find the begging side much more difficult. As mentioned earlier, the not-for-profit begging side requires an enormous amount of creative thinking, excellent writing skills, political and entrepreneurial instincts, a stellar track record with regard to reputation, and strong linkages and positive relationships with government agencies and officials and with community organizations and leaders. The combination of such riches strengthens an agency's ability to successfully develop and win approval of its proposals.

My staff—which includes some of New York City's most talented professional social workers—and I work together as a team. I carefully review the written materials that they originate, and I seek peer reviews of my draft proposals from other agency administrative staff members, professional social work colleagues, authors, and editors to ensure that they are as accurate, complete, and comprehensive as possible prior to their finalization.

To ensure that my staff continue to develop their creative and analytic thinking and their proposal and other administrative writing skills, over the years we have retained many outstanding professionals to provide training in those areas. I reinforce such training by reminding staff to research, analyze, and synthesize throughout their writing assignments. In my ongoing endeavor to create incentives for and to further enhance social work administrators' ability to successfully perform their work and achieve their career goals, my husband, Peter, and I have established an endowment fund at Columbia's School of Social Work that provides for seminars on writing proposals (preferably for government grants) and for the presentation of monetary awards to Columbia social work students who have written the best proposals.

With this philosophy and mission of "good, better, best, never let it rest until the good is better and the better is best," our agency has grown from only a fiscal conduit with no direct social service programs or buildings in 1978 to an organization that has since implemented and now administers 30 New York City social service programs. We have also developed and now manage 10 senior-citizen apartment buildings for the well, frail, and homeless elderly. This growth has occurred as a result of critical thinking, the production of an enormous number of masterfully crafted government grant proposals and administrative documents, and the deployment of entrepreneurial, legal, and political instincts.

Writing is an art form. I believe that strong writing in social work emerges out of education combined with certain instinctive abilities and critical-thinking skills that MSWs and other professionals must possess and continue to build upon throughout their careers. It is my hope that the numerous guiding principles that have been included in *The Columbia Guide to Social Work Writing* will further enhance social workers' ability to think critically and write outstandingly. If social workers marry critical thinking with sound writing, they can compete professionally, serve their organizations ably, and achieve their own career goals.

Reference

Fisher, R., & Ury, W. L. (1983). *Getting to yes: Negotiating agreement without giving in*. New York: Penguin Books.

PREFACE

Jeanette Takamura

PROFESSIONAL SOCIAL WORKERS RELY HEAVILY upon accurate, substantiated, clearly written reports, accounts, and correspondence to facilitate desired changes in the circumstances and behaviors of individuals as well as institutions. The fate of individual clients can hinge upon process recordings that capture the essence of their personalities and the nature of the problems they are confronting for which clinical practice recommendations are formulated. Meanwhile, whole groups and communities, whether they are large or small and whether they are in the United States or other parts of the world, can be affected in significant ways by analyses undertaken to inform social policy formulations and program recommendations. Planning documents, budget justifications, grant applications, formal letters, and e-mail messages constitute some of the other vehicles for written expression that are vitally important in the everyday world of the professional social worker. For those professionals who strive diligently to wed research and practice, articles that they prepare for publication in scholarly journals typically must adhere to even more rigorous writing standards.

Our choice of words bears with it connotations as well as denotations that convey both intended and unintended meanings. Messages and their various meanings can influence how individuals, processes and interactions, situations, and environments are perceived, interpreted, and treated. Today, within our increasingly global context, there are heightened demands for precise communication to ensure that translations from English into other languages and vice versa are not replete with inaccuracies stemming from poorly constructed text. For these and many other reasons, the Columbia faculty concur that students, who are our future social work professionals, must achieve the very highest writing standards.

Professionals who adhere to uncompromised standards of writing excellence know the importance of keen critical thinking. They know how to
extract relevant information, organize thoughts as well as research materials,
and then draft and dispassionately edit subsequent versions as many times as
necessary to produce an impeccable final draft. Because the achievement
of writing excellence typically requires practice, our students are reminded
often that mastery comes from taking every opportunity to write and to build
their proficiency in this important form of communication.

We are fortunate to have Warren Green, our able and dedicated writing center director, who has worked for years with our students to further
strengthen their writing skills, as a co-editor of this book. His imprimatur is
everywhere in the school as our students take what they have learned from
him into their academic and professional lives. He notes and emphasizes
that the quality of one's writing reflects the quality of one's thinking. Hence,
the process of improving writing skills begins with writers' working on their
critical thinking skills in order to crystallize what they are attempting to
communicate. We are fortunate as well to have Barbara Simon as co-editor.
She is a masterful teacher who has seen thousands of papers by students in
her courses. An individual who appreciates the richness of our language
and the many implications of the written word, she could not be a better
co-editor. Warren and Barbara lead a full roster of faculty who contributed
the essays in this book. Each has brought to her or his assignment special
expertise and insights that will benefit both social work students and professionals for years to come. Altogether, the essays that have been gathered
here provide social workers with a comprehensive opportunity to improve
their thinking and writing so that they may clearly communicate the unique
contributions of social work.

We at the Columbia University School of Social Work subscribe to the
highest standards for our students so that they might always put their best
selves forward. We hope that we have contributed in some small measure
toward that end through this publication's specific attention to the realm
of professional writing and the excellence that we believe can be achieved
through the acquisition and lifelong practice of exemplary writing skills.

ACKNOWLEDGMENTS

SOCIAL WORK STUDENTS HAVE INSPIRED this book, and they continue to inspire its two editors.

Vicki Lens, our colleague and a chapter contributor, first suggested the idea for such a book to Columbia University Press. We thank her.

INTRODUCTION

Warren Green and Barbara Levy Simon

WHY A GUIDE TO SOCIAL work writing? Every profession has its unique characteristics, but common to all is a focus on clear, unambiguous prose. Because social work is both an academic discipline and a profession, we have set out to acknowledge and examine writing issues important to both. Also, because contemporary social work practice is increasingly evidence-based, collaboration between practitioners and researchers is ever more welcomed and called for in professional publications. This guide will help social workers write with a keen awareness of the probable expectations of their reader—professor, supervisor, employer, journal article reviewer, grant proposal reviewer, and/or scholarship or admissions reader, to name a few.

The guide presents a collection of essays that highlight writing issues important to social work students (from BSW to PhD), practitioners in the field, scholars, and educators. We've tried to emphasize the issues that will contribute to professionalism in one's writing, whether it be academic and scholarly writing or writing in fieldwork, clinical practice, administration, advocacy, evidence-based practice, or grant and program proposal application. Predominant throughout is a focus on process, that is, on thinking about and approaching one's subject in a manner that will lead to writing that is clear, purposeful, and comprehensive. Case vignettes, descriptions of best practices, and models of good writing, as well as excerpts and author commentary, are presented.

PART I: THE FOUNDATIONS OF GOOD WRITING

Social work practice and writing have been intertwined since the profession began. In the book's first section, chapter 1 explores the history of writing in social work, and then, in the next three chapters, the authors focus on the conceptualization, development, and presentation of key aspects of social work writing, publication, and research.

CHAPTER 1: WRITING IN SOCIAL WORK IN THE UNITED STATES: 1880S TO THE PRESENT

Barbara Levy Simon documents the elasticity and variability that have characterized social work writing, a flexibility that has grown out of the profession's involvement with a multiplicity of methods, activities, clients, contexts of practice, organizational bases, and funding sources since the 1880s. Her chapter tracks the writing that has prevailed over time in the three active realms of social work: daily practice, advocacy, and research and scholarship.

CHAPTER 2: WRITING STRATEGIES FOR ACADEMIC PAPERS

Warren Green discusses the connections between thinking and writing in this chapter on academic writing issues. He posits that free writing, rather than outlining, enhances the entire writing process, from idea to finished paper. He first offers an approach to reading, summarizing, and critiquing journal articles that can quickly and efficiently lead to a sound first-draft paper. He then goes on to discuss the organization of a paper, the editing stage, and APA style. He concludes with tips for international students who may be unfamiliar with the kind of academic writing that is practiced in the United States.

CHAPTER 3: WRITING FOR PUBLICATION IN SOCIAL WORK JOURNALS

Ronald Feldman presents a how-to approach to writing an article for a social work journal—from the initial idea to brainstorming and conducting research through to the writing and publication stages. He gets into the nitty-gritty of writing for publication, right down to the need for a quiet space and regularly scheduled times to write. He organizes the chapter into three phases—pre-writing, writing, and post-writing, carefully and thoroughly delineating each phase along with the distinct issues for work in each.

CHAPTER 4: INSCRIBING KNOWLEDGE: WRITING RESEARCH IN SOCIAL WORK

Denise Burnette reviews the fact-finding, analytic, and argumentative approaches to research. She presents Stephen Toulman's model of structural argumentation as a starting point for shaping a research project. She expands on Toulman's six elements of a strong argument—claim, grounds, warrant, backing, qualifier, and rebuttal—and illustrates their use in a hypothetical study on kinship foster care. She addresses the social science debate over quantitative versus qualitative research, the mixed method approach, and how one's views are affected by one's approach to research. She concludes with a look to research that is increasingly interdisciplinary.

PART II: APPLIED PROFESSIONAL WRITING

Social work is commonly recognized as a profession of numerous methods that serve various populations. Reflecting the field's heterogeneity, Part II probes writing as a necessary element in the profession's practice. Writing as a component of everyday social work is pivotal for students who are entering fieldwork education; therefore, chapter 5 concentrates on student writing in field internships. The following chapters guide readers through writing in five major types of social work that many practitioners consider core forms of the profession: clinical social work, policy practice, program and proposal development, social work advocacy, and social enterprise administration.

CHAPTER 5: STUDENT WRITING IN FIELD EDUCATION

Kathryn Conroy notes two types of writing that predominate in fieldwork education: writing for the purpose of documenting interns' work for agency leadership and reflective writing that is designed to expand students' self-awareness, cultural sensitivities, and practice skills. She discusses chart notes, progress notes, and other forms of agency recordings that undergraduate and graduate students are responsible for keeping up to date. Then she provides an overview of process recordings and fieldwork logs that are favorite educational tools employed by field supervisors and schools of social work. Finally, she reflects on key questions about field education writing that she encourages all social work interns to raise with their field education supervisors and advisors early in their internships.

CHAPTER 6: WRITING FOR AND ABOUT CLINICAL PRACTICE

Mary Sormanti offers guidance on clinical writing. She explains the importance of case notes and how practitioners must be sensitive to the parameters of what to include and what not to include when writing case notes. She discusses clinical writing for treatment plans and for publication, detailing what is called for in each. She poses the question, "Why do clinical social workers write?" and goes on to explore what clinical practitioners can learn about their work and themselves through writing. She then discusses how social work values and ethics influence one's work, offering excerpts from case notes to show how a strengths-based writing approach can positively influence the therapeutic relationship and therefore the client's outcome. She concludes with principles to keep in mind when writing for clinical purposes.

CHAPTER 7: GETTING THE POLICY MESSAGE ACROSS TO DIVERSE AUDIENCES

Shirley Gatenio-Gabel and Sheila Kamerman first define and mark out the roles that both policy analysts and advocates play, showing how their individual roles are critical in effecting social change. They then outline a best approach to writing for policy analysis and advocacy. Leading the reader through a five-step process in analyzing and writing about a policy issue, they show how those five steps can be applied to a variety of policy papers, including reports, briefs, and memos, explaining how structure and purpose differ in each. They conclude with a section on the "dos and don'ts" of effective policy writing.

CHAPTER 8: WRITING IN PROGRAM AND PROPOSAL DEVELOPMENT: THE SOCIAL WORK WRITER AS TRANSLATOR

Marion Riedel illustrates how to best initiate, develop, and write a program proposal by using a personal account of her visit to post-Katrina New Orleans with a group of graduate social work students to develop a proposal for a program that was ultimately funded successfully. Starting with an assessment of the needs of a community along with the inclusion of its members in the development of the proposal, she offers a step-by-step guide on how to move forward with a proposal—from examples of a cover page and an executive summary, through a narrative that presents purpose, background, and the resources needed. She ends with sound advice on how best to implement a successful proposal.

CHAPTER 9: ADVOCACY

Vicki Lens first suggests that success in advocacy calls for appreciating how mainstream society articulates a problem. She then introduces "frames," which are the viewpoints and values from which people think and talk about a problem, and she focuses on the two main frames—liberal and conservative. She discusses the language used to present one's frame, indicating how the terms used to define and denote a problem serve to speak to adherents to that frame and sway others to become adherents to it. She emphasizes the importance of narrative in communicating a position on a problem, using both qualitative and quantitative data to do so. Finally, she notes the importance of choice of writing style to context and audience, whether for a policy brief, an op-ed piece, or a presentation for legislative testimony.

CHAPTER 10: ADMINISTRATIVE WRITING

Sue Matorin notes that with the increasing use of evidence-based methods to enhance efficiency and with face-to-face meetings continuing to give way to written communication, particularly e-mail, writing has become more important than ever before at the program management level of social work administration. After reviewing some basic principles of sound writing, she offers examples and explanations of both poor and exemplary administrative writing, drawn from memos, policy and procedure manuals, mission statements, employee evaluations, minutes, and executive summaries.

PART III: WRITING IN DISTINCT FIELDS OF PRACTICE

Whereas Part II presents core kinds of practice writing that most social workers perform at some points in their career, Part III offers chapters on writing for five discrete fields of practice, designed for specialists who work with particular populations. Each of these five chapters shows a depth of understanding for its respective domain of practice and its writing demands.

CHAPTER 11: WRITING IN FAMILY AND CHILD WELFARE

Brenda McGowan and Elaine Walsh examine recording requirements, mandated by federal and state laws and regulations, that affect professionals involved in protective and foster care services for children and adolescents. They detail the writing choices available to social workers who take part in developmental and preventive services for families and children who are at risk of abuse or neglect. The authors next provide a useful overview of the central components of written intake reports, case assessments and service plans, referral letters, closing summaries, and advocates' public communications. The marked impact of computerization on writing in child and family welfare is also analyzed.

CHAPTER 12: WRITING STRATEGIES FOR SCHOOL SOCIAL WORKERS

Alida Bouris and Vincent Guilamo-Ramos survey the multiple forms of writing regularly done by school-based and school-linked social workers, breaking down the field of practice into four essential parts: (1) consulting on interdisciplinary school-based teams; (2) providing direct services to children, adolescents, and their families in one-on-one, group, or family modalities; (3) pursuing program development initiatives; and (4) conducting assessments. In relation to these four core activities of school-based social workers, the authors discuss letters of introduction to parents and primary caregivers of students, as well as writing called for in workshop designs or curricula for school-based programs organized as efforts to help with the prevention among young children and adolescents of substance abuse, bullying, child abuse or neglect, sexual abuse and sexual delinquency, and the spread of sexually transmitted diseases. Special attention is paid to written communications to and guides for parents and caregivers in prevention efforts.

CHAPTER 13: WRITING ABOUT CONTEMPORARY SOCIAL ISSUES: LESSONS LEARNED FROM WORKING WITH STREET-BASED SEX WORKERS

Susan Witte excavates social work writing in the world of practice that addresses individuals and groups who historically live on the social margins—people affected by homelessness, substance abuse, violence, and HIV and sexually transmitted diseases. In particular, she reports on writing that accompanies work with street-based sex workers. She narrates and analyzes her professional journey as a producer of summary reports, conference presentations, grant applications, and publications about adolescents and adults who make their living in high-risk sexual commerce. Her chapter models her assumption that professional writing is a lifelong process of evolution and improvement, and she provides rich evidence of her steady self-inspection as someone who, like all other human beings, internalizes and inadvertently expresses social biases.

CHAPTER 14: WRITING IN THE FIELD OF AGING

Ann Burack-Weiss's chapter achieves its goal of revealing the uniqueness of the lives of older clients despite the standardization imposed by computerized forms. She pays close attention to the possibilities inherent in the one-paragraph or one-page narratives that are appended to computerized case records in the contemporary field of geriatric social services. Reflecting on her own practice in the recent past with a selection of four older adults and their families, she explores the craft of telling the stories of older individuals through writing intakes and dispositions, referrals, chart notes, and psychosocial assessments.

CHAPTER 15: WRITING IN INTERNATIONAL WORK: POWER, KNOWLEDGE, AND SOCIAL INTERVENTIONS IN THE GLOBALIZED WORLD

Fred Ssewamala and Elizabeth Sperber address the delicacy of intercultural translation in their chapter on writing in international social work in a world still characterized by profound economic, political, and technological disparities. They identify important tenets to take into account when writing about concepts and data across national, continental, and cultural boundaries. The ethical and political pitfalls that are frequently encountered by social development workers in an international context are documented. The authors highlight writing about capacity-building and human agency. They also concentrate on the cultural distance between local understandings of conditions and events and social scientists' conceptions of correlation and causality. The danger associated with writing that implies or expresses value judgments is another of their major themes.

PART ONE

THE FOUNDATIONS OF GOOD WRITING

1

WRITING IN SOCIAL WORK IN THE UNITED STATES: 1880S TO THE PRESENT

Barbara Levy Simon

SOCIAL WORK IN THE UNITED States is a profession about promoting change and offering services. In the three rings of performance that have constituted U.S. social work since its beginnings—practicing with people, communities, and organizations; advocating with and for clients; and creating social work knowledge—there have arisen features of social work writing that are consistent across professional identities and time. Those common dimensions of professional writing have been, necessarily, elasticity and variability. How does a social worker determine which vocabulary, syntax, and format to use in writing, given the triple dimensions of the overall profession?

The particular context and purposes of a social work activity generally shape writing about and within that activity. Since social workers are active in a remarkably wide variety of situations, it follows that we especially privilege flexibility in writing styles and content. The hospital, court, refugee camp, assisted living facility for seniors, group residence for children with severe developmental disabilities, and outpatient mental health clinic constitute just one cluster of many possible work sites, each of which calls for an institutional writing dialect of its own. An effective social worker learns an organization's vernacular and employs it in writing, while concomitantly noting and incorporating the national and sometimes international linguistic requirements of regulatory and accrediting bodies, auditors, and auspices. The elasticity and variability that denote social work writing—be it about practicing with individuals, families, groups, organizations, or communities; advocating for greater social and economic justice; or building knowledge for practice—are a function of the profession's responsiveness to local, national, and, increasingly, global imperatives.

A paragraph from social worker Carol Meyer's first editorial as editor in chief of *Afilia: Journal of Women and Social Work* gives a glimpse of both flexible conceptualization and writing in the profession:

> The term *feminism* clearly means whatever a person intends it to mean, and why not? To some it means bread and butter, the search for equality in jobs, education and access to all social, political, and economic institutions. To others, it means personal freedom to choose one's life-style in matters of relationships, family arrangements, and child care. Perhaps to all, it means a new awareness of oneself as a woman in a patriarchal world and the struggle to help oppressors of women "get it." In spite of the "backlash" and the generational differences among women in their commitments to the feminist cause, the lives of all women are being redrawn as a consequence of the feminist movement. (Meyer, 1993, p. 6)

Though Carol Meyer was writing for a professional audience, she chose everyday terms like "bread and butter" and "get it" to connote the quotidian and gritty nature of the goals and means of the second wave of the women's movement. She also selected a political language ("struggle to help oppressors of women" and "patriarchal world"), for two reasons: She was reflecting the political core of a social movement (feminism), and she was writing as the editor in chief of the first professional journal within the field of social work that featured women and girls as clients, community members, and workers.

Compare the same author's choice of language in a journal article that she wrote 14 years earlier in the flagship journal of U.S. social work, *Social Work*. Here, in contrast with the article partially quoted above, she was writing as a scholar of social work practice and a futurist of the profession.

> From an emphasis on methods, the profession has moved to an orientation in which methods become the servants rather than the masters of practice activities. . . . Perhaps it is now time to apply social work knowledge, values, and skills to an epidemiological orientation. . . .
>
> Social work is presumed by the public and voluntary sectors to be responsible for certain psychosocial problems or conditions of life. Historically, social workers have worked in an institutional framework, thus accounting for their relationships to clients in certain contexts, as in hospitals, clinics . . .

Epidemiology is concerned with the incidence and distribution of disease in the case of public health, but in the case of social work it is concerned with the incidence and distribution of psychosocial adaptations.

This formulation defines social work practice broadly and makes it impossible to limit social work to whatever method social workers happen to know. Practice includes the application of intellectual and assessment skills necessary to understand the social work arena, and, indeed, to individualize need for a range of services. (Meyer, 1979, pp. 269–270)

In this article, Carol Meyer exhibited the elasticity of social work writing in incorporating a public health concept (epidemiology) into her recommendation for a sweeping change in the perspective of social work educators and practitioners. She was both borrowing another profession's technical word and transforming it into a term resonant with social workers' everyday practice (psychosocial adaptations). In that way, Meyer could use an old and familiar concept to retain her professional readers' trust while attempting to rally them to think past an accustomed focus on practice method to a new concentration on professional space and terrain.

As experienced social workers, we generally weigh carefully our readership when committing words to paper, a computer screen, or any other electronic device. We attempt while writing, before finalizing the piece, to anticipate the responses that a client, an agency supervisor, or a colleague might have to a case record, chart note, e-mail message, newsletter article, or publication in a peer-reviewed journal. There are three pivotal questions to ask and answer before finishing any kind of social work writing. First, "What do I think is most important to say?" Second, "Who will be my primary reader(s) of this document?" And third, "What will my reader(s) most likely care about in this written communication?"

Take the example of a social worker in a U.S. Department of Veterans Affairs (VA) vet center who is formally recording her or his use of cognitive processing therapy with a veteran of the war in Iraq that began in 2003. The veteran in question has been grappling with the anguish of post-traumatic stress disorder (PTSD). The vet center social worker follows a writing protocol that is: (1) a function of VA regulations, customs, and expectations; (2) a reflection of the evidence bases and best practices available to trauma specialists; (3) a manifestation of the procedures and terminology of the particular intervention in use, in this case, cognitive processing therapy; (4) an outgrowth of social work's commitment to protecting the confidentiality and

respecting the dignity of each patient, client, or constituent; and (5) an arti-
fact of reporting in a computerized medium.

For example, were the vet center social worker discussed in the paragraph
above writing to secure her supervisor's official support for referring a client
with PTSD to a vet center counseling group made up of veterans of the wars
in Iraq and Afghanistan with PTSD, she might well use the language and
categories of the most recent version of the *Diagnostic and Statistical Manual of Mental Disorders* (currently *DSM-IV-TR*) to document the need for
the referral to a treatment group (American Psychiatric Association, 2000).
Additionally, the social worker would probably cite a recent article or book
on the treatment of PTSD that recommends client involvement in a treatment group as part of a cluster of therapeutic responses to former soldiers or
sailors with PTSD (Zappert & Westrup, 2008, p. 374). Finally the vet center
social worker in this circumstance would emphasize the urgency of the
referral, noting the social isolation of the patient and his stated interest in
joining a group of veterans from the wars in Iraq and Afghanistan who would
know firsthand the experience of both contemporary war and PTSD.

This social worker at the vet center would, in one written message, deploy
and link two of three professional voices. She or he would communicate as
a social work practitioner, drawing on accumulated skills, experience, and
empathy as an experienced cognitive processing therapist and group psychotherapist in pointing out the probable advantages that would accrue for the
veteran in combining group treatment among soldier peers with individual
psychotherapy. Also, this VA social worker would rely, as a practicing professional, on applied social and behavioral science, employing, only after
critical review, the analysis and credibility of *DSM-IV-TR* and recent mental
health peer-reviewed literature from a variety of professions and academic
disciplines in seeking written authorization from a supervisor. Additionally,
the same written request to a supervisor for a referral would advocate quick
action, highlighting the importance of providing the best possible care in
the tradition of the VA and its commitment to former soldiers and sailors.

FINDING SOCIAL FACTS AND ENACTING SOCIAL ETHICS: SOCIAL WORK'S MISSIONS

"Social facts and social ethics," in the words of historian Thomas Bender,
became the focus of social liberals of the western hemisphere, including

most founders of social work, in the last two decades of the 19th century (Bender, 2006, p. 255). To find social facts is to secure accurate and illuminating information about human beings, their interconnections, activities, and contexts across their life course (Elder, 1974). To enact social ethics is to accomplish two different, though related, functions: first, to shape and offer services and programs that meet pressing human needs and support emergent or dormant human capacities; and second, to make demands for a more just society and economy—that is to say, to advocate for specific constitutive elements of social and economic justice.

In other words, social work is at one and the same time a broad continuum of practices, a pursuit of social and economic justice, and an investigatory art and science. Most of the profession's members face daily the rigors of two of these three distinct domains, each of which demands particularized forms of labor and corresponding specialized modes of writing. Frequently, social workers' identities clash in the midst of decisions and actions. Sometimes they coexist necessarily but tensely. On fortunate occasions, social workers' identities as practitioners, advocates, and investigators are enacted in harmony.

To comprehend how pivotal elasticity and variability in social work writing are, whether at a vet center or at one of the many thousands of other venues in which social work in the United States of the 21st century is practiced, it is first necessary to grasp the elasticity and variability of the profession itself. As is often the case, understanding a profession requires that we first delve into its historical roots, evolution, and key components. Only then can we sensibly grasp why its writing shifts shapes so fluidly.

THE CONTEXT OF THE SOCIAL WORK PROFESSION'S EMERGENCE

Political liberals of the early and mid-19th century in the Atlantic and European worlds were inspired by Enlightenment thought and disgusted with the constraints of autocratic and mercantilist rule. Guided by thinkers such as Adam Smith and David Ricardo, liberals of the first three quarters of the 19th century sought freedom for individuals and markets from oppressive and intrusive state control.

The United States became one of the laboratories of political liberalism in the West. During and after the U.S. Civil War, the country experienced an unprecedented increase in the number and size of cities because of rail-roads, industrialization, globalizing commerce, and immigration. Escalating urban concentrations of people, industry, and capital resulted in intensifying crises. Many metropolitan tenements, neighborhoods, and workplaces became centers of destitution, danger, and death. Starting in the 1880s, large numbers of political liberals "lost faith in the capacity of the market to create social justice" (Bender, 2006, p. 255).

Disillusioned political liberals evolved into social liberals, people who surrendered laissez-faire politics and economics for a commitment to an active democratic state that could and would regulate the excesses of unfettered capitalism, industry, and greed. Social work, first as a set of volunteer activities, then as a profession, emerged as one key pathway by which social liberals sought social facts and demonstrated social ethics.

SOCIAL WORK AS A CIVIC PROFESSION

The profession of social work corresponds closely to the concept of civic professionalism that philosopher and educator William M. Sullivan has constructed. He analyzed a cluster of "civic professions," including social work, urban planning, and public administration, among others, which were created during the Progressive era, from roughly 1885 through 1917. Advocates of professionalism in that period, Sullivan argued, found the unexamined faith in capitalism's economic competitiveness far too narrow and shortsighted to serve as an organizing premise for the rapidly growing U.S. society and economy or for the new civic professions. Instead, the leaders of these new professions developed, according to Sullivan, "a conception of highly skilled workers who could bring to a variety of occupations a broader, more socially responsive sense of calling, combining something of religious dedication with the civic ideals of traditional humanism and the scientific virtues" (Sullivan, 1995, p. xvi). Sullivan claims that the concept of civic professionalism forged during the Progressive era offered to individual professionals "a design for living that promised to give individual occupational achievement moral meaning through responsible participation in civic life" (Sullivan, 1995, p. 65). Elizabeth Agnew, a biographer of a prominent social work founder, Mary Richmond, asserts that "professionals and progressives together incorporated into their work principles of scientific expertise and efficiency, while they simultaneously promoted public education and citizen participation as key elements in constructing a morally and politically integrated civic life" (Agnew, 2004, p. 136).

Full participation in moral and political civic life in early social work entailed immediate responsiveness as direct practitioners to underrepresented people's concerns, broad and long-term advocacy, and scientific inquiry in relation to urban poverty and industrial working conditions. Social workers during and since the Progressive era have embraced the interdependent triad of direct practice, systemic advocacy, and social and behavioral scientific inquiry as the three-sided foundation of the profession.

SOCIAL WORK AS PRACTICE

By far the largest and best-known aspect of social work in the United States is that of direct practice with individuals, couples, families, groups, communities, and organizations. As dusk fell on the 19th century, Jane Addams, one of the shapers of social work in the United States, wrote that "the ideal and developed settlement [meaning, settlement house or neighborhood center] would attempt to test the value of human knowledge by action, and realization, quite as the complete and ideal university would concern itself with the discovery of knowledge in all branches" (Addams, 1899, p. 36). For Addams, the founder of Hull House, a prominent settlement house in Chicago, social work was about community-based practice, such as organizing English-language night classes for new immigrants and creating child care and kindergarten classes for preschool children of working parents.

Since Addams helped to inspire the proliferation of social work activities in the late 1880s in the United States, social work practice has mushroomed in kind, size, technique, and social locations. Indeed, many practitioners in the 21st century are drawn to study and join the social work profession because of the rich range of practice opportunities. One hour spent inspecting online Web pages of schools and programs of U.S. social work reveals numerous populations, social issues, fields of practice, and practice methods.

Social workers in the 21st century may be intensive case managers in foster care, community-based gang workers, specialists in helping homeless people find permanent housing, or administrators of after-school or adult education programs. We may lead nonprofit organizations, counsel families of people living with Alzheimer's disease, or help employees manage caregiving responsibilities. We may concentrate on working with children who are grief-stricken or organizations that are struggling with high turnover and low morale among staff members. Professionals in social work may focus on helping recent immigrants find work or manage hotlines for people contemplating suicide. We may counsel youth seeking to be the first in their families to attend college or men and women returning from years in prison. We may work on the staff of an elected official at the local, state, or federal level who is attempting to expand resources for people living with the effects of long-term substance abuse and mental illness. This discussion of social work practice possibilities could continue almost ad infinitum but for page limitations. And each of these myriad forms of direct practice generates writing distinctive to the particular setting, audience, and professionals' function.

SOCIAL WORK AS ADVOCACY

Cheek by jowl with everyday social work practice is the profession's pursuit of greater social and economic justice. For example, the general secretary (that is, head) of the New York Charity Organization Society (NYCOS) in 1902, Edward Devine, believed that as a social worker he needed to launch an advocacy campaign when evidence accrued about the desperate housing conditions of many tenement dwellers in New York City. Therefore he instituted the Special Committee on Tenement House Reform of the NYCOS. Soon thereafter, Devine, "seeing how fertile a cause of poverty tuberculosis is," decided to form a committee of the Charity Organization "to begin active measures for a crusade against the disease" (Hunter, 1902, pp. 86–87).

Edward Devine has countless successors in the universe of U.S. social work advocacy. One illustration of the centrality of advocacy to the social work profession is Greenwich House, a settlement house founded in 1902 in Greenwich Village on the lower west side of Manhattan in a neighborhood of African Americans and Italian and Irish immigrants. Mary Kingsbury Simkhovitch served as its first director (head worker), from its founding until 1946, and led it to become an important site of social work advocacy. Kingsbury's writing details the multiple tiers of Greenwich House advocacy, which campaigned for tenement house inspections and standards, for citywide publicly sponsored day care for babies of working parents, and against "home work" (manufacturing conducted at home) (Simkhovitch, 1938, pp. 155–156). A brief excerpt from Simkhovitch's memoir, published in 1949, reveals practice writing that is steeped in the optimism, political liberals' consciousness, belief in the Social Gospel, and search for common ground amid demographic diversity that characterized most prose by social workers raised as Christians during the first four decades of the profession's history in the United States:

> From 1902 on my work was cut out for me—the building of neighborhood enrichment and integration. Here, too, is the twofold picture of unity and diversity, the struggle against false authoritarianism, and the welcoming of group growth which does not impinge on the freedom and vitality of opposing groups. . . . "Who is my neighbor?" is the old question answered in the Gospel most definitely and with finality. Not power but love, and love through immediate and unquestioned action. (Simkhovitch, 1949, p. 176)

Advocacy concerning social issues, along with case advocacy, have been part and parcel of U.S. social work in the 19th, 20th, and 21st centuries. Indeed, the kinds of issue advocacy within social work have been as various as the forms of professional practice referred to in an earlier section of this chapter. Organizing product boycotts, lobbying, speaking in public, shaping policy, building coalitions, testifying at public hearings, running campaigns for public office, petitioning, and blogging are some of the advocacy activities that social workers regularly engage in concerning topics related to the present and future welfare of client populations (Gamble & Weil, 2010).

Social workers involved in long-term advocacy and direct practitioners recognize the damage that may result if our professional labors are not grounded in and regularly checked against the best available data about societal continuities and discontinuities and human behaviors. Those social workers who concentrate on building knowledge bases in the humanities and the social and behavioral sciences help supply theories, concepts, trend lines, and information without which daily practice and advocacy would be little more than the playing of hunches.

SOCIAL WORK AS AN APPLIED SOCIAL AND BEHAVIORAL SCIENCE

Knowledge, instructing the sense, refining and multiplying needs, transforms itself into skill and makes life various with a new six days' work. . . . Of a truth, knowledge is power, but it is a power reined by scruple, having a conscience of what must be and what may be.

(GEORGE ELIOT, *DANIEL DERONDA*)

Social workers are builders, distributors, and appliers of knowledge. The knowledge that we construct is linked intimately with work, conscience, idealism, and pragmatism, realms suggested in Eliot's quotation. Social workers are, in part, applied social and behavioral scientists. The very names of two of the oldest schools of social work in the United States provide evidence of that commitment to science. In 1915, Bryn Mawr College, near Philadelphia, Pennsylvania, established its Graduate Department of Social Economy and Social Research (now the Graduate School of Social Work and Social Research). That same year saw the creation of the School of Applied Social Sciences of the Case Western Reserve University in Cleveland, Ohio (now known as the Mandel School of Applied Social Sciences). From the earliest decades of its history, professionals in social work sought to ground their planning and actions in ongoing research and reflection. For example, the School of Social Service Administration of the University of Chicago brought into being in 1927 the *Social Service Review*, a leading journal in social work and social welfare, "with the aim of opening 'scientific discussions of problems arising in connection with the various aspects of social work'" (The Historical Context, n.d.). Founders and subsequent generations of social work professionals remained acutely aware that activity guided by the best of intentions (contemporaneous social ethics) might well do more harm than good if those actions were uninformed by the highest quality of available social knowledge.

DIFFERENCES IN WRITING AMONG SOCIAL WORK'S THREE STREAMS

As we have seen, experienced social workers pay close attention to the precise context and purposes of their writing in shaping their messages. And effective social work professionals think carefully about the priorities of their readers when writing for practice, advocacy, or research purposes. As a result, variability and flexibility have been the hallmarks of social work writing across professional roles, functions, settings, and identities.

Notwithstanding this common ground, the writing of social workers who are privileging their work as practitioners often differs in emphasis, word selection, and style from social work writing that is focused on advocacy or knowledge construction. Each major stream of social work, in short, has developed a writing mode that is distinctive despite the shared aspects of professional social work writing.

WRITING AS PROFESSIONAL PRACTITIONERS

The writing of social work practitioners draws upon experience, observation, and published literature. Practice writing focuses on the interrelationships among theory, technique, context, and interpersonal connections with a client or community members. Much writing in and about social work practice involves case studies or vignettes and links practice theory with choices that the author-practitioner makes in selecting, ordering, and timing the use of a technique, method, or competency. Careful attention is paid to explaining the setting of practice, the strengths and needs of a given client or group of clients, and the steps involved in applying a given technique in work with individuals, an organization, or a community. Some form of the evaluation of the efficacy of practice is usually included.

Writing by practitioners commonly highlights the complexity of effective practice. Countless articles and books have noted the interactivity in competent social work among a social worker's abilities to demonstrate authentic caring, call on an up-to-date knowledge of professional literature, and make delicate judgment calls based on prior practice experience. For example, Bertha Capen Reynolds, a social work clinician and educator who published prolifically from the 1930s through the 1960s, emphasized the intimacy of the links among a practitioner's empathy, reliance on a formal knowledge base, and practice wisdom. Reynolds wrote in 1951: "A relationship [with a client] becomes meaningful if it brings to bear on the problem not only the caseworker's warmth but light which is drawn from scientific training, and from experience in dealing with many such problems" (Reynolds, 1975, p. 109).

Offering examples of questions to ask clients is characteristic of writing by professionals immersed in practice and teaching. Illustrations in the form of interview questions help make practice guidelines three-dimensional. As an example, Marion Bogo (2006) provides helpful specificity in discussing interviewing skills:

[*QUESTIONS THAT SEEK CONCRETENESS OR*
REQUEST CLARIFICATION]

Can you tell me what you mean when you talk about respect?

Can you tell me exactly what happens when you say that you feel threatened in your relationship?

You said that you feel uncomfortable with your roommate . . . uncomfortable in what way? (p. 239)

Along a similar line, professional practitioners of social work also insert first-person testimonies into their writing for publication in order to represent in authentic detail the subtleties of experience and perspective reported by clients and constituents. While paraphrasing is an important form of writing often required in effective communication, the original words of clients remain invaluable for relaying the richest possible meanings. In a chapter on practice with people with disabilities, Sisneros, Stakeman, Joyner, and Schmitz (2008) interlace into the text boxes of clients' words. One such box, titled "Disability and Resilience," begins with the sentence "My disability doesn't define me, though it certainly did change my life" (p. 67). Later in the same chapter, another box of testimony appears, this one labeled "My Son is Deaf." It starts with the words "I remember the day in July when I finally received the diagnosis. . . . There was a very loud bang, and all the children jumped except Michael" (p. 72).

Still another dimension of social work practitioners' writing for publication is the inclusion of case examples or case studies that provide a summary of the context and history of a "case," salient slices of client-worker interactions, a portrayal of the sequence of activities undertaken, and copies of materials written by all participants. A case may be focused on an individual, couple, family, small group, service or program, organization, community, or social policy issue. Case studies and their abbreviated cousins, case vignettes, have been at the core of many practitioner publications for more than a century. Multiple illustrations of heuristic case studies, for example, appear in Joan Dworkin's text, *Advanced Social Work Practice: An Integrated Multilevel Approach*. One case study, for example, is named "Outreach to Homeless Youth at Risk." In the case, "Skip" is a case manager in a shelter for runaway, high-risk, and homeless adolescents. "Rhonda" is a fourteen-year-old with circular burns on her right forearm. She had been repeatedly raped by her stepfather, subsequently placed in foster care, and then ran away from her foster family after being molested by her foster father. The case study description ends with the following paragraph:

A week has passed and Skip has not seen Rhonda on outreach or at the shelter. The "crew" [of other homeless youth] she was with said they did not know where she was either. He is getting ready to go home for the evening and, as he turns around, Rhonda is standing outside the doorway and looking down. Her once clean clothes are now torn and dirty. She has multiple bruises on her face and neck. (Dworkin, 2005, p. 38)

Dworkin, the author, leaves the reader at that unfinished and challenging point of the practice story and then poses a list of learning objectives, recommended practitioner activities, and a set of suggested readings (Dworkin, 2005, pp. 38–39). These components that Dworkin places after the narrative are frequently found as part of case studies.

Writing by practitioners of social work additionally includes charts and graphs that track clients' behavioral continuity and change when cognitive behavioral or behavioral approaches are in use. For example, as part of a case study about Bruce, a 12-year-old boy diagnosed with both attention deficit disorder and oppositional defiant disorder, social work practitioners Marlene Cooper and Joan Granucci Lesser present four figures that show: (1) his frequency of temper tantrums before and during a five-week intervention; (2) the forms of rewards for good behavior given to Bruce—with point totals noted for each kind of reward; (3) the trajectory of the peaks and valleys of reward points earned by Bruce over a five-week intervention; and (4) the comparative number of minutes Bruce was able to stay on task during the five weeks of psychotropic and behavioral interventions (Cooper & Lesser, 2005, pp. 200–203).

Another feature that infuses the prose of practicing social workers— whether clinicians or community workers—is attentiveness to clients' or constituents' individual and collective histories. For these practitioner writers, social work on present projects and future possibilities is anchored in discussions of individual and group clients' own narratives of past experiences. The writing of Lorraine Gutierrez and Edythe Lewis, among many others, comes to mind: "Effective multicultural social work is grounded in consciousness-raising. . . . Consciousness-raising on a community level can involve such activities as oral history projects or other activities that capture and tell the stories that are at the crux of understanding vital community issues. Such stories may include tales of exploitation and resistance" (Gutierrez, Lewis, Nagda, Wernick, & Shore, 2005, pp. 346–347). Gutierrez et al. not only encourage an emphasis on oral history taking and sharing in clinical and community practice but also tell many diachronic stories of community participants in their writing.

A final common feature of social work practitioners' writing that is worth highlighting is the presence of the printed or online list of key elements of a practice, intervention, or knowledge base. In a practice world marked by a chronic shortage of time, an excess of tasks, and a multiplicity of extant and emergent theories, perspectives, approaches, and models, social workers rely on compacted and abbreviated renderings of complex applications so that they can act in a timely way and then play catch-up with more in-depth study. For example, social workers who work with immigrants, migrants, and refugees may need to turn for help to a list of documents that are covenants and conventions that elaborate and update the Universal Declaration of Human Rights of the United Nations. Social work practitioners and educators Gamble and Weil have created a list of seven documents, in addition to the Universal Declaration of Human Rights, that are important for practitioners to consult if they have responsibilities with community members and clients whose human rights have been infringed upon or are in danger of such infringement. Without such a list, few social workers, or their clients, would be able to have a comprehensive understanding of the entitlements and protections available to their clients. Two examples from Gamble and Weil's list are the Indigenous and Tribal Peoples Convention and the Protocol to Prevent, Suppress, and Punish Trafficking in Persons, Especially Women and Children (Gamble & Weil, 2010, p. 194).

Social work practitioners' writing features discussion of the complex interplay among empathy, evidence, and insight based on experience. Additionally, writing by practitioners includes questions to ask clients, first-person client testimonies, and case studies. Moreover, charts, graphs, and other figures have become an increasingly important part of social work practitioners' writing as behavioral and cognitive behavioral approaches to practice have flourished. The oral histories and reminiscences of clients and community organization participants are another featured part of practitioners' writing, as are lists—lists of properties of practice models, documents, interventions, and skill sets.

WRITING AS SOCIAL WORK ADVOCATES

A variety of old and newer professions are dedicated to improving the human condition. Only one, however, namely, social work, has as part of its core mission the diminution of economic and social injustices in local and global societies. Not surprisingly, the writing of client, community, and issue advocates within social work reflects that highly demanding, progressive purpose. To illustrate, in 1951, psychiatric social worker and social work scholar Bertha Capen Reynolds, already described and quoted above, wrote:

> Practically all the heroes and heroines of fiction and drama are white people, middle or upper class, able to have interesting experiences. A working man who works, except under exceptionally romantic circumstances, does not appear in an important role. A Negro does not appear unless in a submissive part, or adds so-called comedy relief. . . . Are we, however, sometimes aware that this means that very poor people, and members of minority groups, are not really considered a part of the world that matters, and if the comfortable folk forget them, are we in social work entitled to forget them too? (Reynolds, 1975, p. 5)

Reynolds, alarmed by the increasing neglect of the poorest Americans by nonprofit social work agencies, challenged her profession to return to its original mission. Her advocacy took the form of a question within a book she wrote about her pathbreaking work in helping to create a new social agency, the United Seamen's Service, which she helped establish to serve sailors in the U.S. Merchant Marine during World War II. In so doing, she pilot-tested a new field of practice, social work with workers (industrial social work or social work in the workplace). Reynolds's language is simple and direct: "Are we . . . entitled to forget them too?" The infinitive "to forget" was perhaps chosen in order to resonate with the postwar plea of survivors of the Nazi holocaust to the world to "never forget."

Compare Reynolds's language of exposition and advocacy with that of a modern-day social work scholar, Gordon Pon, published six decades later. Pon wrote:

> The implication of cultural competency in whiteness is evidenced in how it constructs "other" cultural groups, because whiteness is the standard by

which cultures are differentiated. . . . Cultural competency, like *new rac-*
ism, operates by essentializing culture, while "othering" non-whites without
using racialist language.

Cultural competency's disavowal of the postmodern turn, however, ren-
ders cultural competence theoretically and practically obsolete. . . .

Because of the obsolescence of cultural competency and its resemblance
to new racism, I recommend that it be jettisoned by social workers. Letting
go of this discourse would help us to not forget but rather to remember
social work's own modern history. (Pon, 2009, pp. 60, 64, 68)

Pon in 2009 is advocating within a social work profession that, unlike the
profession Reynolds was addressing in 1951, has been immersed for many
decades in a world rocked by racial conflict and social movements, some of
which have been dedicated to obliterating racism and some of which have
been devoted to legitimating it. His language and categories of thought are
those of the postmodern world, an epistemology that he carefully defines in
his article and juxtaposes sharply with the modernity of Reynolds's time.

Advocacy writing in social work is often characterized by a sense of urgency. Authors of advocacy articles, blogs, or op-ed essays ordinarily make
demands of officers and bodies with the authority to make changes in policy,
procedures, or resource distribution. They may frame those demands as suggestions, recommendations, requests, or pleas. For example, in the journal
Social Work, child welfare advocates made "five suggestions for caseworkers,
state trainers, local and state administrators, and social work researchers on
engaging *with* [foster care] youths in relationships that facilitate genuine
system change" (Strolin-Goltzman, Kollar, & Trinkle, 2010, p. 52). Their
recommendations appear in the conclusions of a journal article whose title
itself embodies advocacy rhetoric, "Listening to the Voices of Children in
Foster Care: Youths Speak Out About Child Welfare Workforce Turnover
and Selection." The choice of the verb "speak out" in the subtitle of the
article deploys feminist language of the United States of the 1970s, when
feminists first borrowed an activity from the Maoist revolution in China; it
featured public testimonies by survivors of rape, incest, and domestic abuse
in campaigning against male violence against women and girls. The authors
made explicit and specific calls for change, such as: "Child welfare caseworkers can develop case plans with their clients [and] solicit their clients'
opinions on what services would be most appropriate." Also, "Child welfare
administrators at the state and local levels can solicit youths' opinions on

the causes of and solutions to systemwide problems" (Strolin-Goltzman et al., 2010, p. 52).

The final sentence of journal articles, essays, and other writings shaped by social work advocates usually reaffirms and sharpens their central message. The last words of Strolin-Goltzman et al. in their article in *Social Work* are a case in point: "In sum, child welfare agencies and partnering researchers should be challenged to harness the knowledge and experience of foster care consumers by collaborating *with* them on the development of interventions and innovations that aim to decrease [child welfare caseworker] turnover and ultimately seek to revolutionize systems of child welfare care" (Strolin-Goltzman et al., 2010, p. 52).

Social work advocates who cast their thoughts into written form ordinarily create a discourse of hopefulness and resilience as a necessary counterpoint to the terror, pain, and despair that often spring from the domination, suppression, and violence that too many social work clients and constituents undergo. A representative paragraph of restoration and uplift comes from the book chapter of Colorado advocates Kay Stevenson and Jaime Rall, who specialize in assisting people who have lived through torture, political persecution, or flight from disasters caused by human beings or nature.

> This focus [on the worldwide practice of torture and other human rights abuses] not only is an ethical obligation for social work practitioners but also has the potential for therapeutic value for those who already have suffered such abuses. Effective mental health interventions and community connection restore hope and purpose. Both the individual and community triumph over attempts at deliberate and systematic torture. Torture can, and does, fail. Survivors can and will be victorious. (Stevenson & Rall, 2007, p. 256)

WRITING AS SOCIAL AND BEHAVIORAL SCIENTISTS AND HUMANISTS

All social workers depend upon multiple knowledge bases—those of the natural and physical sciences, mathematics, the social and behavioral sciences, the humanities, and other professions. Some social workers choose to add to those foundations as scholars, researchers, and authors.

Writing by social workers who contribute to the evidence bases upon which practitioners, advocates, and other researchers rely is, most of the time, shaped in accordance with one of two major scholarly tradition~ ¹¹

of the social and behavioral sciences and that of the humanities. While the first category unquestionably undergirds the preponderance of current journal articles, books, monographs, and reports in U.S. social work publications, the second form of scholarship, work that is rooted in philosophical, political, literary, linguistic, and historical approaches, also has figured prominently and continues to play a significant—though now minority—role in U.S. social work knowledge building. (By contrast, throughout Europe and the 54 independent nations that are part of the Commonwealth of Nations, the influence of the humanities in social work publications remains far greater than in the contemporary United States.)

Social worker Stanley Witkin has noted that the writing of literature and that of science diverged by the 17th century.

> The former, associated with the arts, culture, and humanities, was concerned with the language itself, how it might be used to express, explore, analyze, and create. For science, however, language simply was a vehicle for recording the regularities of nature and the methods for producing those regularities. By and large, academic journals, including *Social Work* [in which this quotation appeared], have adopted the writing format developed for scientific writing. (Witkin, 2000, p. 389)

Social workers who have written in a social or behavioral scientific mode tend to place a high premium upon methodological consistency, standardization, and predictability. They are usually, though certainly not always, quantitative researchers. One example comes from the work of social worker Edna Wasser, who understood the research interview to be a pivotal scientific component of social work.

> Reliability of the data is increased by standardization of procedures in research interviewing. Standardization enables the research-interviewing staff to function consistently, with each person having a knowledge of each other person's activity, and to achieve uniformity of practice. Standardization does not imply automatic or rigid practice, but it provides a framework within which the research interviewer can perform tasks imaginatively and sensitively. Use of a structured schedule according to specific instructions is an example of standardization. (Wasser, 1962, p. 290)

Statistical sophistication has grown noticeably within social work research and within most social work publications since Dr. Wasser's comments of 1962, thanks to an increasing emphasis in social work education on embedding the teaching and learning of the methodologies of the social and behavioral sciences at the bachelor's, master's, and, especially, doctoral levels of education. The need on the part of social work faculty and independent researchers to obtain governmental and foundation funding for their research is one of several causes of enhanced attentiveness to statistics and quantitative methods. Forms of quantitative analysis popular in social work journals of the 21st century are both more advanced and far more numerous than in those of earlier times. Writing in social work journals, reports, and books has, on the whole, become suffused with the "lingo" as well as the epistemology of social and behavioral science methodology.

The abstract that social work researcher Yoonsook Ha wrote for an article that she published in *Social Service Review* in 2009 gives the reader a preliminary glimpse of the high level of literacy in statistical knowledge and research design that one needs in order to read her article in a thoughtful manner. The article is titled "Stability of Child-Care Subsidy Use and Earnings of Low-Income Families."

> This article explores the duration and effect of child-care subsidy use among low-income working mothers in Wisconsin. Using an event-history model, the study finds that mothers are likely to cycle on and off subsidy systems and that their subsidy spells tend to end relatively quickly. Results from a Tobit model with a lagged independent variable suggest that long-term use of child-care subsidies is associated with increases in mothers' earnings. (p. 495)

Turning briefly to a potent though minority strain of U.S. social work writing for publication in the 21st century, that written in the vein of the humanities, one finds a rich array of essays, editorials, agency and professional newsletters, letters to the editor, journal articles, books, and blogs. Social work authors whose research and writings are rooted in the humanities tend to employ considerable imagery and care in language usage as they study, document, and interpret social work practice, culture, and human interrelationships with other people and their built and natural environments. Frequently, the dissection of theories and concepts and contemplation of their application in professional work, close study of historical contexts, and self-reflection in practice are woven into social work writing of this kind.

Social worker and historian Michael Reisch provides an example of interpretive scholarship steeped in the habits of the humanities.

In contrast to debates over social justice, the discourse on what is now termed "multiculturalism" occurred in a variety of contexts, often without a clear or consistent focus. In the U.S. its central concern has been in relation to race ... Ironically, at the turn of the 20th century, when social welfare leaders first proposed re-orienting the field toward social justice, the nation was more thoroughly racialized ... than at any other point in American history" {Foner, pp. 12–13} (Reisch, 2007, pp. 70–71)

CONCLUSION

A profession devoted to behavioral and social change has markedly modified its forms and ways of writing over time. Compared with our 19th-century predecessors, U.S. social workers in the 21st century write in a far more compact and measured fashion. The condensation of social work writing has grown out of the speed-up in social work practice, the increasing dominance of the social and behavioral science paradigm, bureaucracies' needs for efficiency, and the rise of computer technology. Our challenge as social worker writers — whether we are performing as practitioners, advocates, researchers, or as amalgamators of those roles — is a demanding one. Our duty is to retain empathy, authenticity, precision, and accuracy as we describe, analyze, and interpret the facts about and consciousness of clients and their local and global neighbors.

References

Addams, Jane. (1899). A function of the social settlement. *Annals of the American Academy of Political and Social Science, 13*(3), 33–55.

Agnew, E. N. (2004). *From charity to social work.* Chicago: University of Illinois Press.

American Psychiatric Association. (2000). *Diagnostic and statistical manual of mental disorders* (4th ed., text revision). Washington, DC: Author.

Bender, T. (2006). *A nation among nations: America's place in world history.* New York: Hill & Wang.

Bogo, M. (2006). *Social work practice: Concepts, processes, and interviewing.* New York: Columbia University Press.

Cooper, M. G., & Lesser, J. G. (2005). *Social work practice: An integrated approach* (2nd ed.). Boston: Pearson Education.

Dworkin, J. (2005). *Advanced social work practice: An integrative, multilevel approach.* Boston: Pearson Education.

Elder, G. H. (1974). *Children of the Great Depression: Social change in life experience*, chaps. 1 and 2. Chicago: University of Chicago Press.

Eliot, G. (1984). *Daniel Deronda*. New York: Oxford University Press, Clarendon ed. (First published in 1876)

Foner, E. (1999). Expert report of Eric Foner to the Federal Court of Appeals. 6th Circuit. *Gratz et al. v. Bollinger et al.* and *Grutter et al. v. Bollinger et al.* Web site http://www.umich.edu/~urel/admissions/legal/expert/foner.html. Cited in Reisch, 2007.

Gamble, D. N., & Weil, M. (2010). *Community practice skills: Local to global perspectives*, chaps. 5, 10, 11. New York: Columbia University Press.

Gutierrez, L., Lewis, E., Nagda, B., Wernick, L., & Shore, N. (2005). Multicultural community practice strategies and intergroup empowerment. In M. Weil et al. (Eds.), *The handbook of community practice* (pp. 341–360). Thousand Oaks, CA: Sage Publications.

Ha, Y. (2009). Stability of child-care subsidy use and earnings of low-income families. *Social Service Review, 83*(4), 495–523.

The Historical Context. (n.d.). Retrieved from the University of Chicago School of Social Administration Web Site, http://www.ssa.uchicago.edu/aboutssa/school-desc.shtml#history, on April 30, 2010.

Hunter, R. (1902). The relation between social settlements and charity organizations. *Journal of Political Economy, 11*(1), 75–88.

Meyer, C. H. (1979). What directions for direct practice? *Social Work, 24*(4), 267–272.

———. (1993). The many faces of Eve [Editorial]. *Affilia: Journal of Women and Social Work, 8*(1), 6–8.

Pon, G. (2009). Cultural competency as new racism: An ontology of forgetting. *Journal of Progressive Human Services, 20*, 50–71.

Reisch, M. (2007). Social justice and multiculturalism: Persistent tensions in the history of U.S. social welfare and social work. *Studies in Social Justice, 1*(1), 67–92.

Reynolds, B. C. (1975). *Social work and social living: Explorations in philosophy and practice*. Silver Spring, MD: First NASW Classic Edition. (First published in 1951 by Citadel Press.)

Simkhovitch, M. K. (1938). *Neighborhood: My story of Greenwich House*. New York: W. W. Norton.

———. (1949). *Here is God's plenty*. New York: Harper & Brothers.

Sisneros, J., Stakeman, C., Joyner, M. C., & Schmitz, C. L. (2008). *Critical multicultural social work*. Chicago: Lyceum Books.

Stevenson, K. M., & Rall, J. (2007). Transforming the trauma of torture, flight, and resettlement. In M. Bussey & J. B. Wise (Eds.), *Trauma transformed: An empowerment response* (pp. 236–258). New York: Columbia University Press.

Strolin-Goltzman, J., Kollar, S., & Trinkle, J. (2010). Listening to the voices of children in foster care: Youths speak out about child welfare workforce turnover and selection. *Social Work, 55*(1), 47–53.

Sullivan, W. M. (1995). *Work and integrity: The crisis and promise of professionalism in America.* New York: HarperBusiness.

Wasser, E. (1962). Research interviewing in social work research: Some formulations. *Social Service Review, 36*(3), 286–294.

Witkin, S. L. (2000). Writing social work [Editorial]. *Social Work, 45*(5), 389–394.

Zappert, L. N., & Westrup, D. (2008). Cognitive processing therapy for posttraumatic stress disorder in a residential treatment setting. *Psychotherapy Research, Theory, Practice, Training, 45*(3), 361–376.

2

WRITING STRATEGIES FOR ACADEMIC PAPERS

Warren Green

THINKING AND WRITING

How can I know what I think until I see what I say?

E. M. FORSTER

FORSTER REFERS TO NOT KNOWING what he is thinking until he sees what he has written. His statement resonates with me, as I'm often surprised when I notice a line I've just written causing an "aha!" moment; that is, I instantly realize something I had not known, at least consciously. These moments occur when I make a connection between two thoughts that had seemed unrelated—when writing a report on what a student presented in a writing center session, or an e-mail message to a friend, or a few reminder sentences to myself about some issue that's been lurking about my mind. I'll ask students whether they've had similar experiences when writing; many will first consider the question and then slowly come to an affirmative reply, as though realizing it themselves for the first time. What I want to convey in this chapter is that writing and thinking go hand in hand and that writing itself spurs thinking about and engagement with the subject being considered. We begin with our thoughts, of course, but gathering them and stringing them together to express and communicate meaning—perhaps even the aha! moment—is what we're after.

You've heard it before: Good writing does not just appear, like wise Athena bursting out of the head of Zeus. Many of us view improving our writing as a lifelong activity. Writing assumes an intelligence hard at work, struggling to get at and then form thoughts and ideas into a coherent whole.

Writing is dynamic and personal work, as it helps uncover, or discover, our selves, so it includes some process of self-awareness. Writing brings into play the handling and expression of our thoughts, feelings, experiences, and even assumptions. But any such demanding expression of the self can put us in a vulnerable state. Though we tend not to choose this state, it is where much learning takes place, and as writers we are sensitive to it, welcoming it, exploiting it to our own benefit and growth. Good writing may come out of thinking about and taking notes on our reading, then discussing the issues and ideas raised (e.g., in class, on Web forums and blogs, with friends and family), then organizing our notes and research material, and then writing up a draft—a first draft. We may follow with writing another draft and another before even beginning to think about editing, proofreading, and the ubiquitous APA style.

My perspective is that of a writing center consultant and director who has worked for many years with Columbia MSW and PhD social work students on a wide range of writing issues, so the focus of this chapter will be on the most widespread and most important issues that students have presented. Typical responses when asked what brings someone to the writing center tend to be all-encompassing: *The paper doesn't flow. . . . The paper's all over the place; I need help organizing it. . . . I've written too much, and all of it's research; there's nothing of me!* Coming from the front lines, sitting with students, brainstorming our way through one idea after another, trying to better understand and communicate a pressing issue, I've learned that engaging with and thinking about the issue can lead to writing that inevitably captures what the writer wants to say. And, correspondingly, engaging with what's been written leads to further thinking, leading to more and better writing. This journey of discovery, of writing your way into a final draft, will ultimately help you produce a paper that will be at the least adequate and possibly exemplary.

The link between thinking and writing has been much discussed (Bean, 2001; Becker, 2007; Flower, 1993; Fulwiler, 1997; Howard & Barton, 1986; Ruggiero, 1991), and my space is limited, so my intention is try to convey this bond in a way that complements what other chapter authors in this collection have to say. I will offer an approach to the academic writing that social work students are usually called upon to produce. In doing so, I will focus on how reading and thinking and discussing and writing are interwoven elements that go into the development of a completed paper.

I'll first state the obvious. Most of the work of writing involves thinking, whether it be in the initial stages, when associative thinking and creativity are most active, or in the editing stage, when our critical thinking takes over. We know that reading journal articles and book chapters and writing notes and discussing content all involve thinking, and we know that writing is the expression of our thinking. Howard (1990), a noted philosopher of education, stated that "the primary goal of writing, like reading, is to *understand* and then to make that understanding *available* to others in writing" (p. 84). Thinking entails how we understand a reading and how we apply that understanding, the way in which we proceed to express our view. Writing reveals the thinking behind our beliefs, opinions, ideas—from first draft and onward, as we gradually shape and form our writing into a finished work that can be communicated to others. My attempt here to dissect thinking and writing as qualities of our comprehension and expression is meant to introduce an approach to achieving a synergy of these qualities, an approach referred to as free writing.

FREE WRITING

What is free writing? Elbow (1998), who first articulated the approach, noted that free writing consists of committing to writing continuously for a prescribed period of time (e.g., 5, 10, 15 minutes) without regard to grammar, punctuation, or any kind of evaluation. The goal is to identify, to discover, what you are thinking, and this is done by writing about the subject at hand. Free writing literally connects thinking and writing. As we first read and write about a subject, our thinking tends to be associative and random; that is, we make connections between and among various ideas and thoughts that come to mind. Free writing sets out to deliberately take advantage of this state, as it fosters the process of both getting in touch with our thoughts and writing them down without concern for the form the writing takes. Free writing is most helpful in the initial stages of work, when we need to tap into our resources. After this point, it varies. Ideally we will go right on to a first draft, using the free writing as a basis; however, some may want to first create an outline.

Why focus on free writing? In my work the most important issues students present are structural—how the writing is organized, how it is put together. But the major impediment to addressing this issue sits in front of us—the computer. Word processing predisposes us to focus on surface issues (i.e., spelling, grammar, punctuation) rather than on the core concerns (Dave & Russell, 2010; Hass, 1989). Free writing can take us away from this hypercritical concentration on form in the early stages of writing. When we stop writing too soon and too often—to review, to edit—we lose a sense of flow, which Csikszentmihalyi (1991) defined as a state of focused concentration in which one is deeply and successfully immersed in some productive activity. This loss of flow can hinder both our forward movement and our voice, our uniqueness as a writer.

Academic writing, unlike personal writing of any kind (e.g., fiction, memoir, personal narrative) demands a clear, direct, unambiguous style that expresses the writer's thinking, not his or her feelings, sensibility, or even speculations, although these qualities may certainly be present and inferred by the reader. But in free writing, thoughts, beliefs, feelings, assumptions, speculations all carry equal weight for the purpose at hand, which is to identify, locate, and express what it is you think about the issue under discussion. After two or more drafts, editing will take care of the ideas that did not pan out, the personal asides, the ambiguous statements.

At this point, some may be thinking about outlines. For many, the traditional outline structure (I, II, A, B, 1, 2, a, b, etc.) stifles curiosity and associative and creative thinking, forcing a compartmentalized, dividing approach to thinking and to writing (Elbow, 1981; Kellogg, 1990; Sharples, 1999). For example, you may squash your idea A if you cannot think of a B, and that A may be a valuable theme or concept. Because writing itself stimulates thinking, write as much as possible. Once you have a draft that appears close to what you want to say, get feedback—from peers and instructors and supervisors—before your paper is evaluated and judged. Discussions with others will help you to further hone and better mold your subsequent writing (Rivard & Straw, 2000). And, of course, revise. Keep in mind that everything you read in any book or journal has been read, rewritten, edited, copyedited, and proofread many times and by any number of people. Writing as a developmental activity values active thinking over a focus on presenting the perfect essay. The writer's interest is stimulated through reading and experiential learning and, again, by talking about the issues and ideas raised in both. In this manner the writer draws sustenance.

PRODUCING AN ACADEMIC PAPER

An academic paper (for an assignment, an article, even a dissertation) starts with your idea, issue, or topic. Next comes thinking through the choice of terms and phrases to use when conducting a search of the literature; you'll notice how one term makes you think of another. This search leads to titles of articles, from which you'll decide which abstracts to read, and then which articles to read, all leading directly to the first and subsequent drafts of your paper. And I want to suggest an approach to this work that can be used for any and all academic writing work—whether it be a short paper in which only reading and summarizing are called for or a formal research paper.

Students at Columbia (and I'm sure elsewhere) take five and sometimes more classes per semester, plus perform an internship in the field of 20 hours a week (though usually more) throughout the academic year, all making for a life that is both exciting and exhausting. It is not unusual for an instructor to assign 100 to 300 pages of readings per week, so multiply that by 4 or 5 to appreciate where this thought is leading. These readings are usually 20- to 30-plus-page articles or chapters from peer-reviewed journals or books, and students must usually provide a 1-to-4-page summary and/or critique for such an assignment. Having so much to read while carrying on with all the other demands of life can quickly overwhelm the best of students; therefore, rethinking how to go about your reading assignments may be in order.

Let's assume you're writing a 15-page research paper. You've chosen your issue, and you've conducted a search through the library's databases (e.g., Social Work Abstracts, ProQuest, Social Services Abstracts), so you know what literature is available on the subject. You can clearly articulate your research question on the issue you want to explore. You may have had to expand or narrow your topic of interest. Getting to know what issues are important entails immersing yourself in the material and developing a discriminating eye. One way of doing this is to stay flexible with regard to the issue under study. Always be open to expanding or narrowing your search criteria. For example, you're having trouble finding either enough or up-to-date articles on your population: early adolescent Latinas from urban low-SES single-mother households. Maybe you'll add all adolescent Latinas; maybe you'll delete the term "urban."

The literature review will inform you on the issue. For this 15-page paper, you may be asked to provide 20 to 25 citations, which means you'll read as many as 200 abstracts, from which you'll choose to read perhaps 30 to 50 articles before you select 20 of those to use in your paper. This process will enable you to clearly articulate the problem, the issue under study, the focus of interest. However, such a project takes time, so skimming becomes important, and it is a skill you can develop by first understanding how journal articles are generally put together, or constructed; that is, they follow a formula. For example, empirical articles will usually consist of an introduction that states the purpose of the study, followed by a literature review, the methods used to conduct the study, a results section, a discussion of the results, and a conclusion. Clearly identifying each of these sections will enable you to quickly determine what is essential to know and therefore needs to be noted. Though there are other types of articles (e.g., review, methodological, theoretical, case), each of which also follows a distinct pattern, empirical social science articles are the dominant type that instructors will want to see.

It's 1 A.M., and your mind is on the 15-page paper, but you still have three articles to read, summarize, and critique for another class before trying to get some sleep so that you can arrive promptly (and alert) at 9 A.M. at your internship. Keeping in mind what you must produce for your instructor (e.g., a 2-page summary and a 2-page critique of three journal articles, each 30 pages long) and that you intuitively know more than you might be willing to admit to yourself, what follows is a method, derived from the work of Pauk and Owens (2010), that can be applied to the reading and summarizing of articles, though it's not one you'd use for an article written in a traditional narrative form or an essay with an opening position, followed by supporting details, arguments, and conclusion. And by reading, I don't mean the approach we use when reading a story, a novel, or a magazine article; I mean an active approach, that is, with pen or marker in hand, jotting down notes, highlighting passages as you read. This simple method is one that most of your instructors adapted to get through their own graduate programs.

1. Reread the abstract, note the length of the article, and scan through all the headings, subheadings, graphs, tables, and pictures. Doing so will provide you with a needed preview.
2. Read the introduction: Of critical importance is to identify the author's purpose or intent, and thesis.

3. Skip to the end and read the conclusion: It should elucidate what you noted in the introduction and inform further on the issues involved.

4. Return and read the first and last paragraphs of the section immediately following the introduction, usually the methods section, though there may be a literature review preceding it. The essential elements of the methods section will usually be found in these two paragraphs. Then read the middle paragraphs.

5. Follow this same pattern with the results and conclusion sections: Read the first and last paragraphs of each section, followed by the middle paragraphs.

As you read, highlight or jot down notes—key points, relevance to your subject of interest, your reactions, other readings it reminds you of. Ask yourself questions, ask the author questions, write down your responses. You'll be looking for and noting the substantive content the abstract described and the most important details: the author's intent, the methods used, the results, and the conclusions and discussion. After applying this method to a few articles, you'll quickly grasp what's important to note for your summary or research paper, and you'll soon be able to dispense with reading the middle paragraphs altogether, as they will usually provide unneeded detail. Gradually, reading article after article, you'll be able to forgo reading them through; you'll know exactly where to look for what you need, making it easier to gather data from these usually highly structured articles. Make a pile of the articles that particularly interest you, and during the winter or summer break you can read them at your leisure.

Whether for the 15-page research paper or that 4-page summary/critique, taking this approach to reading and summarizing articles leads directly into the first draft of your paper. And perhaps most important, by identifying the author's thesis, intent, or purpose, you are both engaging with the larger issue—your subject—and preparing for your summary and critique of that author's article. You are connecting with the larger assignment, making associations among the various issues. As you work your way through the articles, you're gaining strength and certainty. You're already engaged in building your paper. Your thinking is stimulated, ideas flow, and the more problematic questions you had are now within reach. This process should enhance both your ability to determine what to take note of in your readings and your critical thinking skills. You are learning how to discriminate between what's important and what's not.

A NOTE ON APPROACHING A GROUP OF ASSIGNED ARTICLES

Assignments often call for reading a group of four or five articles. Here's a suggestion similar to the above approach: Scan through all the articles in the group; that is, read the abstracts and skim through the intros. Order the readings according to accessibility—the one that most appeals to you or the one you already know something about to the one that seems most difficult or problematic. Read them, moving from user-friendly to most difficult. When you finally take on that most difficult, most abstract and dense article, you may very well decide it's not so challenging after all, because you've prepared yourself well for it. This same approach can be successfully applied to writing responses to exam questions. Review all the listed questions, begin writing on those most easily within your reach, and proceed to the most difficult.

A NOTE ON WRITING A LITERATURE REVIEW

Most articles in social work journals include a review of the literature, usually just after the introduction. This review is an up-to-date report on the work that scholars have conducted on a subject. The purpose in writing the review is to both convey and critique the published knowledge and thinking about that subject. A well-executed literature review might well include a statement of what research still needs to be done.

When you're writing a literature review, your objective is to gather and organize your material around the issue, research objective, or problem statement you plan to address. Because you want to include only pertinent work, it is essential to develop a discriminating eye for what to include and from which articles. As you make these decisions, think of categories (e.g., thematic, chronological, demographic) in which you can place the various articles; this way, you are already beginning to "write" your paper; that is, the thinking and organizing aspects have begun. Also, keep in mind that although we may strive for an unbiased view on a subject, we are each drawn to certain theories, models, and approaches, any one of which will no doubt influence the categories we set up, the articles we choose, and the rhetorical presentation we make.

If you find an abundance of material, you will likely want to narrow the range of your subject (e.g., by limiting your population in terms of age, gender, ethnicity, SES, etc.). While reading abstracts and skimming through articles, deciding on what to include, keep in mind that most social work research builds on what has preceded it; therefore, look for recently published articles, as they will more likely have considered the most recent data and findings on your subject. However, you will also want to include pioneering research, which you should quickly be able to identify, as it will likely be featured in many of the articles you peruse.

SOME TIPS FOR GATHERING ARTICLES

- Identify and find the big names and the best publications in your research area. Ask your professors for names.
- Conduct an online literature search, using, for example, ProQuest, Social Sciences Abstracts, and Social Work Abstracts.
- Look in bibliographies (reference lists) of the most recently published books and journal articles related to your work; copy the references out in APA style or use software programs such as EndNote.
- Check out the most recent journals in the field, as the articles therein may not yet be in other reference and bibliographic sources.
- Do not rely on one author's description of another essential study or its findings. That one author may have cited the source erroneously or summarized and highlighted that essential study in a skewed manner. Look up the original article.
- Avoid popular press—New York Times, Wall Street Journal, Newsweek—and Internet sources such as Wikipedia and Google and blogs. These are good starting places for identifying terms and learning about issues, but they are no substitute for scholarly work.

SOME TIPS FOR A CRITICAL ASSESSMENT

1. List three questions you want answered by the material.
2. Summarize the major points the author makes.
3. How does the author support his/her position (specific facts, details, etc.)?
4. Were the three questions raised concerning the article answered? List answers. If not, what questions did the author subsequently raise and answer?
5. Evaluate the article, with consideration for the following:

A. What are its strengths and/or weaknesses?

B. Is the subject covered adequately?

C. Is the author's position adequately supported?

D. Is it biased, balanced, etc.?

E. Do you agree or disagree with the author's position and why?

USING ELEMENTS OF FREE WRITING IN THE FIRST DRAFT

Most papers can first be approached using some type of free writing, where your thinking and writing are most connected. Again, Forster's line—"How can I know what I think until I see what I say?"—is in play, pointing to the link between thinking and writing. Using free writing for the first draft immediately puts you in touch with your own ideas, and you'll write them down without editorial commentary from the critic within you. You'll deal later with APA style rules and grammar and punctuation. The first draft is for your eyes only, so don't worry what it looks like. The activity involves getting in touch with your thoughts, keeping in mind that all writing is rewriting. Very, very few people can sit down and knock out a perfect, done, finished paper. According to Weinstein (2010), the Nobel laureate William Faulkner wrote *As I Lay Dying* in an astonishingly fast 47 days, from midnight to 4 a.m., while working at the Oxford, Mississippi, power plant. However, Nobel laureate Toni Morrison has stated that she may think about prewriting issues for up to two years before even putting pen to paper. In music, Mozart could write a masterpiece rather quickly, but Beethoven needed to labor on and on to produce one of his magnificent wonders. Would anyone doubt the genius of any of these four artists?

A NOTE ABOUT WRITER'S BLOCK

For those who experience writer's block and those who say they can't stop their critical self from emerging (e.g., a focus on grammar and/or APA style while writing a first draft), free writing can help you begin the writing without regard for form. If you are blocked, then your thinking is blocked, so free writing can be used to engage with yourself in a dialogue that stimulates your thinking. Another suggestion is to view your writing project as comprising two distinct papers. In the first paper you'll be getting in touch with what you think. This is writing that is creative, free, flowing. Your critical self is nowhere to be found. You're not focused on grammar, punctuation, or APA style, and you know that no one else will read the paper in its present form. Once you feel you've addressed the content issues, which may entail one or two more drafts, you go on to the second paper. Here is where you first work on the organization, the structure of your paper, where you make it fit the criteria laid out by the instructor, and where you pay attention to the length, to headings and subheadings, to transitions, to how well you've developed the issues. Once you've taken care of all these aspects of the paper, then, finally, you move on to address grammar, punctuation, and APA issues. One argument that favors putting off proofreading and APA concerns is that you could easily have 25 first- or second-draft pages of a paper for which the instructor has already stated she'll read no more than 15 pages. You don't want to be editing and formatting 25 pages if you've ultimately got to cut it down to something at least close to the required 15-page length.

INTRODUCTIONS COME LAST

What's most important in social work writing is knowing what's most important—and stating that clearly in the introduction of your paper. Once you've completed the paper, write the introduction—after you've covered all the questions, even after the conclusion. Again, Forster's line is at work. Starting with the intro often slows you down, because at this point you don't know exactly what the paper's about. A major problem among procrastinators and blocked writers is getting stuck in the introduction. They're stuck because they've not yet done the real work of the paper. Once you're finished with your paper, you'll know what you've done, so it will be easier to write your introduction, stating the purpose, the issues to be discussed, and, perhaps, the layout of the paper. However, it is certainly fine to produce a rough, free-writing introduction in your first draft, one that includes a working thesis and a statement of intent, as doing so will provide you with enough structure, direction, and guidance to proceed. Just don't get bogged down writing it.

And in that introduction, along with your purpose and thesis, you will want to state why your subject is an important one. Why should the reader take the time? You may want to provide your most compelling data as early as possible—in the introductory paragraph. Doing so immediately engages the reader to believe that the subject is an important one. For example:

"According to the UN (2008), in a country of 6.8 million people, 80% live below the poverty line." This statement sets the context for the subsequent, more detailed data on the author's intent. "Since 2000, the rate of men leaving the country to find work . . ." Which leads to the issue under discussion: "The effect of the loss of the traditional wage earner on the family . . ." Provided with such information, I, as a reader, already have a sense of both the importance of the subject and what the writer is going to focus on.

MAINTAINING A BOND WITH YOUR READER

In a writing center meeting I may ask the meaning of a particular term, phrase, or issue that suddenly appears, without antecedent and without apparent basis in the subject under discussion. The student will often tell me to read on further in the paragraph to get at the idea she's trying to express, or she'll say that the question I'm raising will be dealt with later—in the next paragraph, on the next page, or in another section. No. You must explain immediately. For example: On page 5 of a paper on a client, a child not previously identified is mentioned. I'll have to ask the age of the boy because he's sharing a bed with his 15-year-old sister, who has already been identified. Is the boy 4 or 14? You do not want the reader wondering about or distracted by such matters. When you bring up a new point, a new client, a new idea, you must immediately clarify or explain it; otherwise the reader is left wondering and/or gets sidetracked, which you don't want.

It is the writer's responsibility to guide, to lead the reader through her paper. A reader wants to believe in what he's reading; he wants to feel that the writer knows of what she writes, that he is in the hands of an expert as he follows the narrative. And the reader needs to trust that what he's reading warrants attention now, not further on in the paragraph or in the following paragraph, not on the next page or in another section. So, for example, when introducing a client and any other people associated with that client and about whom you'll be writing, set the context early on: "The client, who will be referred to as Karen (all client names are pseudonyms), is a single white 32-year-old woman with three children—Jenny, 15, Sue, 10, and Tyler, 4. The family lives in a two-bedroom apartment in a lower-income, ethnically diverse neighborhood in Brooklyn." Not doing so risks losing the reader's attention and/or confidence in the writer. If you want to bring up an issue that you'll explore in depth later, state this clearly upon introducing the issue, and state why you're bringing it up at present.

EDITING YOUR PAPER

Yes, there are a few people who can sit down and write a paper in one draft, but they have invariably first thought it all out in their heads—from beginning to end—spending much time doing so. Most of us need to read, rewrite, read again, and edit two, three times, at least. Here is Toni Morrison on revising:

> I love that part; that's the best part, revision. I do it even after the books are bound! Thinking about it before you write it is delicious. Writing it all out for the first time is painful because so much of the writing isn't very good. I didn't know in the beginning that I could go back and make it better; so I minded very much writing badly. But now I don't mind at all because there's that wonderful time in the future when I *will* make it better, when I can see better what I should have said and how to change it. *I love that part!* (Bakerman, 1978)

Assuming you've written two decent drafts in which you haven't worried about grammar, punctuation, or APA style, editing comes after you're confident about what you've written.

Of great consequence when editing your paper is to keep the following elements in mind, and in descending order of importance: Content, Organization, Development, and Form (APA style, grammar, and punctuation). The order is important because if you've not addressed the most important aspects of your subject (content, etc.), perfection in grammar and APA style will not matter. Some questions to ask yourself:

1. Content: Have I clearly stated the main idea or purpose of the paper, and addressed all the issues? Is the thesis or focus clearly presented and appropriate for the reader (audience)?
2. Organization: How well is it structured? Have I validated the main idea with supporting material? Is it well-thought-out (e.g., general to specific, sequential, significance)? Also, keep in mind that headings and subheadings can help you—and the reader—gain a broad awareness of the substance and direction of the paper.
3. Development: How well does it flow? Have I integrated the various elements, from the literature to class lectures and discussions? Are supporting data sufficient?

4. Form—APA style, grammar, and punctuation: Check for APA style issues, redundancy, problematic wording and terminology (always know
the definition of any word you use!), flawed sentence constructions and
selection, spelling, and punctuation.

Academic writing, and social science writing in particular, calls for short
sentences—one idea per sentence. Because social science writing strives to
present objective data about people and their behavior, it demands clear,
unambiguous expression. But at the same time it must acknowledge and
respect the human subjects under study, so there will always be exceptions,
nuances, distinctions. For example, when making a claim, try to stay away
from what may be called 100 percent words, such as *proof*, *fact*, *truth*, *all*,
and *everyone*. So, rather than using "It is a fact that children with autism . . ."
try "The study shows that children with autism tend to . . ." Rather than
"The author's proof that single mothers . . ." try: "The author presents single mothers as . . ." And remember that the word *most* means more than
half. Also, restrict your use of unneeded modifiers: *kind of*, *type of*, *really*,
definitely, *basically*, *generally*, and, particularly, *very*. And refrain from colloquial language: For example, don't use *a lot*—use *much* or *many*, depending on the context; and don't use *besides*—use *in addition to* or *except for*.
Also, though I'm using contractions here to save space and to help establish a direct, informal voice, don't—do not—use them in formal academic
writing.

So, first, take a ten-minute break between writing and proofreading, especially if it's two o'clock in the morning. Stare out the window, drink a
cup of tea or coffee, phone a kindred classmate who you know is up and
working on the same paper. And keep this in mind: Editing on the computer
screen is quite different than editing on paper (Mantex, 2009). We tend to
be merged, at one, with the computer screen, as though we're reading from
inside our own brain; that is, there's a lack of distance, objectivity, and dis-
crimination that paper, in contrast, allows. To save paper, and the forests,
print out your paper double-sided and in a smaller type size. After all, the
finished product will usually be presented on—and read from—paper, so
take up a pen, make corrections, and enter them into the electronic file.
And, yes, do automatic spelling and grammar checks, but keep in mind that
most grammar-check programs are far from accurate, so if yours flags some
term or line that you intuitively feel is the right one, trust your own judgment, as you'll likely be correct (Bishop, 2005). And never submit a paper

if you haven't read the final draft in your hands (i.e., a paper copy), even if you're turning it in electronically.

Finally, take another five- or ten-minute break, even if it's now 4 a.m. and you're hyped. Change your position, to another room or another chair. Read the paper out loud—it's easier to hear the mistakes in the flow of words. Read the paper from the perspective of your audience—imagine your instructor. And, to focus your attention for a line-by-line review, take a clean sheet of paper and slide it down the page as you read.

APA STYLE

Writing style is understood by the reader as the writer's use of language, from word choice to phrasal patterns and voice (i.e., your personality expressed). Consistency in style is important because you want to maintain a trusting bond with your reader, and you do not want the reader to become distracted from the substance of your writing. In addition, for consistency in appearance and clarity in meaning, all professional writing adheres to one publication style or another, and social work, along with psychology, education, nursing, business, and other social science fields, uses the style of the American Psychological Association ([APA], 2001). Following APA rules governing the citation of reference sources will enhance your ability to communicate effectively; therefore, it is best to know and use these rules. In addition to the importance of knowing who wrote what and when, documenting allows you to build credibility with your audience—you are participating in a conversation in a way that shows you understand the accepted method of discourse.

Much of social science writing can be seen as cumulative. On any given subject, you are both acknowledging, by way of citing, what has come before and trying to add something new (e.g., a new perspective, additional data), so the literature is constantly being replenished and enhanced. And this is why APA style calls for citing the year of your source: The date when a study was done carries much weight, as it assumes, and often incorporates, knowledge already published on your subject; therefore, those articles most recently published will more likely have the most up-to-date data.

The use of proper citation will also help you to avoid plagiarizing a source. Some writers incorporate information from an article into their own writing without referencing the author. This kind of plagiarism often occurs when writers genuinely cannot tell the difference between what they think and what they have read about a subject, or they may think that the author's words, the author's language, express the idea much better than what they would be able to achieve using their own words. Here is a guide to keep in mind: In a 10- to 15-page paper, one with 20 or more reference sources, quotations from the literature will be kept to a minimum. Such a paper will have no more than three well-chosen quotations, and they will be used only to state an essential theory or to capture how an important concept has been expressed. Of course, you will be summarizing and paraphrasing—and therefore providing citations—throughout your paper. In a sentence of 15 to 20 words gleaned from some source, you will paraphrase the author and use 3 or 4 of her key words, terms, and no more than 3 words verbatim.

And even when presenting your own ideas, you will always want to find an authoritative source to cite, because doing so will confirm, back up, and give legitimacy to your own position. Underlining reading texts helps, as does jotting down summaries of the ideas in the reading. Noting your own response to what you've read will help you become aware of the differences between your ideas and those in the text, allowing for a dialogue to develop between you and the author, and this engagement will become the starting point of your first draft.

IN CONCLUSION

Finally, let me offer a quick checklist that you may find helpful when writing any paper that entails research:

1. Formulate your idea, subject, or issue
2. Begin the exploratory research—searching through the databases
3. Narrow or expand your topic as needed—your search criteria
4. Focus in, read abstracts, make choices as to readings
5. Skim through articles, choosing and eliminating
6. Summarize what the chosen authors have stated
7. Decide what to include and from which articles—constructing piece by piece
8. Write the first (free writing) draft(s)—editing for content
9. Write the second draft(s)—editing for organization and development
10. Write the third draft(s)—editing for language issues and APA style

STUDENTS WHOSE FIRST ACADEMIC LANGUAGE IS NOT ENGLISH

Of greatest importance: Become aware of the similarities and differences between the American academic approach and the academic approach from which you come—in thinking, writing, organizing material, reading, and studying. The more you understand these variations, the more control you'll gain over your academic life.

In working with international students, I'll sometimes notice broad thematic methods that diverge from what the instructor has called for. In discussing the issue, what often comes up is an approach to the writing that will appear unfamiliar to a reader trained in the American academic tradition. What follows are a few examples of writing styles that differ from the American approach that I'm referring to.

Some international students and students whose primary language is not English use a writing style that might be described as indirect and/or subtle when compared to the American direct style (Ames & Rosemont, 1998; Fox, 1994; Mao, 2006). An indirect approach may be one that states no clear position or statement of purpose at the onset but that implies one throughout or at the end, or the author's intent may be reached in some circuitous—and for the American reader, confusing—manner. In a more homogeneous culture, such writing may not need to be stated directly, perhaps being the result of shared assumptions between the writer and the reader, but it risks being interpreted as ambiguous to an American reader. Again, it may not be stated due to shared cultural assumptions that the writer holds with his or her audience on the issue being discussed. Some cultures emphasize writing that puts the burden of understanding, of meaning, of interpretation, on the reader—that is, again, not stating directly what is intended (Fox, 1994; Nisbett, 2003). In a review of the literature, Steinman (2003) noted that some cultures emphasize what might be referred to as beautiful writing, in which the emphasis, from an American perspective, may be skewed more toward style than content. Some cultures call the writer to first establish a bond, an intimate relationship, with the reader before addressing an issue under discussion. Also, some cultures may discourage critiquing an author's work and asserting one's opinion, which can lead to writing that lacks both a clearly stated thesis and any detailed, accurate support in one's writing.

All these styles of and approaches to writing have their place, but not in American academic writing, particularly writing in the social sciences. At times I like to think that perhaps because the United States is a heterogeneous society, one in which people hold assumptions that are widely divergent from one another, the dominant writing style, though coming out of the Greek tradition of rhetoric, developed into a particularly direct one so that the various groups of people could better understand one another. The simply structured and uncomplicated five-paragraph essay—with its thesis, position, or premise stated clearly in the first paragraph, followed by arguments and details supporting that clearly stated position in the next three, finishing off with a neat concluding paragraph—may most exemplify this direct American style.

Regarding plagiarism, some cultures maintain standards that are different from those in the United States. Some students have been taught to restate that which has already been stated by the instructor or to find a relevant passage in the literature and copy it into a paper without referencing the author (Shi, 2004; Sutherland-Smith, 2005). We know such practices are not allowed in U.S. academic writing and that one can be expelled from a program for using them. A writer who plagiarizes usually does not intend to deceive but is expressing some uncertainty with the subject. We know that to search out and find research material and then to summarize and critique it means to come to understand the original piece, determine what concepts and terms are essential, and finally transform this knowledge into our own words, without losing the meaning of the original. This thinking/writing task is hardly an easy one for American students, and most of us have struggled to acquire the skill. For someone whose first academic language is not English, developing such a skill can be an even greater challenge.

WRITING IN YOUR FIRST LANGUAGE

If you find yourself thinking through an assignment in your first language, it's a good indication that you should be writing your first draft in that language as well, as a number of studies have indicated (Bean et al., 2003; Friedlander, 1990; Hawras, 1996; Kern, 1994; Lay, 1988). Also, the more intellectually challenging the assignment is, the more reason to write the first draft in your first academic language. Don't assume it will mean more time spent on the assignment because of the need to translate. Grappling with a difficult subject is enough of a burden, but thinking about the issue in one language and writing about it in another can interfere with the thinking/writing process. You could easily spend more time thinking and then writing and rewriting the paper if you stick to English. Rather than struggle through the paper using only English, write the first and/or second draft in your first language, then translate it and work on the editing issues mentioned previously. We are all well aware that language learning is an ongoing process. No one can instantly perform at a high level in a new language, as if he or she were a native speaker.

WRITING ABOUT YOUR OWN CULTURE

In your assignments, always be looking for ways to write about your own culture and/or country, particularly in policy and research papers, where you may not have the familiarity with U.S. social policy issues that an American student may have. Also, most instructors will not know as much as you do about your own country's social policy system, its laws, and the social issues it faces. And if you don't know either, such an assignment will give you the opportunity to conduct research in your primary academic language. In addition, most instructors will welcome your desire to write about your own country. They will learn something new, which is always stimulating. And remember, they read many papers on the same issue, written by American students who will not be stating much that the instructor has not already read, probably many times.

RECOMMENDED READINGS

There are excellent reference books that cover everything from grammar and punctuation to critical thinking and writing research papers. A short list follows, but look through a bookstore's reference section, as authors vary widely in style and expression, and in what they emphasize.

The Bedford Handbook, by Diana Hacker. My favorite all-purpose reference book. Clearly written and user-friendly. Also by Diana Hacker: *A Pocket Style Manual* and *Rules for Writers*.
The McGraw-Hill Handbook of English Grammar and Usage, by Mark Lester and Larry Beason.

Grammar Girl's Quick and Dirty Tips for Better Writing, by Mignon Fogarty. Ms Grammar Girl keeps it simple, engaging, and fun.

Rhetorical Grammar: Grammatical Choices, Rhetorical Effects, by Martha Kolln, sounds heady but is written in a lucid, engaging, intimate voice, as though the author is having a conversation with the reader, making the subject more accessible.

These two books are both informative and fun to read, so they may even stimulate your interest in writing:

Woe Is I: The Grammarphobe's Guide to Better English in Plain English, by Patricia T. O'Conner, is full of sound advice on grammar, punctuation, usage, and style. It's written in a tongue-in-cheek manner, making it a fun read as well.

Eats, Shoots & Leaves: The Zero Tolerance Approach to Punctuation, by Lynne Truss. A number one best seller in the UK, where its author resides, this book is all about punctuation, its history, and its essential place in our lives.

Two classics:

The Elements of Style, by William Strunk, Jr., is a gem of a book covering usage, composition, voice, form, and word choice.

Fowler's Modern English Usage, by H. W. Fowler (R. W. Burchfield, editor), will help you solve prickly questions of grammar, style, syntax, and usage.

Dictionaries and thesauruses:

The Social Work Dictionary (5th ed.), by Robert L. Barker, is the essential dictionary for the practicing social worker.

The Synonym Finder, by J. I. Rodale, is an excellent and user-friendly synonym dictionary. Unlike a thesaurus, which groups words according to meaning, this book arranges its entries in alphabetical order.

Merriam-Webster's Collegiate Dictionary (11th ed.) is the American English language dictionary of choice:

The New Shorter Oxford English Dictionary [CD-ROM] is a shorter, though excellent, version of the OED

Dictionaries and reference books for English-language learners:

The Cambridge Dictionary of American English

The Longman Advanced Dictionary of American English

The Macmillan English Dictionary

The Oxford Advanced Learners Dictionary

A Practical English Grammar, by A. J. Thomson and A. V. Martinet, gives explanations and examples for all grammar points that ESL students might find problematic. This book helps the students formulate their own reasons when they have to tackle ESL scripts that are full of errors that "just don't sound right."

Writing Clearly: An Editing Guide has chapters on all the most common errors that ESL students are likely to make, and all sorts of charts and tips on how to avoid those errors.

The Essentials of English: A Writer's Handbook, by Ann Hogue. A book focused on the needs of non-native writers.

Listening to the World: Cultural Issues in Academic Writing, by Helen Fox, provides a clear view on what international students face in a U.S. academic environment. Her chapter "Worldwide Strategies for Indirection" is must reading for anyone not familiar with U.S. academic life.

References

American Psychological Association. (2001). *Publication manual of the American Psychological Association.* 5th ed. Washington, DC: Author.

Ames, R. T., & Rosemont, H. (1998). *The analects of Confucius: A philosophical translation.* New York: Ballantine.

Bakerman, J. (1978, summer). The seams can't show: An interview with Toni Morrison. *Black American Literature Forum.* Retrieved July 8, 2010, from http://grammar.about.com/b/2008/12/05/toni-morrison-on-writing-without-whining.htm

Bean, J. (2001). *Engaging ideas: The professor's guide to integrating writing, critical thinking, and active learning in the classroom.* San Francisco: John Wiley & Sons.

Bean, J., Cucchiara, M., Eddy, R., Elbow, P., Grego, R., Haswell, R., et al. (2003). Should we invite students to write in home languages? Complicating the yes/no debate. *Composition Studies,* 31(1), 25–42.

Becker, H. S. (2007). *Writing for social scientists: How to start and finish your thesis, book, or article.* Chicago: University of Chicago Press.

Bishop, T. (2005, March 28). A Word to the unwise: Program's grammar check isn't so smart. *Seattle Post-Intelligencer*. Retrieved March 19, 2009, from http://seattlepi.nwsource.com/business/217802_grammar28.asp

Csikszentmihalyi, M. (1990). *Flow: The psychology of optimal experience*. New York: Harper & Row.

Dave, A. M., & Russell, D. R. (2010). Drafting and revising using word processing by undergraduate student writers: Changing conceptions and practices. *Research in the Teaching of English, 44*, 406–434.

Elbow, P. (1981). *Writing with power: Techniques for mastering the writing process*. New York: Oxford University Press.

———. (1998). *Writing without teachers*. New York: Oxford University Press.

Flower, L. (1993). *Problem-solving strategies for writing*. Fort Worth, TX: Harcourt Brace Jovanovich.

Fox, H. (1994). *Listening to the world: Cultural issues in academic writing*. Urbana, IL: National Council of Teachers of English.

Friedlander, A. (1990). Composing in English: Effects of a first language on writing in English as a second language. In B. Kroll (Ed.), *Second language writing: Research insights for the classroom* (pp. 109–125). Cambridge, UK: Cambridge University Press.

Fulwiler, T. (1997). *College writing: A personal approach to academic writing*. Portsmouth, NH: Boynton/Cook

Hass, C. (1989). How the writing medium shapes the writing process: Effects of word processing on planning. *Research in the Teaching of English, 23*(2), 181–207.

Hawras, S. (1996). *Towards describing bilingual and multilingual behavior: Implications for ESL instruction*. Double Plan B Paper, English as a Second Language Department, University of Minnesota.

Howard, V. A. (1990). *Varieties of thinking*. New York: Routledge.

Howard, V. A., & Barton, J. H. (1986). *Thinking on paper*. New York: William Morrow.

Kellogg, R. T. (1990). Effectiveness of prewriting strategies as a function of task demands. *American Journal of Psychology, 103*(3), 327–342.

Kern, R. G. (1994). The role of mental translation in second language reading. *Studies in Second Language Acquisition, 16*, 441–461.

Lay, N. (1988). The comforts of the first language in learning to write. *Kaleidoscope 4*(1), 15–18.

Mantex. (2009). *Editing on screen and paper*. Retrieved March 31, 2009, from http://www.mantex.co.uk/samples/editing.htm

Mao, L. M. (2006). *Reading Chinese fortune cookie: The making of Chinese American rhetoric*. Logan: Utah State University Press.

Nisbett, R. E. (2003). *The geography of thought: How Asians and Westerners think differently . . . and why*. New York: Free Press.

Pauk, W., & Owens, R. J. Q. (2010). *How to study in college*. Beverly, MA: Wadsworth.

Rivard, L. P., & Straw, S. B. (2000). The effect of talk and writing on learning science: An exploratory study. *Science Education, 84,* 566–593.

Ruggiero, V. R. (1991). *The art of thinking: A guide to critical and creative thought.* New York: HarperCollins.

Sharples, M. (1999). *How we write: Writing as creative design.* New York: Routledge.

Shi, L. (2004). Textual borrowing in second language writing. *Written Communication, 21*(2), 171–200.

Steinman, L. (2003). Cultural collisions in L2 academic writing. *TESL Canada Journal, 20*(2), 80–91.

Sutherland-Smith, W. (2005). Pandora's box: Academic perceptions of student plagiarism in writing. *Journal of English for Academic Purposes, 4,* 83–95.

Weinstein, P. (2010). *Becoming Faulkner: The art and life of William Faulkner.* New York: Oxford University Press.

3

WRITING FOR PUBLICATION IN SOCIAL WORK JOURNALS

Ronald A. Feldman

THERE ARE TWO COMPELLING REASONS for social workers to write for publication: for personal enjoyment and fulfillment and to advance the knowledge base of the social work profession. The optimum conditions for writing are obtained when both of these motivating forces converge in the course of a single writing project. The absence of either can greatly reduce the likelihood that the other will be fully realized.

With the expectation that both of these forces motivate readers of this chapter, the following discussion sets forth guidelines and recommendations for writers who wish to prepare a manuscript for publication in a social work journal. It views professional writing as a *process* that consists of three discrete phases: the pre-writing phase, the writing phase, and the post-writing phase. Central considerations for each phase are discussed below.

THE PRE-WRITING PHASE

Myriad challenges emerge as one considers whether to write a manuscript for journal publication. These include selecting the topic of your manuscript, delineating and refining the goals of the manuscript, choosing the preferred form of publication, identifying the most appropriate journal, reviewing relevant background literature, collecting and organizing pertinent data, and envisioning the final draft. Each of these tasks warrants special attention.

SELECTING THE TOPIC

The first challenge in preparing a journal article is to identify a topic that is both engaging and likely to constitute a meaningful contribution to the social work literature. This is no small matter given the fact that one can select from among a potentially limitless universe of topics. When contemplating a journal publication, it is first and foremost essential to recognize that your substantive interests need to correspond closely with the publication priorities of the journal's editors. Once shared interests have been identified, you must be cognizant of the particular decision-making criteria that editors of that journal employ when reviewing a manuscript for publication. Two overarching goals prevail: (1) does the manuscript advance the knowledge base of social work, and (2) does it advance the interests and stature of the journal itself?

Within these parameters, the process for evaluating manuscripts submitted for publication may vary from one journal to another. For the most part, however, it includes such factors as the originality and innovativeness of the submitted manuscript, the extent to which it builds upon the existing literature and promotes further advances, the rigor of logic and analysis, the practical utility of its formulations and findings, and, of course, the clarity and persuasiveness of exposition. Nevertheless, perhaps your paramount consideration when deciding whether to write a manuscript is to identify a topic that you consider interesting, engaging, and important.

DELINEATING AND REFINING GOALS

The next challenge entails defining the cardinal goals that you wish to achieve by preparing a manuscript for journal publication. You must clearly conceptualize the specific contributions that you desire to make to the professional literature. In what particular ways do you want to advance the knowledge base of professional social work? Do you seek to formulate or test one or more practice interventions? Do you want to improve a particular type of research methodology? Do you intend to codify or synthesize a particular body of knowledge? Do you aim to apply knowledge drawn from the social sciences or allied health professions toward social work practice? Or do you perhaps wish to bring to readers' attention the intricacies and practice implications of a particular case illustration?

The goals that underlie preparation of a manuscript can be myriad, just as the possible topics for it can be virtually limitless. Therefore, precision and clarity are essential when delineating a manuscript's publication goals. Your ability to clearly specify and articulate those goals will substantially determine the extent to which your written product can advance social work's knowledge base and, therefore, be received favorably by a journal's reviewers.

Furthermore, the clarity and specificity with which you articulate the manuscript's goals will shape the structure, substance, and focus of your manuscript as well as define the particular venues where it can be published.

CHOOSING THE PREFERRED VENUE FOR PUBLICATION

Integrally related to the preceding challenge is the question of whether you should aim to write your manuscript for publication as a book, a monograph, a journal article, or something else. Journals usually are the preferred venue for publication when the ideas or findings that one wishes to introduce to the professional literature can be directed toward a narrowly defined group of readers with shared substantive and professional interests. Moreover, they are the preferred venue when the writer's formulations or findings can be explicated adequately within the severe length constraints usually imposed by journal editors.

Even though this chapter focuses primarily on journal publication, it would be remiss not to affirm that the knowledge base of social work also can be advanced through groundbreaking books, monographs, and other forms of knowledge dissemination. Importantly, however, the number of journal publications in social work has grown dramatically in the last three decades. This increase has resulted from numerous factors, including the rapid growth of specialized fields of practice in social work, the considerable weight accorded peer-reviewed journal publications by academic promotion and tenure review committees, the comparatively short turnaround time between submitting a manuscript to a journal and its subsequent publication, and the formidable complexities and time demands of writing much lengthier book manuscripts.

Yet, given the rapid proliferation of journal publications in social work, there is a concomitant need to codify, analyze, synthesize, translate, and apply the publications in ways that can enhance the competencies of practitioners. Often this need can be addressed most readily through the publication of well-developed books and monographs, which may appear in the form of original treatises or as edited compilations examining a given topic. In both formats, however, the preponderant content that is presented or referenced is likely to have appeared previously in the form of a published journal article. In view of the determinate role of journal publications in furthering the knowledge base of social work, then, this chapter focuses primarily upon writing for professional journals.

IDENTIFYING THE MOST APPROPRIATE JOURNAL

A vast array of journals can be found in social work, the allied health professions, and the social sciences. As the number of journals burgeons, it becomes increasingly difficult to select the most appropriate one in which to publish any given article. Yet the selection of a journal will inevitably shape the way you write your manuscript. Journals vary in their respective guidelines for content, format, and length. They also vary in terms of prestige, impact, number of manuscripts received, and selectivity.

Perhaps the paramount criterion for selecting a particular journal for publication is the fit between your topic and the journal's substantive priorities and, correspondingly, the interests of its readers. In addition, factors such as journal selectivity and impact in the field may be of considerable importance for writers whose publications will be scrutinized by academic review committees as evidence for a promotion or a tenured appointment.

When the latter considerations are central, writers are well advised to become acquainted with the extensive literature that seeks to rate the differential impact of various professional journals (see, for example, Garfield, 1998, 2006; Lindsey, 2002). It is necessary to realize, though, that impact ratings often are significantly flawed. Most are predicated merely upon the number of times that published articles have been cited in the literature, without accounting for the fact that the citations of a particular journal article may reflect assessments of its content that range from extremely positive to extraordinarily negative. Because ratings seldom take such crucial variations into account, they can be misleading and of limited value in determining the actual "impact" of a journal's articles or authors (for further discussions of journal selection and impact ratings, see Coleman, 2007; Doreian, 1989; Moed & Van Leeuwen, 1995; Nisonger, 2004; Saha, Saint, & Christakis, 2003; Seglen, 1997; and Thyer, 2008). Hence, a writer's subjective decision about a publication venue must balance such considerations as the manuscript's fit with a journal's particular priorities; the likelihood of acceptance; and the journal's readership, stature, and impact, however it is defined.

REVIEWING RELEVANT BACKGROUND LITERATURE

Before you begin to write your manuscript, it is essential that you review the professional literature about your selected topic. If nothing else, this exercise enables you to determine whether someone else has already published a version of the contemplated manuscript. Nothing better assures rejection of a manuscript than a reviewer's realization that it has essentially already been written by someone else or that it contributes little or nothing new to the literature.

A comprehensive literature review enables the writer to identify crucial gaps, inconsistencies, limitations, and unresolved issues in the pertinent literature. This, in turn, helps the writer to delineate a promising topic, focus the manuscript with greater specificity and clarity, and pinpoint for readers exactly how the manuscript will advance current knowledge. Even more, significant portions of the literature review are likely to be incorporated into the manuscript itself so as to document or dramatize the importance of the selected topic and elucidate how the writer aims to advance the profession's knowledge regarding it.

COLLECTING AND ORGANIZING PERTINENT INFORMATION

Writing a manuscript involves collecting and organizing relevant background information. In the case of manuscripts that are based upon quantitative or qualitative research, writing will be made easier if the requisite data are organized in ways that are logical, inclusive, retrievable, and directly related to the substantive areas being addressed. Useful discussions in this regard appear elsewhere in the social work literature (see, for instance, Grinnell & Unrau, 2008; Holosko, 2008; Reid, 2008; and Rubin & Babbie, 2006).

The preparation of journal articles can be facilitated greatly if the author keeps logs or notebooks that permit the recall and retrieval of ideas, events, and data that can inform the manuscript. More than ever before, these tasks can be expedited by contemporary computing and data storage technologies. Without such systematic efforts, promising insights and innovations are lost or forgotten and thus fail to find their way into the professional literature.

ENVISIONING THE FINAL DRAFT

Before you begin to write, it is especially helpful to outline your vision of a final draft. Without an outline, your early drafts may be disjointed, rambling, or poorly focused, and critical aspects of the topic could be neglected or overlooked. The most expeditious way to develop an outline is to succinctly list the key headings and subheadings that you intend to discuss. This process enhances the likelihood that all of the major considerations will be addressed in your manuscript and that they will be presented logically, incrementally, and in ways that make the manuscript more comprehensible and engaging for readers. The typical components of such an outline for journal manuscripts are described in the next section.

THE WRITING PHASE

As you commence the actual writing of the manuscript, you need to address operational, substantive, and stylistic considerations. The foremost operational consideration entails creating a physical and social environment that is conducive to writing. The key substantive issues are the structure, format, and specific content of the manuscript. Stylistic considerations pertain to your choices from the wide range of possible writing styles, from formal and regimented to informal and spontaneous. Although journal editors generally prefer manuscripts with a clearly defined structure, their respective preferences and requirements can vary considerably. Hence, before you begin to write, it would be a good idea to become well acquainted with the specific guidelines for substance and style that are required by the particular journal to which you wish to submit your manuscript.

CREATING A POSITIVE WRITING ENVIRONMENT

Authors too often neglect the conditions under which they will write. Yet undue constraints within the immediate physical or social surroundings can make the writing process much more difficult than need be. Since individuals respond differently to different environments, the same set of working conditions will not necessarily fit all writers, but several basic factors ought to be regarded as environmental prerequisites.

Perhaps foremost is the actual physical setting where the writing is done. It should be a place that affords sufficient quiet for serious thinking and writing. There should be adequate heat, light, and fresh air. Likewise, there should be easy access to materials that are needed for the manuscript, including books, data sets, supplies, and a computer. Comfortable seating must be available if you expect to write for protracted periods of time. And it is essential that the setting offer few distractions, such as noisy office mates, frequent meetings, or a blaring television set. In the absence of a readily accessible writing environment, it may be necessary to seek other places to write. For instance, public and private libraries can provide most of the supports needed for serious writing.

Time is another key variable that must be considered. For the actual writing of the article, it is helpful to set aside blocks of two, three, or more hours on several days or evenings each week. The question of schedules and deadlines also falls into this category. When a publisher or coauthor wishes to impose a deadline for completing a manuscript, it must be realistic. Deadlines that are inordinately short can force one to unduly rush the writing process and prepare a manuscript that is underdeveloped or otherwise inadequate. The writer ought not to accept such deadlines. However, once a realistic deadline has been agreed upon, the writer should establish a timetable and identify specific interim milestones by dividing the process into discrete phases and assigning a date for the completion of each. If done appropriately, this exercise will set reasonable working goals and provide a mechanism for monitoring and, if need be, modifying the rate of progress. Even more, this process introduces a system of self-reinforcement, since the achievement of each interim goal increasingly motivates the writer to proceed apace toward the next marker.

STRUCTURING CRITICAL COMPONENTS OF THE MANUSCRIPT

Professional journals often require that manuscripts submitted for publication conform to a specific structure or format. Authors should carefully review in advance the particular priorities and guidelines of the journal to which they wish to submit their manuscript. In the absence of clear guidelines, a detailed examination of articles that have appeared in recent issues of the journal may clarify and expand the available options with regard to structure, format, and style. In general, research-oriented journals encourage structures that include all or most of the following components.

ABSTRACT   Nearly all professional journals require that an abstract precede the text of a published article. It must concisely describe the main goals, features, findings, and results of the manuscript. The American Psychological Association (2001) recommends that abstracts be limited to 120 words. Key words or descriptors may be highlighted in order to direct readers to the article and expedite electronic retrieval. Although the abstract usually is not written until the manuscript has been completed, you may find it useful to prepare a rough draft even before you begin writing. This exercise may help you to better formulate and organize the writing process, even though you will need to redraft the abstract after the manuscript is completed.

INTRODUCTION AND BACKGROUND Your manuscript typically should begin with an introductory section that states concisely why you selected that particular topic. It should indicate why you deem the topic to be important and of particular interest to the journal's readers (such as social work practitioners, administrators, researchers, or educators). You should point out how your manuscript will extend or deepen the knowledge base of professional social work and how it will address critical gaps, inconsistencies, or dilemmas in the literature. In addition, you can indicate how, if at all, the manuscript builds upon your prior research and publications or will lay the groundwork for future work in the field. This section is especially important, since it provides the initial impressions that may largely shape the reader's decision about moving on to the entire text.

LITERATURE REVIEW AND PROBLEM FORMULATION In large part, the literature review section of your manuscript will reveal the extent to which you are, in fact, an expert in the area being addressed. This section should briefly summarize previously published formulations, issues, findings, and trends related to your topic. In turn, it should lead to your own conclusions and formulations regarding the literature. While your literature review should be concise, it must nevertheless encompass most or all of the central considerations that pertain to your topic.

The literature review should be inclusive, logically ordered, and, above all, constructively critical. By using it to specify significant deficiencies of the literature, you will lay the groundwork for the advances that you wish to propose. It should culminate in a clear explication of the core topics and issues that you intend to address in your own manuscript. Ultimately, it should indicate how you have formulated the problems to be examined and, in doing so, prepare readers for the next sections of your manuscript, where the interventions and methods for addressing those problems will be elucidated in detail.

DESCRIPTION OF PROGRAM AND INTERVENTIONS Key attributes of the pertinent interventions and programs discussed in your manuscript should be described in sufficient detail to permit readers to learn precisely how they were designed and delivered and, if need be, how to implement them on their own. However, if these details are excessively complicated or extensive it may be advisable to explicate them more fully in an appendix to the manuscript, or even in a companion monograph that is referenced in your article manuscript. Either of these strategies can be employed to reduce the extent to which such content detracts from the overall cogency and impact of your narrative.

METHODOLOGY   If your manuscript reports the findings of a research study, the methodology section may pose a special challenge. Depending upon the size and complexity of the study, reviewers will want to know crucial methodological details in order to judge its rigor and suitability for publication. First and foremost, they will want information regarding the actual research measures employed in the study. For instance, is the study based upon interviews, survey data, or time-sampling observations of subjects' behavior? Regardless of the measures selected, the writer must address a wide range of issues. With regard to behavioral observations, for example, how was the time sampling conducted? Who performed the observations? How were the observers trained? At what junctures were the time samples acquired? What coding categories were employed? Were the measures subjected to tests regarding their validity and reliability? Were the observers evaluated for the accuracy of their judgments? And can the resulting data be regarded as useful for social work practitioners, educators, and/or researchers? Similar questions can be posed for most other types of research-oriented publications, including surveys, field experiments, and case studies. In the methodology section it also is advisable for the writer to articulate significant limitations— as well as strengths—of the interventions and research methods employed in the study. Doing so will convey to the reader the extent to which the study has, in fact, been conducted with skill and integrity.

Likewise, attributes of the subjects and sampling procedures should be described in detail. Was random sampling used? If not, what types of sampling procedures were utilized? What are the key demographic features of the sample with regard to such important attributes as gender, race, age, ethnicity, and related variables? How representative is the sample of the larger community or universe from which the subjects were drawn? Will it be possible to validly generalize the findings from the sample studied to other populations?

If the manuscript is based on research that examines one or more treatment interventions or independent variables, it will be strengthened considerably if you articulate the precise nature of the interventions and specify the procedures employed to develop them, train the intervention agents, and determine the extent to which the interventions were applied faithfully. This section of the manuscript should also describe the human subjects review procedures that were used.

The methodology section is also the place for detailed specification of the study's data analysis procedures. Advances in computing technology and software development have yielded a wealth of new methods for analyzing research data. Your manuscript will be strengthened to the extent that it can describe your rationale for selecting the particular data analysis procedures that you used and demonstrate how they were applied appropriately. If this information is inordinately complex, it may be advisable to present some of it in an appendix.

RESULTS   Many readers view the results section as the most important component of a published article. Indeed, the main reason for writing an article is to share the singular findings of your study with a journal's readers. Nevertheless, the results section has little meaning if you have not already done a credible job of drafting the antecedent portions of the manuscript. No matter how striking the results of your study, they will gain little acceptance if the manuscript lacks crucial background information about subject selection and the measures, interventions, and data analysis methods employed.

When the results section presents findings about multiple variables or complicated statistical interactions, it usually is necessary to provide considerable detail about them. In such instances, the key to keeping the reader engaged is to organize the results section in a logical, orderly, and lucid way that incrementally sheds light on your findings. Here the generous use of headings and subheadings can be helpful. Likewise, emphasizing key findings by means of italics, underlining, or boldface type can be useful. Explanations of complex findings may also be facilitated by visual aids, such as figures, graphs, and tables.

DISCUSSION   The discussion section of a manuscript enables the writer to progress beyond the sometimes dry and dispassionate findings that appear in the results section. It is in this part of the manuscript that the author can elucidate the nuances and, more important, the various practice and policy implications that emerge from the study. Careful writing of this section can energize both the manuscript and the reader. Many readers who find it daunting to interpret the research methods and data analysis techniques of a journal publication may read only this section. Therefore, you should make every effort here to articulate clearly the implications of your manuscript for social workers who may wish to apply its results in their practice. It is also important to specify significant caveats, concerns, and issues that may somehow limit application of the findings or require that they be modified or adapted for practice.

SUMMARY AND CONCLUSIONS   Nearly all journal articles offer a summary section or, alternatively, both summary and conclusions sections. This part of your manuscript should be as concise as possible. It succinctly informs the reader about the main findings and conclusions of your manuscript. Typically, this section of the manuscript is no lengthier than several paragraphs.

REFERENCES   All sources that have been cited in the text of your manuscript should be listed in the references section. While many different formats may be employed, perhaps the most widely accepted is the one promulgated by the American Psychological Association (2001).

APPENDIXES   Appendixes are especially useful when the writer wishes to present detailed information that might perhaps be distracting or of secondary importance if it appears in the main body of the manuscript. In research-based articles, for instance, a full copy of a questionnaire, survey instrument, or diagnostic measure is often presented as an appendix. Likewise, as noted above, if a section of your manuscript requires unusually detailed explication or interpretation that, too, might best be placed in an appendix.

STYLING AND EDITING THE MANUSCRIPT

Regrettably, many manuscripts that have the potential to introduce significant innovations to the social work literature fail to find their way into print merely because their writers pay insufficient attention to critical stylistic and editorial concerns. Four stylistic considerations are particularly important.

First, it is essential that the author adopt a writing style that is appropriate for the specific type of article. The first-person style of a personal memoir, for instance, will be very different from that of a research report. Second, the author should employ the same style of writing consistently throughout the article. Third, the writing should be as straightforward, jargon-free, and concise as possible. And fourth, the author should recognize that prose is not always the best means for conveying exceptionally complex ideas and information to readers. Consequently, he or she may need to complement the expository material with figures, graphs, tables, and other visual aids that can enhance the clarity and efficiency of the presentation. As the time-honored maxim states, a well-designed picture can, in fact, eliminate the need for thousands of superfluous words.

Above all, it is essential to edit, proofread, and continuously refine your manuscript as it progresses toward a final draft. Even a few instances of poor grammar, awkward sentence structure, incorrect spelling, or careless typographical errors can doom its chances for publication. Common examples of such errors are described extensively elsewhere (see, for instance, Furman, 2007 and Glicken, 2008).

In short, then, when drafting a manuscript one needs to write concisely, avoid jargon, compose lucid sentences, and attend as closely as possible to editing and typographical oversights. You can gain invaluable assistance with these issues by sharing an early draft of your manuscript with one or more colleagues who are willing to provide constructive feedback. This strategy can be especially beneficial if they have published previously in your preferred journal or have served as journal reviewers or editors themselves.

POLISHING THE MANUSCRIPT

Though completion of the first draft of your manuscript presents legitimate cause for celebration, you should realize that it is highly improbable that the project will require no further attention. Nevertheless, at this juncture you may find it helpful to take a short break. You may want to turn your attention to other manuscripts or projects and then return to the first draft with renewed objectivity and vigor. Upon doing so, you may discover significant—if not altogether startling—omissions, misstatements, or oversights that you did not notice before.

When you have completed the second draft, it is again prudent to ask a colleague to review and constructively critique it. This can be especially beneficial if the colleague is not only a skilled writer but an expert in the particular area that is the subject of your manuscript. Although some writers are reluctant to prepare multiple drafts of a manuscript, each and every version is likely to result in noteworthy improvements. Usually the greatest gains are realized in the first several drafts; at some point you will reach a point of diminishing return, where the additional effort that can be put into a manuscript is not offset sufficiently by accompanying gains. That point is different for every writer, in every project, and you are the only one who can judge when it has been reached.

THE POST-WRITING PHASE

The author's work may not be finished even after the manuscript has been submitted for review by a journal. In fact, some of the most challenging issues may emerge at this point.

RESPONDING TO REVIEWERS' CRITIQUES

Typically, feedback about your submitted manuscript will be provided by an editor after it has been reviewed. Whether the manuscript has been accepted or rejected for publication, the editor will usually send the reviewers' anonymous comments to you. Some manuscripts are accepted for publication without requests for further revision. In other instances, the editor will either reject the manuscript or recommend that it be revised and resubmitted for further consideration. In either case, the reviewers' comments can aid you in preparing a revised draft that is likely to be superior to the original. Even when a first draft has been accepted for publication, editors sometimes will request certain modifications so that the manuscript conforms more readily to the journal's standards or better addresses the particular interests of its readers. The author should respond to each of the reviewers' criticisms and suggestions individually and thoroughly.

MONITORING POST-PUBLICATION REACTIONS

Once your manuscript has been published, it is likely to elicit responses— both positive and negative—from the journal's readers and from others. Some reactions may reflect misinterpretations or misrepresentations of your findings. Others may reveal differing theoretical, methodological, or ideo-logical orientations. And still others may represent entirely valid concerns about your manuscript. It is prudent to closely monitor *all* of the reactions and to respond to them promptly and forthrightly. Failure to do so is likely to be viewed as disinterest or inability on the writer's part.

PREPARING FOR THE NEXT MANUSCRIPTS

When you are writing an intervention-based manuscript, it is important to appreciate the value of diligently maintaining your original database and de-vising ways to sustain or augment it in the future. The utility of studies that are based upon data acquired from an original sample of subjects can be increased substantially if ongoing contacts with the subjects are maintained over a period of many years. This will enable you to acquire long-term follow-up data from them and to evaluate the extent to which any improve-ments in their outcomes have been maintained over time.

One frequently employed mechanism for attaining such goals is to mail a birthday card or send an e-mail message every year to each person who participated in the study, along with a request that he or she provide up-dated information about any changes in residence or contact information. This will make it easier to locate your subjects if you should want to obtain follow-up data from them. Failure to implement such a procedure virtu-ally precludes the possibility of conducting fruitful longitudinal research with your sample and, consequently, of writing subsequent manuscripts that might build upon your previous work.

Writing for journal publication is a skill that develops incrementally, like most other competencies. Consequently, the feedback and constructive cri-tiques that emanate from one's early efforts can lead to significant improve-ments over time. A writer's visibility and stature in the scholarly world is likely to grow as his or her publications further advance the profession's knowledge base about a given subject. This does not mean that writers ought to limit themselves to scholarship on a single topic throughout their career. To the contrary, as one builds a scholarly agenda, both the writer and the profession are likely to benefit when interests are developed in related realms that can complement the author's core areas of expertise. Indeed, the advances that evolve in one field of inquiry often can facilitate breakthroughs in others. Some of the most profound advances in a given realm have resulted not from an original and dramatic intellectual breakthrough but from insights that were borrowed from one field of endeavor and applied laterally to another.

Finally, after your manuscript has been published and subjected to the reactions of readers, it will be advantageous if you contemplate how subsequent manuscripts might be able to build upon it to further advance social work's knowledge base. Writers often do not realize how this can be accomplished until the reactions of reviewers and others have raised the critical questions that sometimes are needed to galvanize further advances in a field of inquiry. Hence, social workers should appreciate the fact that publication of a manuscript is but one important step in the continuous process not only of developing and refining one's writing skills but also of advancing one's intellectual leadership within the profession.

SUMMARY

Writing for publication in a professional social work journal is a process that consists of three distinguishable phases, namely, the pre-writing phase, the writing phase, and the post-writing phase. Each phase requires that the writer attend to a wide array of tasks. If the writer accomplishes those tasks efficiently and effectively, he or she can maximize the probability that a manuscript will receive favorable reviews and will be accepted for publication.

Among the tasks of the pre-writing phase are selecting the topic, delineating and refining the goals of the manuscript, choosing the preferred venue for publication, identifying the most appropriate journal for the manuscript, reviewing relevant background literature, collecting and organizing pertinent information or data, and envisioning the final draft.

The writing phase requires that attention be directed toward creating a positive writing environment, structuring critical components of the manuscript, styling and editing the manuscript, determining whether and how to incorporate visual aids, and refining and polishing the manuscript. Among the typical structural components of a journal manuscript are sections that discuss introductory and background considerations, describe key features of the pertinent programs or interventions, explicate the research methodologies that have been employed, present the results of the writer's research, discuss and further explicate the practical implications of the findings, and summarize the manuscript's overall findings and conclusions.

Central features of the post-writing phase include responding to reviewers' critiques, monitoring post-publication reactions, and preparing for subsequent manuscripts. Through careful attention to these tasks and others, social workers are bound to improve their writing skills incrementally, heighten the likelihood that their written products will be accepted for publication, contribute significantly to the knowledge base of social work, and consequently advance their own professional and personal development.

References

American Psychological Association. (2001). *Publication manual of the American Psychological Association* (5th ed.). Washington, DC: Author.

Coleman, A. S. (2007). Assessing the value of a journal beyond the impact factor: Journal of Education for Library and Information Science. *Journal of the American Society for Information Science and Technology, 58*, 1148–1161.

Doreian, P. (1989). On the ranking of psychology journals. *Information Processing and Management, 25*(2), 205–214.

Furman, R. (2007). *Practical tips for publishing scholarly articles: Writing and publishing in the helping professions.* Chicago: Lyceum Books.

Garfield, E. (1998). Long-term vs. short-term journal impact: Does it matter? *Scientist, 12*(3), 10–12.

———. (2006). The history and meaning of the journal impact factor. *Journal of the American Medical Association, 295*(1), 90–93.

Glicken, M. D. (2008). *A guide to writing for human service professionals.* New York: Rowman and Littlefield.

Grinnell, R. M., & Unrau, Y. A. (Eds.). (2008). *Social work research and evaluation: Foundations of evidence-based practice* (8th ed.). New York: Oxford University Press.

Holosko, M. J. (2008). Evaluating quantitative research studies. In R. M. Grinnell & Y. A. Unrau (Eds.), *Social work research and evaluation: Foundations of evidence-based practice* (8th ed., pp. 423–444). New York: Oxford University Press.

Lindsey, D. (2002). Building a research journal in child welfare. *Children and Youth Services Review, 24*, 881–883.

Moed, H. F., & Van Leeuwen, T. N. (1995). Improving the accuracy of the Institute for Scientific Information's Journal Impact Factors. *Journal of the American Society for Information Science, 46*, 731–732.

Nisonger, T. E. (2004). The benefits and drawbacks of impact factor for journal collection management in libraries. *Serials Librarian, 47*(1/2), 57–75.

Reid, W. J. (2008). Writing reports from research. In R. M. Grinnell & Y. A. Unrau (Eds.), *Social work research and evaluation: Foundations of evidence-based practice* (8th ed., pp. 409–422). New York: Oxford University Press.

Rubin, A., & Babbie, E. (2006). *Research methods for social work* (5th ed.). Pacific Grove, CA: Wadsworth.

Saha, S., Saint, S., & Christakis, D. A. (2003). Impact factor: A valid measure of journal quality? *Journal of the Medical Library Association,* 91(1), 42–46.

Seglen, P. O. (1997). Why the impact factor of journals should not be used for evaluating research. *British Medical Journal,* 314(7079), 497.

Thyer, B. A. (2008). *Preparing research articles.* New York: Oxford University Press.

4

INSCRIBING KNOWLEDGE: WRITING RESEARCH IN SOCIAL WORK

Denise Burnette

The corpus of scientific writing is one of the more remarkable of human literary accomplishments. Innovation, complexity, intricacy, social influence, and simple extensiveness of the corpus make scientific writing interesting as an object of study and important as part of human society.

BAZERMAN, *SHAPING WRITTEN KNOWLEDGE*

SETTING ASIDE THE OBVIOUS REPRESENTATIONAL challenges of being twice removed from the lived experiences that are the bases of most research in social work, the task of writing about writing research poses a host of unruly demands. These challenges stem at least in part from the multiple purposes, myriad forms, and thorny political issues that tend to accompany any effort to bring order and meaning to an always messy, at times chaotic, social world.

To manage the breadth and complexity of this topic, I begin by stating what I will and will not attempt to cover about writing research. To further delimit the scope and sharpen the focus, I then offer a working definition of research and slightly narrower operational descriptions of three main types of research: informational, analytical, and argumentative. From there, I introduce British philosopher Stephen Toulmin's influential model of structured argumentation and use it to describe and illustrate the processes of formulating and writing argumentative inquiry. Finally, building on the implications of this model for multiple approaches to argumentation, I conclude with a discussion of the purpose, structure, content, and style of writing in quantitative, qualitative, and mixed methods research.

I will not address grant writing or writing for scholarly publication, nor will I speak to writing research on specialized methods or fields of social work practice. Other chapters in this volume thoroughly attend to these topics. Rather, I will concentrate on questions of why, how, and to what ends social workers inscribe new knowledge and fresh conceptualizations of existing knowledge to inform and advance social work practice, public policy, and professional education. To facilitate the application of concepts, I will use examples from the field of kinship foster care throughout the discussion.

INFORMATIONAL, ANALYTIC, AND ARGUMENTATIVE RESEARCH

As with all research writing, we must first establish a workable definition of our topic. A University of Idaho (2008) information literacy Web site cites a 2003 Cambridge dictionary definition of research as: "a detailed study of a subject, especially in order to discover (new) information or reach a (new) understanding." Authors of this Web site go on to note that the term "research" is used to describe a number of similar and often overlapping activities, all of which involve a search for information but differ in major ways. Table 4.1 depicts three such research activities, each with its own distinctive features and related implications for writing.

The overall purpose of writing research is to convey knowledge by situating it in a broader context and, in the case of social work, by linking this knowledge to practice, policy, and professional education in an effort to improve the quality of human life. The first type of research involves straightforward factual reporting, while the second requires the skillful use of evidence to synthesize relevant facets of an issue. In the third approach, argumentation, the researcher poses an open-ended question that lacks a ready answer, then uses evidence to convince readers of a particular stance on a debatable topic.

The compilation of accurate, timely factual information and the careful synthesis of high-quality evidence are certainly essential features of professional writing. However, the bulk of social science research is ultimately concerned with how best to use such information and evidence to craft a strong argument and to translate it effectively into real-world applications.

TABLE 4.1 Types of Research and Their Essential Characteristics

RESEARCH QUESTION	ESSENTIAL CHARACTERISTICS
1. How many kinship foster care placements took place in the United States in 2007?	A search for **individual facts or data**. May be part of the search for a solution to a larger problem. Concern is with facts rather than with knowledge or analysis, and answers can normally be found in a single source.
2. How did relatives become part of the formal U.S. foster care system in the late twentieth century?	A **report** or **review**, not designed to create new information or insight but to collate and synthesize existing information. Usual sources are books, articles, and Web sites. [*Note*: Often includes activities like #1]
3. What factors influenced the rapid growth of kinship care providers in the U.S. foster care system?	Involves gathering and analyzing a body of information or data and **extracting new meaning** from it or **developing unique solutions** to problems or cases. [*Note*: Always includes #2 and usually includes #1; may also involve gathering new data]

Source: Adapted from University of Idaho (2008). *Information literacy*. Retrieved May 28, 2008, from http://www.webs.uidaho.edu/info_literacy/modules/module2/2_1.htm

Let us consider the issue of integrating relatives into the child welfare system's foster care program. Valid, timely facts about growth of the foster care population and the program's carrying capacity are clearly needed. This information is instructive in its own right, and it can be used to develop or strengthen an argument for a program or policy to address the unmet needs of children in need of foster care and their caregivers.

In analytic research, one would develop further expertise on the topic by breaking it down into its component parts, carefully studying each part, then reorganizing the parts into a new whole from a novel perspective. Examples of components might be the responsibilities and training of foster parents and their relationships with the child, the child's parents, and the child welfare system. After critically examining existing information and perspectives on these and other salient aspects of the topic, one would synthesize the findings so as to make an original contribution to academic and professional discourse on this topic.

An argumentative research paper, by contrast, takes a stand on an issue and uses evidence to substantiate that position. The position serves as the thesis of the written account. It is conventionally stated early on in order to set the stage for the developing argument. It is then revisited at the end of the paper within the context of the larger body of knowledge on the topic. The study topic should be worth arguing, which is to say that the thesis statement should be sufficiently engaging, important, and controversial. Asking whether relatives should be involved in the lives of foster children may not be worth arguing, for instance, since they fill a sizable gap in the traditional foster care program, and most people are likely to endorse the ongoing support of relatives in the lives of children.

A more suitable argumentative research question might be: "Do children who are placed in kinship foster care, a program that permits relatives of children in need of out-of-home care to serve as foster parents, fare better socially, emotionally, and academically than those who are placed in traditional foster care?" Or a researcher might wish to examine the lived experiences of children in kinship and/or traditional foster care. She would still need to critically review and evaluate existing information on salient aspects of the topic. However, these phases of the research process would serve more as evidence to support the theses of an argumentative report. The current emphasis on evidence-based practice in the applied professions in many ways represents an effort to strengthen the sources, strategies, and outcomes of argumentation.

British philosopher Stephen Toulmin's (1958, 1969) classic (and many times revised and reworked) model on structured argumentation may help to clarify and advance our thinking here.[1] Essentially, this model is used to establish a claim that is based on facts. In an effort to bring together the best current thinking on the Toulmin model and its uses, Hitchcock and Verheij (2006) described the model as "a process that has a field-invariant pattern of analysis that is designed to do justice to the process of defending a particular claim against a challenger" (p. 1). The fact-finding activities and the process of collating and synthesizing relevant data described above are incorporated into the argumentation process via "micro-arguments," which constitute a series of successive articulations and challenges (Toulmin, 1958, p. 94).

Toulmin, Rieke, and Janik (1984) identified six elements of a good argument. I present each here, with illustrative examples from a hypothetical study on whether federal and state governments should establish subsidized guardianship programs for kinship foster parents. The purpose of such programs would be to better equalize the level of financial stipends and other supports for these two types of care.

1. **Claim.** The first step in an argument is to make a claim. The claim is the thesis statement. It answers the question "What are you trying to prove?"

Example: Kinship foster families and traditional foster families should receive comparable levels of support.

2. **Grounds.** The grounds (data) provide the support or evidence for the claim. They answer the question "What have you got to go on?" Grounds may comprise one's own theoretical or empirical data or that of others.

Example: The number of children in need of foster care roughly doubled between 1982 (262,000) and 2005 (513,000).[2] During this same period, the availability of traditional foster homes declined markedly. To help fill the resultant gap, the child welfare system introduced kinship foster care programs, whereby children are placed with relatives and, in compliance with a Supreme Court decision in *Miller v. Yoakim* (1979), provided with financial and other types of support. Yet the level of support is typically set lower for kinship foster parents. Indeed, in some states, the differential is nearly threefold.

3. **Warrant.** The warrant is the reasoning (rule or principle) that connects the claim and its grounds, legitimizing the claim by showing the grounds to be relevant. It answers the question "How did you get there?" A warrant may be explicit or unspoken and implicit.

Example: Most children enter foster care because of parental maltreatment or neglect. Kinship foster parents have basically the same level and types of responsibility and care for these children as traditional foster parents do.

4. **Backing.** The backing is further facts or reasoning used to support or legitimize the warrant. Backing is what we come up with if asked "why in general this warrant should be accepted as having authority" (Toulmin, 1958, p. 103). Warrants can be established by claims of fact or value and are often backed by cause and effect or comparative reasoning.

Example: The Adoption and Safe Families Act (Public Law 105–89) of 1997 recognized that reunifying children with their parents—a major goal of the Adoption Assistance and Child Welfare Act of 1980 (Public Law 96–272)—is not always in the best interests of the child. Moreover, the stability and familiarity of kinship placement may help to mitigate the trauma associated with placement.

5. **Qualifier.** Many arguments are valid only if qualified or accepted with reservations. A good argument thus makes these qualifications explicit and reasonable. Qualifiers can apply to the claim or the warrant and are often expressed by adverbs such as "probably," "possibly," or "certainly."

Example: Not all kinship options are equally viable. There will always be some relatives who are willing but unable to care for young kin, even with a lot of external supports.

6. Rebuttal. A good argument considers both sides.

Example: Children whose relatives are willing and able to care for them may differ in important ways from those who lack this option. Traditional foster care placements are less stable than kin placements, for example, and multiple moves may well exacerbate children's emotional, behavioral, and academic problems. Children in traditional foster care may thus need more intensive supports.

This discussion of Toulmin's model of structured argumentation is intended to demonstrate the significance of the argumentative process in writing research. It is also meant to illustrate how this model can serve as a useful vehicle for evaluating the relative strengths and weaknesses of the sources and arguments we use in our own writing.

In addition to laying the groundwork for argumentation, Toulmin is credited with helping to "move epistemology away from formal, technical logics and toward informal, applied, and rhetorical logics—working methods of argument that recognize rhetoric's epistemological power . . . and the complex and complementary natures of human rationality and language" (Clauss, 2008, ¶ 5; see also Sujan, Smith, & Harrison, 2006). Contending that research is incomplete unless it considers informants' cognitions (processes) *and* the causes of social practice (outcomes), Toulmin (1982) references the value of quantitative and qualitative data in argumentation and in assessing the relative worth of conflicting claims. A researcher might use numeric data to rule out alternative hypotheses in a quantitative study, for example, or he might need to choose from multiple plausible interpretations of qualitative data.

To recap, I began this section with a definition of research as the study of a subject that aims to discover new information or achieve new understandings of a phenomenon. I then described three basic types of research, each with a unique purpose: the factual report, the analytical study, and the argumentative approach to systematic inquiry. Toulmin's structured model of argumentation, which incorporates all three types of research, requires one to identify the parts of each argument that one makes, systematically comparing and evaluating the claims, the data, and the warrants along with any qualifiers, rebuttals, or backing that pertain.

The thesis of a research project, the arguments used to develop the thesis, and the evidence used to support the arguments are all grounded in a philosophical paradigm. Schwandt (1989) referred to a paradigm as a "worldview" that encompasses beliefs about the nature of reality, knowledge, and values, whereas Morgan (2007) preferred to mix the "worldview" version of paradigms with that of "epistemological stances." Paradigms influence a researcher's methodological decisions, and these in turn contribute to the purpose, structure, content, and style of writing. I will return in a moment to a consideration of how these four elements of writing play out in quantitative, qualitative, and mixed methods research. A brief note on the "paradigm debate" in the social sciences will help to establish a context for that discussion.

THE PARADIGM DEBATE AND SOCIAL SCIENCE RESEARCH

Two distinct approaches to social science inquiry, one quantitative and the other qualitative, have competed for dominance since the early 20th century. The 1962 publication of Thomas Kuhn's *The Structure of Scientific Revolutions* is widely regarded as a watershed in social science research. Asserting that research is "a strenuous and devoted attempt to force nature into the conceptual boxes supplied by professional education" (p. 5), Kuhn did much to catalyze the academic "paradigm wars" of the latter half of the twentieth century.[3]

Guba and Lincoln (2005) provided a thorough treatment of the history, nature, and implications of this debate. The reader is referred to a series of succinct tables in which Guba and Lincoln compared a number of defining features of five major philosophical paradigms for social science inquiry: positivism, post-positivism, critical theory, constructivism, and participatory. Suffice it to say here that the conflicts are rooted in differing philosophical paradigms that in the extreme (e.g., positivism vs. critical theory, constructivism or participatory) hold fundamentally incompatible views on all major aspects of research, including written reportage.

To extend the earlier example, a researcher may wish to know how children in kinship foster care fare during their placement. Arguing from a post-positivist stance and using quantitative methods, she might test the hypothesis that a group of children in kinship care will fare better on certain dimensions of well-being than a comparable group of children who are in traditional foster care. Using a quasi-experimental design, she would compare standardized numeric data on samples of children in each setting to test this hypothesis.

In contrast, a critical or constructivist approach would highlight social and cultural contexts of kinship foster care, including historical antecedents (critical theory) and locally constructed understandings (constructivist) of the experience. These approaches are transactional and dialectic, meaning that they are deeply embedded in the contexts of and interactions with study participants. In addition, these two approaches have chiefly instrumental aims in the sense that they aspire, albeit in different ways, to effect change in the "real world."

A critical theorist might study the political economy of public foster care in order to equalize supports for foster parents in different types of placements, maintaining that this would affect how foster children fare. A constructivist might seek the same distal and proximal changes in the system and its clientele through a careful and compelling report of the narrated experiences of various stakeholders in each type of care.

There is now a general acceptance of the relative merits of variant approaches to social science research. Paradigmatic features continue to shape the research process, of course, but their influence only partially accounts for writing decisions. Oakley (1999) observed that the interplay of epistemological position and methodological decision is also affected by contextual factors such as peer behavior, funding sources, publishing prospects, and professional politics— "both in its commonly understood sense and as applied to power relations between academics and those who take part in research" (p. 247). Writers must thus seek outlets that are compatible with paradigmatic assumptions and features of their work *and* with their personal and professional proclivities and commitments.

In sum, disputes over a range of philosophical paradigms, each with a particular worldview, have fueled a vigorous debate on two major approaches to social science inquiry, one quantitative and the other qualitative. The value of both approaches is now widely acknowledged. But their differences will be evident in the discussion on writing quantitative, qualitative, and mixed methods research that follows, since the purpose of a study guides one's choice of methodology, which in turn influences the structure, content, and mode and style of representing findings.

WRITING QUANTITATIVE RESEARCH

The quantitative research tradition emanates from positivist and, more typically of the social sciences, post-positivist paradigms. This worldview espouses a realist epistemology, ascribing to notions of an independently existing, value-free social reality; a correspondence of truth between words and this impartial reality; and a belief that developing propositional knowledge is a worthy goal per se. Consistent with the tenet of objectivity in quantitative methods, the post-positivist researcher attempts to maintain neutrality through enumeration, aggregation, and causation (Reichardt & Rallis, as cited in Abusabha & Woelfel, 2003).

Apropos of these foundations, quantitative study designs are in effect detailed operational plans for testing predetermined hypotheses (see Piergiorglo, 2003). Their purpose is for the most part to determine the relationships between one or more operationally defined independent variables and a dependent (outcome) variable in a population. Statistical sampling is used, usually in conjunction with descriptive or experimental designs, to establish associations or causality between these variables.

Written accounts of quantitative research are highly systematic and tightly scripted, and the structure, content, and style of writing reflect the philosophical underpinnings and purpose of the study. In keeping with an objectivist epistemology, for instance, the language, tone, and voice are scientific, matter-of-fact, and impersonal, and the writing style is frank and terse. The *Publication Manual of the American Psychological Association* ([APA], 2010) dictates standards for academic writing in most social and behavioral sciences. In addition to requirements for a title page, abstract, references, and appendixes, the section of the manual titled "Structure and Content" calls for an introduction, followed by methods (subjects, participants, apparatus, design, and procedure), results, and discussion. This layout reflects the standard format of an experimental study and is consistent with the steps of the traditional scientific method. The quantitative report must also conform to the conventional space limitations of 18–20 pages in peer-reviewed journals.

Finally, when writing a research report it is important to know how its quality will be assessed. Quantitative studies are mostly judged on appropriateness and sophistication of the methodology and on the logic and consistency of the argument or analysis. Russell (2005) offered a helpful checklist of criteria for evaluating the written quantitative report.

WRITING QUALITATIVE RESEARCH

With roots in critical theory and postmodern thought, qualitative research relies on relativist epistemologies to discover new insights and to develop novel understandings of social phenomena. The subjectivist and contextualized perspectives of this approach have inspired the time-honored traditions of interactionism (Atkinson & Housley, 2003; Denzin, 2001) and interpretivism (Denzin, 1997; Hiley, Bohman, & Shusterman, 1991) that are forerunners of more-contemporary feminist, ethnic, and "alternative" approaches.[4]

There are no standardized ways to organize qualitative research for publication, and, as Ponterotto and Grieger (2007) noted, the guidelines that do exist often provide inadequate space or flexibility to fully present the content. Qualitative researchers are often advised to either adjust to prescribed APA sections (Choudhuri, Glauser, & Peregoy, 2004; Drisko, 2005) or modify writing within sections. Morrow (2005) suggested that qualitative reports be framed as follows: introduction, methods (orienting paradigm, specific research design or approach, researcher-as-instrument note, participants, sources of data and data analysis), results, and discussion.

Drawing on Morrow (2005) and Elliott, Fischer, and Rennie (1999), Ponterotto and Greiger (2007) proposed an outline for writing qualitative research that integrates post-positivism and constructivism. They suggested 35–45 double-spaced pages—the APA manual simply urges brevity and parsimony. Following a title page and abstract, Ponterotto and Greiger called for an *introduction* of 6–7 pages in which post-positivist writing is guided by theory and previous research and constructivist writing draws on theory and research to inform, but not stifle, innovation and discovery.

A *method* section 6–7 pages in length then describes and references one's paradigmatic approach and uses thick description[5] to address pertinent aspects of the methodology. Whereas post-positivist writing focuses more on managing researcher subjectivity and highlighting procedures for achieving consensus in data analysis, constructivist writers should address researcher positionality, researcher as instrument, researcher subjectivity and reflexivity, and data adequacy (Morrow, 2005). In this section, writers should own their perspective; describe participants' characteristics, study context, and sampling procedures; address quality control and ethical considerations; and report analytic methods. Writers of constructivist studies should also provide evidence of data saturation.

A *results* section of 9–11 pages is meant to provide a robust account of study findings. Ponterotto and Greiger (2007 asserted that thick description of the methods used in post-positivist *and* constructivist studies should easily lead into thick description and thick interpretation[6] for both paradigms in this section. As noted, post-positivist studies will lean toward testing theory or findings that were reviewed in the *introduction* section. By contrast, constructivist studies should report on researcher-participant relationships, co-construction of findings, and participants' experiences of the phenomena being studied. There is often an expectation of discovery, and quotes are useful for supporting thematic findings. Using these data, readers should be able to assess the "adequacy-of-data" and the "adequacy-of-interpretation" (Morrow, 2005).

Finally, a *discussion* section of 5–6 pages should further summarize and integrate study findings and link the results to the broader field of inquiry and to professional practice, policy, education, and future inquiry. This section should also discuss study limitations and any procedural and ethical challenges. References, tables and figures, and appendices, as indicated and permitted, conclude reports of research in the post-positivist and constructivist paradigms.

Analytic strategies such as coding and thematic analysis are geared toward organizing, managing, and making sense of large bodies of data, often using a software program. Qualitative data are principally narrative, but may also take other, more sensate forms such as photographs or sounds. Data collection, data analysis, and writing are iterative and recursive processes that fundamentally inform one another.

The discovery-oriented purpose of qualitative projects influences the structure, content, and style of writing. However, these approaches pose unique opportunities and challenges. On the one hand, freedom from the lockstep strictures of the scientific method opens possibilities for creativity, innovation, and emotional expression. Likewise, there is less social and intellectual distance between the researcher and participants, which can encourage a more reflexive and dialogic writing style. Attention to power dynamics is made explicit, and participants' voices feature prominently, individually or in concert with the researcher's voice, in the text. Finally, overt, value-laden commitments to advance social change characterize many types of qualitative research, especially those that arise from critical theory.

On the other hand, the qualitative umbrella is so broad and its methods so diverse that the writing task can be bewildering. Consider a grounded theory study in which a researcher seeks to understand how foster children's relationships with their caregivers develop. The structure of qualitative articles is flexible, yet many grounded theory reports hew more or less to the traditional research process. Prescribed sampling and coding procedures are thus reported along with data from field notes and memos, all with an eye to developing a substantive theory on the phenomenon of interest.

Another researcher might wish to engage kinship foster parents in a participatory action project designed to teach them advocacy skills for changing local or statewide supports. The content and tone of this type of article would likely be more explicitly political and the language more rhetorically charged. Study participants or community advisors might well join the researcher in authoring a report on the study.

The growing use and wider acceptance of the panoply of qualitative research methods have complicated the assessment of quality. This is particularly the case with innovative approaches that overlap with the humanities—for example, linguistics, dramaturgy, and poetry (Caulley, 2008). Central to this complication is a fundamental disagreement about whether and how standardized criteria should be used to assess the quality of interpretive research.

Sandelowski and Barroso (2002) submitted that practice disciplines should replace epistemic criteria for evaluating written reports with aesthetic and rhetorical concerns (see also Sandelowski, 1998). In contrast, Barbour (2001) called for the judicious use of criteria-based checklists in assessing qualitative research. From a more middle ground, Choudhuri, Glauser, and Peregoy (2004) and Ponterotto and Grieger (2007) offered a modified checklist and a set of process-oriented guidelines respectively for qualitative manuscripts.

Regardless of whether qualitative writers use standardized assessment criteria, they, like their quantitative counterparts, should attend diligently to the strength, relevance, and coherence of their thesis, the arguments they use to develop it, and the evidence they use to buttress their arguments—and all of these components should be consistent with the tenets of the particular philosophical paradigm on which they draw.

MIXED METHODS RESEARCH

An increasingly common strategy for capitalizing on the advantages of both quantitative and qualitative methods and, when possible, compensating for their respective disadvantages is to combine, or mix, them in the same study. Rocco, Bliss, Gallagher, and Perez-Prado (2003) described two "positions" on the "mixed methods" approach. The first, a pragmatist stance, suggests the selection of "whatever philosophical and/or methodological approach works for the particular research problem under study" (Tashakkori & Teddlie, as cited in Rocco et al., p. 21; see also Hanan, 2006 and Tashakkori & Teddlie, 2003). The second, a dialectical position, aims to achieve "a synergistic benefit" by integrating post-positivist and constructivist paradigms. This approach appeals to a plurality of interests, voices, and perspectives (Greene & Caracelli, as cited in Rocco et al., 2003).

Greene and Caracelli (1997) proposed five purposes for mixing methods:

1. Triangulation, or convergence on the same phenomenon to improve validity;
2. Complementarity, which aims to get at related but different facets of a phenomenon;
3. Development, or the use of results from one phase of a study to develop another phase;
4. Initiation, or the intentional analysis of inconsistent qualitative and quantitative findings to derive new insights; and
5. Expansion, or using multiple components to extend the scope of a study.

Rocco et al. (2003) noted that design options increase as the purpose of mixing methods moves from triangulation to expansion.

The level of complexity inherent in these multiple purposes and myriad designs suggests that the structure, content, and style of writing in mixed methods research are variable and depend at least partly on whether the main purpose of the investigation is quantitative, qualitative, or of equal weight. A focus-group study to develop and validate measures for a system-wide survey of kinship foster parents (developmental purpose) might be more qualitative, explaining the process of developing the measures via focus-group methodology and analysis. A second article might privilege survey results and use the focus-group data to verify or support these findings (triangulation purpose). Either way, the writer must be fluent in and able to effectively communicate the rationale for mixing methods and the multiple methodological aspects of the study.

CONCLUDING THOUGHTS AND FUTURE DIRECTIONS

I began this chapter with a review of three major types of research: informational, analytic, and argumentative. Using Stephen Toulmin's model of structured argumentation as a basis for crafting research reports, I then laid out the major points of this process together with illustrative examples. Finally, I highlighted several key points of the paradigm debate in the social sciences as a context for discussing how worldviews influence the purpose, structure, content, and style of writing research. I conclude with a look to the near future of writing social work research in terms of the implications of three current contexts—interdisciplinary collaboration, globalization, and translation—for writing. These directions, both singly and together, may well require new paradigms and new models for the conduct of research and its writing.

In the first instance, knowledge development and the technologies to apply it are increasingly interdisciplinary. This trend will require social work researchers to clearly articulate and effectively communicate the vital contributions they are able and obligated to make to interdisciplinary research teams. Interdisciplinary research heightens the need for negotiated roles in dissemination, including writing, and the need to publish and read more widely in interdisciplinary journals. The content, structure, and style of writing interdisciplinary research depend, as in other approaches described above, on the purpose of the study and on the paradigmatic assumptions that apply in it.

With respect to these assumptions, pervasive globalization is rapidly rendering inadequate the paradigms that have shaped knowledge development in Western societies. As we have seen, research reports are essentially stories based on argumentation. In this way, they resemble writing in other genres, as the products of all are deeply embedded social, cultural, and politically situated narratives. Kee (2004) argued that methodology, ways of knowing, and culture are inextricably linked. Demonstrating the ill fit between Western research methodologies and her work in Malaysia, she concluded that the theoretical development of culturally appropriate social work practice needs to be situated within indigenous research paradigms.

If research and practice are to be truly mutually informative,[7] authors of accounts that emanate from indigenous research paradigms must be able to sufficiently comprehend, adequately capture, and meaningfully communicate the elements of writing in local contexts. Moreover, research and practice are located within a particular time, space, and place, and both activities reflect societal conditions that are continuously changing. Writers who use indigenous paradigms and culturally specific research methods that draw on local knowledge and conditions may thus need to set their work within both local and rapidly changing global contexts.

Finally, there is now widespread emphasis on the translation of research, or the meaningful application of research knowledge in real-world settings. To a considerable extent, this trend overlaps the current stress on evidence-based practices and policies in the professions. Assuming that these emphases will continue—and indications are that they will at least for the immediate future—the timing for modifications or alternatives to current paradigms may be especially propitious.

Morgan (2007) critically reviewed the theory and practice of mixing qualitative and quantitative methods over the past few decades. He used the interdisciplinary perspective of "science studies," which defines a paradigm as "the consensual set of beliefs and practices that guide a field" (Zammito, as cited in Morgan, p. 48). He concluded with a compelling appeal for social scientists to revisit a "pragmatic approach" as a way to redirect attention toward the methodological and away from the metaphysical concerns that have dominated this literature for several decades. Morgan's advice is surely worthy of the studied attention of social work researchers.

Finally, regardless of the purposes, paradigms, and methodologies of social work research, written reports should be guided by elements of good reportage. Roscigno and Hodson (2007) listed the following uniform and rigorous standards for reporting: (1) clarity in writing, interpretation, and organization; (2) theoretical development and insight; (3) empirical rigor and focus, as defined by a particular methodological tradition; and (4) innovation and creativity in research questions, theoretical argument and development, and/or research methodology and analysis design. The clearer this focus is, the more purposeful, engaging, and influential the writing of social work research will be.

References

Abusabha, R., & Woelfel, M. L. (2003). Qualitative vs. quantitative methods: Two opposites that make a perfect match. *Journal of American Dietetics Association*, 103(5), 566–569.

Adelman, L., Lehner, P. E., Cheikes, B. A., & Taylor, M. F. (2007). An empirical evaluation of structured argumentation using the Toulmin Argument Formalism. *Systems, man, and cybernetics*, Part A, *IEEE Transactions*, 37(3), 340–347.

American Psychological Association. (2009). *Publication manual of the American Psychological Association* (6th ed.). Washington, DC: Author.

Atkinson, P., & Housley, W. (2003). *Interactionism: An essay in sociological amnesia*. Thousand Oaks, CA: Sage.

Barbour, R. S. (2001). Checklists for improving rigour in qualitative research: A case of the tail wagging the dog? *British Medical Journal*, 322(7294), 1115–1117.

Bazerman, C. (2000). Shaping written knowledge: The genre and activity of the experimental article in science. WAC Clearinghouse Landmark Publications in Writing Studies: http://wac.colostate.edu/books/bazerman_shaping/ Originally published in print, 1988, by University of Wisconsin Press, Madison.

Caulley, D. N. (2008). Making qualitative research reports less boring: The techniques of writing creative non-fiction. *Qualitative Inquiry*, 14, 424–449.

Cheikes, B. A., Lehner, P. E., Taylor, M. F., & Adelman, L. (2004). *An empirical evaluation of structured argumentation using the Toulmin Argument Formalism*. Bedford, MA: MITRE Corporation, Center for Integrated Intelligence Systems.

Choudhuri, D., Glauser, A., & Peregoy, J. (2004). Guidelines for writing a qualitative manuscript for the *Journal of Counseling and Development*, 82, 443–446.

Clauss, P. J. (1999). Stephen Toulmin's *The uses of argument: A contextual re-reading*. Unpublished doctoral dissertation, Ball State University, Muncie, Indiana.

Denzin, N. K. (1989). *Interpretive biography*. Newbury Park, CA: Sage.

———. (1997). *Interpretive ethnography: Ethnographic practices for the 21st century*. Thousand Oaks, CA: Sage.

———. (2001). *Interpretive interactionism* (2nd ed.). Thousand Oaks, CA: Sage.

Denzin, N. K., & Lincoln, Y. S. (Eds.). (2000). *The SAGE handbook of qualitative research*. (2nd ed.). Thousand Oaks, CA: Sage.

Drisko, J. W. (2005). Writing up qualitative research. *Families in Society*, 86(4), 589–594.

Elliott, R., Fischer, C. T., & Rennie, D. L. (1999). Evolving guidelines for publication of qualitative research studies in psychology and related fields. *British Journal of Clinical Psychology*, 38, 215–229.

Fulkerson, R. (1996). The Toulmin Model of argument and the teaching of composition. In B. Emmel, P. Resch, & D. Tenney (Eds.), *Argument revisited, argument redefined* (pp. 45–72). Thousand Oaks, CA: Sage.

Geertz, C. (1973). Thick description: Toward an interpretive theory of culture. In *The interpretation of cultures: Selected essays* (pp. 3–30). New York: Basic Books.

Greene, J. C., & Caracelit, V. J. (1997). Defining and describing the paradigm issue in mixed-method evaluation. In J. C. Greene & V. J. Caracelli (Eds.), *Advances in mixed-method evaluations: The challenges and benefits of integrating diverse paradigms* (pp. 5–17). (New Directions for Evaluation, No. 74). San Francisco: Jossey-Bass.

Guba, E. G., & Lincoln, Y. S. (2005). Paradigmatic controversies, contradictions, and emerging confluences. In N. K. Denzin & Y. S. Lincoln (Eds.), *Handbook of qualitative research* (3rd ed.) (pp. 191–216). Thousand Oaks, CA: Sage.

Hanan, A. A. (2006). A view from somewhere: Explaining the paradigms of educational research. *Journal of Philosophy of Education, 40*(2), 205–221.

Hiley, D. R., Bohman, J., & Shusterman, R. (Eds.). (1991). *The interpretive turn: Philosophy, science, culture.* Ithaca, NY: Cornell University Press.

Hitchcock, D., & Verheij, B. (Eds.). (2006). *Arguing on the Toulmin Model: New essays in argument analysis and evaluation.* New York: Springer.

Kee, L. H. (2004). The search from within: Research issues in relation to developing culturally appropriate social work practice. *International Social Work, 47*(3), 336–345.

Kuhn, T. S. (1962). *The structure of scientific revolutions.* Chicago: University of Chicago Press.

———. (1970). *The structure of scientific revolutions* (2nd ed.). Chicago: University of Chicago Press.

Miller v. Yoakim, 440 U.S. 125 (1979).

Morgan, D. L. (2007). Paradigms lost and pragmatism regained: Methodological implications of combining qualitative and quantitative methods. *Journal of Mixed Methods Research, 1,* 48–76.

Morrow, S. L. (2005). Quality and trustworthiness in qualitative research in counseling psychology. *Journal of Counseling Psychology, 52,* 250–260.

Oakley, Ann. (1999). Paradigm wars: Some thoughts on a personal and public trajectory. *International Journal of Social Research Methodology, 2*(3), 247–254.

Piergiorglo, C. (2003). *Social research: Theory, methods, and techniques.* Thousand Oaks, CA: Sage.

Ponterotto, J. G. (2006). Brief note on the origins, evolution, and meaning of the qualitative research concept "thick description." *Qualitative Report, 11,* 538–549.

Ponterotto, J. G., & Grieger, I. (2007). Effectively communicating qualitative research. *Journal of Counseling Psychology, 35*(3), 404–430.

Proctor, E. K. (2005). The question of questions: An agenda for social work practice research. International Practice Research Symposium, University of Albany, Albany, New York. June 2, 2005.

Reichardt, C. S., & Rallis, S. F. (Eds.). (1994). *The qualitative-quantitative debate: New perspectives.* Thousand Oaks, CA: Sage.

Rocco, T. S., Bliss, L. A., Gallagher, S., & Perez-Prado, A. (2003). Taking the next step: Mixed methods research in organizational systems. *Information Technology, Learning, and Performance Journal, 21*(1), 19–29.

Roscigno, V. J., & Hodson, R. (2007). Engaging sociological audiences: Editors' comment. *American Sociological Review, 72*(2), iii–v.

Russell, C. L. (2005). Evaluating quantitative research reports. *Nephrology Nursing Journal, 32*(1), 61–64.

Sandelowski, M. (1998). Writing a good read: Strategies for re-presenting qualitative data. *Research in Nursing & Health, 20*(4), 375–382.

Sandelowski, M., & Barroso, J. (2002). Reading qualitative studies. *International Journal of Qualitative Methods, 1*(1), 1–47.

Schwandt, T. (1989). Solutions to the paradigm conflict: Coping with uncertainty. *Journal of Contemporary Ethnography, 17*(4), 379–407.

Sujan, M. A., Smith, S. P., & Harrison, M. D. (2006). Qualitative analysis of dependability argument structure. In D. Hitchcock & B. Berheij (Eds.), *Arguing on the Toulmin Model: New essays in argument analysis and evaluation* (pp. 1–20). Netherlands: Springer.

Tashakkori, A., & Teddlie, C. (2003). *The handbook of mixed methods in the social and behavioral sciences.* Thousand Oaks, CA: Sage.

Toulmin, S. E. (1958/1969). *The uses of arguments.* Cambridge: Cambridge University Press.

———. (1982). The construal of reality: Criticism in modern and post-modern science. *Critical Inquiry, 9,* 93–111.

Toulmin, S. E., Rieke, R., & Janik, A. (1984). *An introduction to reasoning* (2nd ed.). New York: Macmillan; London: Collier Macmillan.

Tumposky, N. R. (2004). The debate debate. *The Clearing House, 78* (2), 52–56.

University of Idaho. (2008). *Information literacy.* Retrieved May 28, 2008, from http://www.webs.uidaho.edu/info_literacy/modules/module2/2_1.htm

PART TWO

APPLIED PROFESSIONAL WRITING

5

STUDENT WRITING IN FIELD EDUCATION

Kathryn Conroy

FIELD EDUCATION IS THE PLACE where social work theory and practice come together. Social work education is a two-part endeavor. Alongside courses in the classroom, students are assigned to a field placement, an organization or agency, where social work students (interns) practice implementing, under the watchful eye and trained ear of a seasoned social worker, the values, theories, and skills introduced in the classroom.

Student writing in fieldwork also falls into two basic parts. Some writing is formal reporting and communication that takes the form of case notes, chart notes, progress notes, other records, letters, memos, and e-mails. Other student writing is reflective in nature and is designed to stretch a student's general self-awareness, cultural sensitivities, professional vocabulary, and developmental competence with clients, citizens, patients, or other students. The purpose of this chapter is to identify and explore both reporting and reflective social work writing in fieldwork.

Many field placements (internship assignments) are set in social service and social welfare advocacy organizations. For example, a student may be placed in a settlement house, a child welfare program, or a senior center. In general, each of these settings is run by a social worker, who is usually the executive director, and the entire organization is governed by social work philosophy and practice. However, a significant proportion of social work students are also assigned to agencies where social workers are not in charge and where the ethos of the organization may be quite different from that of a social work organization. Some examples include hospitals, schools, legal services, governmental offices, and labor unions. These sites are referred to as "host" settings, meaning that social workers are hosted by professionals who are not social workers. For example, they may be health care professionals, lawyers, or educators.

FIELDWORK WRITING: A THREE- OR FOUR-PERSON ENDEAVOR

Three parties generally participate in fieldwork writing: the social work student, the social work supervisor at the fieldwork site, and the fieldwork advisor, who is the social work school or program's representative to the fieldwork site and is responsible for supporting the educational work of both the student and the organization-based supervisor. Sometimes a fourth person is also involved in the student's fieldwork writing—a task supervisor who may or may not be a social worker. The task supervisor works with a social work intern on one particular project or activity, while the fieldwork supervisor is responsible for monitoring, offering feedback, and evaluating all parts of the social work intern's performance. This chapter will focus primarily on students' fieldwork writing, while giving some attention also to the perspectives of the cast of characters who study that writing—the fieldwork supervisor in the fieldwork agency, the school's fieldwork advisor or liaison, and, sometimes, the task supervisor in the field organization.

FORCES THAT SHAPE THE FORMS OF STUDENT WRITING IN FIELDWORK

Social workers and social work interns in the twenty-first century are called upon to honor each field agency's reporting requirements, as well as the respective social work school's or program's field writing stipulations. Like the profession of social work itself, field writing requirements shift with the times. Much of agency- and organization-based reporting today is actually dictated by governmental and private funding sources. These recording and reporting mandates generally mean, in our computer-rich world, that brevity is important and accuracy is paramount in order to ensure that reimbursement, refunding, and reauthorization are sustained. More importantly, clients' lives may be negatively affected if fieldwork recording and reporting are inaccurate, verbose, or unclear. Case record keeping takes a shape that is specific to the purpose and auspices of its organizational setting, be it a mental health clinic, a drug rehabilitation program, a school, or a center for new immigrants and refugees. Many organizations run their own extensive in-service training on the keeping of case notes and case records in order to meet the demands of their funding and licensing sources, as well as to protect their clients, whose records run the risk of being subpoenaed. For example, a husband involved in divorce proceedings might try to subpoena the notes of his wife's psychotherapist to help build his case for gaining child custody. It is therefore necessary that social work students understand the ways in which their own case or chart notes, process recordings, and field logs could influence clients' interests and welfare, as well as the service and legal priorities of their field internship organization.

Meanwhile, each social work school and program creates a fieldwork manual (which in the twenty-first century is usually online) that outlines the expected forms of reflective fieldwork writing that are pedagogically inspired. These forms of written reflection are distinct from the case notes, chart notes, progress notes, or reports that organizations require of all workers as well as interns. Appendixes A, B, C, and D, which follow the text of this chapter, represent the current reflective writing requirements of the Columbia University School of Social Work. Just as case or chart notes that a social work intern writes serve as a report to the supervisor, fieldwork agency, its funders, and governmental and professional auditors about the nature of work being done with a client or group, so reflective fieldwork writing offers the fieldwork supervisor and fieldwork advisor (liaison) evidence of the student's thoughts and feelings, ethics, fieldwork relationships, and applications of classroom learning and supervisory input.

VARIED METHODS IN FIELDWORK WRITING

Students themselves emphasize different methods in their study. Some pursue the clinical method, while others study policy, administration, organizing, or advanced generalist practice methods. Each method has its own curriculum and course of study, in addition to the fundamentals that all social work students learn. The context of the field placement is defined by the intersection of the type of setting (social work service vs. profession of the host) and the method of study (clinical, advanced generalist, policy, etc.). Regardless of the setting of the placement or the method pursued by the student, writing is an indispensable skill. It will have a particular emphasis, format, and flavor derived from the setting or method, but the essentials, covered in this chapter, will be the same across social work methods.

PROCESS RECORDINGS

Foremost in field writing is that which is done purely for an educational purpose: writing as learning/teaching activity shared by the student and the field instructor. This form of writing is most typified by *process recordings*, an instrument used in teaching both basic social work skills and advanced methods of practice. Some history of process recordings is helpful. In 1979 Esther Urdang, who began writing about field education in 1964 and is an expert on process recording, faculty advising, and field instruction, stated that "process recording has long suffered a bad press" (p. 1). She went on to point out that process recordings were dreaded by both students and field instructors. However, she insisted on their utility, stressing that they (1) teach students the necessity of recall, thus keeping them sharp and attentive during an interview; (2) enhance the process of active integration as the student relives the interview; and (3) provide an opportunity for analytical reflection, which in turn provides the basis for a supervisory exchange. Twenty years later, Fox (2000) pointed out the many advances in recording technology, including audio and video, which at this point are fairly easy to implement with the proper equipment, informed consent, and safeguards. However, process recordings remain the simplest and maybe the best way for students to track their progress and to analyze their work and the best tool for field instructors to use in teaching.

One need only surf the Web to find examples of process recordings, from almost every school of social work in the country (mostly, but not exclusively, from master's programs). What these examples have in common is that students must:

1. Reconstruct the interview.
2. Describe the words they spoke and actions they took.
3. Reflect on the way in which they used themselves in the interview.
4. Assess their practice; and, in some examples.
5. Name the specific skill they were using at the time.

There is some literature about format, but not much. Graybeal and Ruff (1995) argued that process recordings should be done as a continuum of techniques that emphasize skills acquisition, and then they proposed a method for doing so. Today that method is referred to as "three-column process recording." Walsh (2002) suggested a structured format for process recordings that took into account the development of the strengths perspective. The author provided a format to enable students to analyze a client's strengths as part of the total assessment and a checklist for students to analyze their own interventions in relation to those strengths.

Several formats may be used in fieldwork instruction. The first is purely narrative: The student writes paragraph after paragraph, first describing the client(s) and their context, noting client-worker interactions, and incorporating their reflections as students (see Appendix A). The two-column format is another option: The first column is for the interaction between the client and student, and the second is for the thoughts and feelings that were running through the student's mind while the interaction was occurring. The three-column format takes the two columns and adds a third in which the student identifies the specific skill she was using at the time and/or the skill that she should have used (see Appendix B).

Black (2006) suggested a thematic model for students to follow. A theme, selected by the student and/or the field instructor, is identified as key to classroom learning, agency structure, or the individual student's learning needs. The theme organizes the focus of the process recording and provides a way for students to home in on a particular learning objective, which allows for better field instructor assessment of that learning aim.

The use of process recordings may be more of an art than a science. Bembry (1992) pointed out that practitioners, field instructors, and students are without an evaluation instrument to assess interviews that are reconstructed after the fact through process recordings. This claim is both true and not true. What is true is that the field instructor is using the reconstructed interview as remembered by the student. It is also true, as Bembry noted, that this retrospective account does not address the fact that students forget some of the things they said and did during the interview, nor does it address the fact that students may remember things they wish they had done and said but did not actually do and say. One way around these problems of omission and wishful remembering is to have a student tape-record (with the proper permissions) an interview and then immediately give the tape to her field instructor. The student then proceeds to write the process recording as she usually would. Later, the field instructor listens to the tape while reading the process recording. What clearly emerges is a picture of anything in the interview that the student missed or added when she wrote the account later. If this taping process and comparison are done several times during the semester, the field instructor can ascertain whether the student is beginning to make progress on the issues that are most challenging for her in work with her clients. And while Bembry (1992) was right that the participants in field education lack a validated assessment tool for evaluating a process recording, every school has its own list of skills that should be evident in a student's work with clients. In fact, these skills are highly similar from school to school. Field instructors should be reading the process recording with an eye to the skills acquisition that is the target of their teaching at that point in time and looking for evidence of degrees of progress, stasis, or regression in student practice competencies.

Interestingly, the use of process recordings is not limited to social work. In 1976 Baker wrote about the disadvantages of using process recordings in nursing for teaching and evaluating communication. However, more recent nursing literature values process recordings as a means for teaching self-reflection and increasing the quality of interventions. As O'Connor (2006) and almost everyone involved in social work field education would acknowledge, process recordings, since they are written after the act, are by their very nature reflective. The structure of writing about the interview and the process of describing one's own actions offer students the opportunity to be self-reflective. The insights developed in this endeavor help students become aware of their actions and the meanings and impact of those actions, thereby improving their competencies. As in social work practice itself, the student's process recordings are reviewed by the supervisor, who then becomes aware of components of the practice that the student himself may be unaware of, allowing the supervisor the opportunity to teach from that information.

ADDING REFLECTIVE NARRATION TO PROCESS RECORDINGS

Process recordings are not the only writing tool available for the learning/teaching partnership. In medicine, the work of Rita Charon (2006), of Columbia University on narrative medicine has much promise for social work education. Dr. Charon runs writing workshops with doctors, nurses, social workers, and physical and occupational therapists who stop in the midst of their busy days for an hour to write about a patient, not as a collection of symptoms but as an individual with human rights, unique capacities, and aspirations. This reflective and narrative process helps these health professionals better view their patients as human wholes, thereby enhancing their own humanity and adding reflection to their own practice. Process recordings, as currently employed in social work education, require the student to describe the client and the client's context before the intervention is described. This introductory paragraph is the perfect opportunity for student and field instructor to incorporate some of the aspects of narrative medicine: Describe the client in detail, as a person, in his or her own life context, *before* labeling the person as "client" and listing her or his needs for social work activity.

CRITICAL INCIDENT TECHNIQUE, RECORD OF SERVICE, AND THE PROJECT LOG

Other forms of written records for the purpose of social work education and practice have also been used over time. Social work borrowed from psychology the use of the "critical incident technique" of Flanagan (1954). The technique includes four components: (1) the general aim of the activity; (2) specific plans for collecting the material or data about the incident; (3) the actual collection of the data; and (4) an analysis of the data. This format could be applied to a one-on-one session, a therapeutic group, a meeting, or a policy or social administration intervention. Another format, this one developed by social workers for use in community centers and with groups, is the "record of service" (Garfield & Irizarry, 1971), which also includes four components: (1) identification of the problem and how it is known about; (2) a summary of the professional support work to date; (3) an assessment of the human service work already accomplished; and (4) specific next steps to be taken. While the record is primarily an accountability device, it does have utility as a supervisory instrument since it clearly describes problem identification, intervention, and outcome. However, like the critical incident technique described above, in its pure form the record of service does not elicit the self-reflection that is required of students when they write process recordings. The Columbia Department of Field Education has adapted these models for its own use, referring to its version as the project log (see Appendix C).

REFLECTIVE JOURNAL

Another format for teaching/learning in the field through writing is the reflective journal (see Appendix D). This device is most useful for students in the areas of policy, administration, and community organization. In its simplest form, the student makes one entry per week, following this outline:

a. Write a narrative of salient moments, activities, or events during this past week in your work with colleagues and in your work on programmatic assignments.

b. Reflect on the conscious use that you have made of your professional self in the moments, activities, or events you have identified. Pay particular attention to excellent and poor uses you have made of your professional self.

c. Comment on any parallels that you notice between your way of working on programmatic tasks, your way of working with colleagues, and your use of supervision.

d. Comment on any disjuncture that you notice between your way of working on programmatic tasks, your way of working with colleagues, and your use of supervision.

e. Articulate some implications of these reflections for your field education and practice in the immediate future.

Process recordings and reflective journals are *not* static learning tools (this is also true of records of service and the critical incident technique). They are meant to be interactive and dynamic. The interactivity and dynamism come when the field instructor first reviews and comments on the document and then uses it during the supervisory session. Just as any teacher prepares for a class, so the field instructor prepares for meeting with the student. From the comments made in the process recording (or record of service, critical incident technique, etc.), the field instructor should build an agenda of topics to be covered in the supervisory session. At the same time the student should review her process recordings before the session and identify those topics she would like to discuss. If the supervision is going well, and the field instructor is sensitive to the student's learning style, the field instructor's agenda and the student's agenda will become more similar to each other over time.

PEDAGOGICAL USES OF REFLECTIVE WRITING

The use of the process recording during supervision essentially depends upon the teaching style of the field instructor and the learning style of the student. For some, the best teaching/learning is done line by line. Together the field instructor and student go over each interaction and discuss its meaning and effect. For others, the best supervisory session is one in which

the field instructor and the student use the material in the process recording to role-play. Sometimes the field instructor is the client; sometimes the
student takes that role. In this way the field instructor can model for the
student different approaches to the work, and the student can practice different interventions, particularly those she may be uncomfortable with in
her work with clients.

Field advisors/liaisons also use process recordings, but for a different
purpose than does the field instructor. While the student and field instructor use the reflective writing component of process recordings for learning
and teaching, the advisor/liaison uses it to measure the supervisory progress.
Advisors/liaisons do not comment on the practice described in the recordings but look at what the student has written and what the field instructor
has commented on in order to measure positive educational movement
and the degree of acquisition of specific skills. In most schools it is the
advisor/liaison who grades the student in fieldwork, and reflective writing
is the primary basis for internship grades. It is important that the student understand this and remain open to being fully transparent about his practice,
as the sole goal here is to make sure that he is learning and achieving.

All field-based recording is done for multiple reasons: (1) for the student's
learning; (2) for ensuring the field instructor's accountability to the student;
and (3) for determining whether the student is learning the skills required in
the field curriculum and grasping the several dimensions of the professional
role. In addition, field-based recording can identify any impediments to the
student's learning or ability to practice. The student should be forthright,
honest, open, and self-critical in what she records. Unfortunately some students have difficulty discerning the nuances inherent in self-disclosure, the
conscious use of oneself, and boundary setting with clients. Therefore a
supervisor's timely written and oral responses to a student's process recordings and other written reflections on practice are especially pivotal in both
undergraduate and graduate fieldwork. Learning about the subtleties of self-
disclosure, the conscious use of self, and boundary setting with clients is a
complex process that involves trial and error, dialogue, and steady practice.

QUESTIONS AND PRECAUTIONS ABOUT
WRITING IN FIELDWORK

Much as clinicians know that one should self-disclose with a client only
when it is necessary in service to the client, so students would do well to

self-disclose in fieldwork writing only when it is in service to their learn-ing. Students need not disclose previous conditions or episodes in their lives unless it is essential that the field instructor know such information for teaching purposes. Under that rubric, there is actually little that has to be shared—which does not, however, mean that students should be closed and withholding. It is not necessary for students to disclose that they had an eating disorder in high school that is now ameliorated, or that they had an episode of cutting in junior high school, or that they were date-raped in college. If, however, they are working with a client who has had similar experiences, it is important to be open with the field instructor if they feel their past experience may be impeding the services they are providing to the client. And it is important for students who have had such experiences and for whom the work with a client is raising old issues to find the support they need outside of fieldwork to address the issues.

Social work students would be wise to obtain clarification from their field instructors early in field internships about ground rules governing issues of written documentation. What portion of a student's work with a client, for example, must be entered into the case record? Of particular concern is the widespread use of electronic case records; a student should insist, with the support of the school field placement liaison if necessary, that he receive his own agency e-mail account if he is expected to insert documentation directly into the electronic case record. In some systems, a student's signing on as the primary caseworker to enter documentation of his own work with a client would be considered fraud. In other systems, case plans must be submitted by someone who supervised the direct hands-on work in the case. The student (and other workers) may be supplying significant content to the case plan, but that substance must nonetheless be submitted under the case planner's name for acceptance by the overseeing entity. It is important that the student understand situations like these at the outset of the field placement.

Memos, letters, and e-mails that are fieldwork-related are professional documents. The acceptable degree of informality is dictated by the culture of the organization and one's place in it. While the supervisor may not ask to see all communications before they are sent, the student should always strive for a professional tone and avoid use of overly casual greetings, jokes, or emoticons. The agency also may have a preference concerning what title the student uses in these communications, such as using "intern" to specify the student's role in the agency and in the case.

With regard to e-mail and other social media, a student needs to know the guidelines of the agency, academic school, or program, and the ethics of the profession. Not all agencies have specific policies for the use of e-mail, but in general one should remember that once an e-mail message is sent, it may end up in the in-boxes of many different people—sometimes in error. The National Association of Social Workers (NASW), as part of its definition of informed consent, cautions all social workers to explain to clients the risks attached to communications provided via electronic media. In the case of e-mail, maintaining confidentiality is a real concern. The NASW Code of Ethics states: "Social workers should take precautions to ensure and maintain the confidentiality of information transmitted to other parties through the use of computers, electronic mail. . . . Disclosure of identifying information should be avoided whenever possible." For the student, this caveat means that e-mails about the client should contain *no* information that makes the client identifiable by anyone who does not have a role in the case. The student should review the contents of all electronic communications and determine this: If the message was erroneously sent to a distribution list of 50 people, would recipients know who was being discussed? Case numbers and other identifiers that can be used by other people working with the client are acceptable, but names, addresses, and extensive details about the client should never be transmitted via e-mail. A student being directed to use e-mail in a way that may place client confidentiality at risk should discuss the situation with the field instructor and field placement liaison. Students should refrain from contacting clients or other stakeholders from their personal, private e-mail accounts and should not supply a personal e-mail address. Finally, they must be sure never to use an agency's e-mail for personal correspondence or sharing jokes, inspirational stories, photographs, or anything else not related to business. All electronic communications that a student sends via the placement agency's e-mail system may be subject to archiving and electronic discovery should the agency be party to any type of lawsuit.

While many agencies do not have detailed policies regarding e-mail, even fewer have policies about the use of social media. Students should be exceedingly alert to maintaining professional standards while discussing their experiences in field placements on social media platforms like Facebook or Twitter. Best practices include *never* mentioning the names of one's field placement agency in social media and public forums and *never* speaking about case specifics or client names. The concerns here are multiple.

First, the student does not want to violate client confidentiality or discuss the client in a way that would be detrimental to the client if he/she or his or her family members or friends were to see what was written. Second, the student will damage his or her own professional reputation with potential employers and colleagues if they find that the student posted material that was unflattering to a field placement agency on the Internet. A student's behavior on the Internet may also cause friction between the student's school and the field placement agency, which could create problems for the student or jeopardize present or future student placements. Finally, a student's glib or negative comment about fieldwork, in a blog, for example, written spontaneously after a frustrating day, could also reflect poorly on the student's school or academic program if readers were to interpret the remark as evidence of a less-than-serious and empathic approach to clients or social work practice.

CONCLUSION

This chapter addresses student writing in social work field education, emphasizing the learning and teaching aspects of field education, the critical location where theory meets practice, and how writing helps to document their integration. A cluster of reflective writing formats and tools are described. Additionally, case notes and records, e-mails, letters, memos, and progress reports are discussed as important learning devices that are at the same time reporting and accountability mechanisms. They instruct the social work student in the language and repertoire of the activities of engagement, assessment, intervention, and evaluation that take place in his or her fieldwork agency.

Fieldwork writing, in sum, enhances students' overall self-awareness, including their cultural self-awareness. Writing in field placement expands students' knowledge about clients, the context of the field agency, and the relationship between a social work practitioner and a client. Fieldwork writing helps students grasp the reporting and accountability requirements of agency-based professional practice. Writing in fieldwork expands students' grasp of the relationship between a supervisor and supervisee and the art of professional communication. Writing for accountability and for reflection in fieldwork also serves to enhance students' practice of skill clusters and exposure to professional ethics.

Appendixes A, B, C, and D provide illustrations of forms of fieldwork writing that are currently used at the Columbia University School of Social Work. The forms represented are taken from the Columbia University School of Social Work (2011) *Handbook for Student Social Work Recording* (http://www.columbia.edu/cu/ssw/field/documents/Recordings.pdf).

REFERENCES

Baker, J. (1976). An alternative to process recording. *Nursing Outlook, 24*(2), 115–118.

Bembry, J. (1992). Evaluating the interrater reliability of process recordings. *Research on Social Work Practice, 2*(2), 198–206.

Black, P. (2006). Process recordings revisited: A learning-oriented thematic approach integrating field education and classroom curriculum. *Journal of Teaching in Social Work, 36*(3/4), 137–153.

Charon, R. (2006). *Narrative medicine: Honoring the stories of illness.* New York: Oxford University Press.

Flanagan, J. C. (1954). The critical incident technique. *Psychological Bulletin, 51*(4), 327–358.

Fox, R. (2000). Process recording: A means for conceptualizing and evaluating practice. *Journal of Teaching in Social Work, 20*(1/20), 39–55.

Garfield, G. P., & Irizarry, C. R. (1971). The record of service: Describing social work practice. In W. Schwartz & S. R. Zaiba (Eds.), *The practice of group work.* New York: Columbia University Press.

Graybeal, C. T., & Ruff, E. (1995). Process recording: It's more than you think. *Journal of Social Work Education, 31*(2), 169–181.

O'Connor, A. (2006). *Clinical instruction and evaluation: A teaching resource.* Sudbury, MA: Jones & Bartlett.

Urdang, E. (1979). In defense of process recording. *Smith College Studies in Social Work, 50*(1), 1–15.

Walsh, T. C. (2002). Structured process recording: A comprehensive model that incorporates the strengths perspective. *Social Work Education, 21*(1), 23–34.

APPENDIX A

PROCESS RECORDING (NARRATIVE MODEL)

Social Work Intern Name: _____

Date: _____

THIRD SESSION WITH CLIENT

RELEVANT BACKGROUND INFORMATION

A is a 17 y/o female, born in the United States but immigrated to the Dominican Republic when she was 12 years old to live with her father's wife (not her mother). She went to school in the Dominican Republic until her sophomore year in high school. She recently immigrated back to the U.S. and now lives with her mother and older sister in a two-bedroom apartment. Both caretakers receive public assistance. A has not had much contact with her father but presently is working on rebuilding that relationship. A's initial presenting problem was stress in connection with academic failure. Presently A is working on issues of self-esteem, body-image, and stress in connection with a variety of variables.

SOCIAL WORK INTERN'S PURPOSE

Continue to build client-counselor relationship; identify areas of strengths of and challenges faced by client; begin to develop goals and objectives determined by client.

SESSION (ENTIRE ACCOUNT)

A entered the office with a look of panic and concern on her face. She slumped down in the chair next to my desk and let out a deep and resounding sigh. She quickly informed me that she was extremely stressed. This concerned me, because though stress was her initial presenting problem, she had never come into the office appearing so distraught. While she told me she had a problem, she was continually rubbing her stomach. I immediately thought she might be pregnant. When I tried to elicit what the problem was, she blurted out, "I think I am pregnant." I explored with her what she had done to verify this and where she might go, to help her determine what resources were available to her. My goal with her was to help her see there were options. During this time, her body language revealed how stressed she was partially in response to how this would be seen by her mother, who is traditional. My struggle during this was to keep her talking about what was a very scary discussion. In an effort to clarify with her, I asked her, "What makes you think you are pregnant?" When she responded that she "just had that feeling" along with symptoms that could accompany a host of different illnesses—headaches and stomachaches—I was relieved. However, given her pattern of not anticipating possible problems, I suggested that if she was late next week, we could talk about next steps. I hoped by doing this I could take some pressure off her and let her know that (1) I would be there for her and (2) she did not have to feel overwhelmed. Her nonverbal communication throughout this portion of the interview continued to be pressured and to reflect her sense of being out of control. During this conversation I realized A was the third girl this semester to face a possible pregnancy and that we were not doing a very good job in educating the kids on safe and healthy sex practices. From her narrative, it was clear that A felt there were no supports for her either at home or with the young men she had been dating. While I wanted to shake her and say, "Why didn't you use a condom?" I struggled to maintain my non-judgmental stance and said to her, "I am not here to judge you." I think this helped me re-focus on her and her dilemma. I realized she would not be facing this dilemma if she had been using condoms regularly, so I chose to explore this with her. When she told me it broke, it was hard to believe. Knowing how important safe sex is for her and the other young women in the program, I keep thinking about how we can address this need with them. As we talked, she did reveal that she didn't always use condoms, for a variety of reasons; the spur of the moment, boys don't always have them, etc. I mentioned that the consequences could be extremely harmful and then realized that this might increase her sense of panic. It made me wish she was part of the group where we could discuss healthy choices and safe sex, since the group support could help her, and the others, better understand the consequences of behavior. With A, I felt I needed to empower her, and so I offered her condoms that she could have available in the event of a situation where she needed protection. On a couple of occasions she talked about not wanting to keep the baby if she was pregnant; here it was easy for me to reassure her that she needed to think about the best decision for her even though it might be a difficult one. I will have to remember she faces some religious and cultural issues that have an impact on the decision to pursue an abortion or not. This seemed to help her calm down and reflect on what she needed to consider. I reinforced this by telling her that she did need to think about our discussion. At the same time I did not want to minimize what she might be facing, so I said to her, "I am not going to tell you not to worry over the next week, because you will. If you find yourself really stressing next week where you can't focus, come and see me and we can discuss next steps." She said she'd try.

ASSESSMENT (CLIENT AND SESSION)

A responded well to the session. She is often abrasive and confrontational when discussing personal topics, but there has been progress. This was not our first meeting, and she felt comfortable enough to come and share this with me. At first she was very tense, but by the end of the session, though still stressed, she was a bit more relaxed. I am very worried for A. I am concerned about her age and maturity level. A has a very strong personality. She is able to communicate her feelings without much probing. However, she does have challenges in establishing healthy relationships. She is extremely trusting of men in particular and at times does not use good judgment. The session went well. The first goal was achieved. However, due to A's objective for the session, the second was not met (but will be revisited in another session). A was responsive and engaged in the dialogue. I was understanding and non-judgmental of her situation. The questioning was non-threatening and non-critical.

NEXT STEPS

- Determine if A will go to _____ Clinic for a pregnancy test
- Determine the next steps to take after results are known
- Discuss A's options if she is pregnant
- Discuss safe sex practices/consequences of risky behavior
- Offer opportunity to join the upcoming "safe sex" discussion group

AGENDA

- Develop focus groups (girls, boys, coed) to discuss topics regarding safe sex, facts and myths about sex, and teenagers' knowledge and values around sex (Part of Needs Assessment)
- Create a proposal for a student-designed, -implemented, and -managed sex education program
- Collaborate with _____ Health Van personnel
- Establish training sessions for "Safe Sex Educators"—students

FUTURE CONSIDERATIONS / QUESTIONS

- Can we discuss birth control options with the clients?
- If A is pregnant and decides to have an abortion, should I discuss other options?
- Because of her relationship with her mother and her mother's beliefs, would bringing in her family / sister be beneficial or detrimental?
- The possible child's father is also a client. If it is determined she is pregnant, how should we proceed?

APPENDIX B

PROCESS RECORDING (VERBATIM MODEL)

Social Work Intern Name: _____

Date: _____

Identifying/Background Information

Client: A, 17 y/o, female, born in the United States, first language is English (fluent in Spanish — both written and verbal), lives with her mother and older sister in a two-bedroom apartment. Both caretakers receive public assistance. A appeared very distraught, concerned, and anxious.

Referral Source and Reason: Services were self-selected by client; in need of counsel in regard to possible medical situation.

Location of Session/Event: Counseling office

Date of Session: September 17, 2007

Purpose/Goals for the Session

SWI's Session Purpose:

Engage client; continue to develop a counseling relationship
Identify areas of strengths of client and challenges faced by client
Discuss client's goals and objectives

Client's Session Purpose:

Discuss possible medical situation
Explore possible options concerning medical situation

VERBATIM TRANSCRIPT (ENTIRE SESSION)	SWI'S (SOCIAL WORK INTERN'S) FEELINGS, THOUGHTS	ANALYSIS: INCLUDE CASE TO CAUSE ISSUES
A (client): I am mad stressed!	I was a bit concerned b/c A had an extremely troubled look on her face.	
N (social work intern): What's going on?		
A: I may have a problem.	She rubbed her stomach as she said this.	
N: What's the problem you think you may have?	I think she may be pregnant. In my head I was thinking, "Oh my gosh. She cannot be pregnant. She is only 17 and a bit immature!"	I notice that this is the third pregnant student this semester and begin to wonder if a group could be developed for support and information.
A: I think I am pregnant.		
N: Why do you think you may be pregnant? Have you taken a pregnancy test?		
A: No. I can't go to my doctor b/c I don't have my card yet. Plus, I am not going to my doctor. My mom and my sister go there.		Mom is very traditional and religious. A and her sister have a good relationship. I need to probe this connection a bit.
N: Have you ever heard of the _____ Clinic?		
A: No. What's that?		
N: It is a clinic that you can go to and you don't need a Medicaid card. It only costs $5. Would you like the information?		
A: Yeah.		
N: How do you feel about this?	I can only imagine how she is feeling. Her face is telling a lot. She looks stressed, disappointed, and scared.	

(continued)

VERBATIM TRANSCRIPT (ENTIRE SESSION)	SWI'S (SOCIAL WORK INTERN'S) FEELINGS, THOUGHTS	ANALYSIS: INCLUDE CASE TO CAUSE ISSUES
A: I'm stressing out. I cannot be pregnant!		
N: This can be an extremely stressful thing to deal with, especially for someone your age.	I wanted her to feel that I understand that she is in a scary and stressful situation.	
A: I really messed up! What am I going to do?		She needs to know all options available to her.
N: You don't know for sure yet. Do you have time tomorrow before classes to go to the clinic?	I could tell by her tone and facial expressions that she was blaming herself. I really didn't know how to ease that for her.	
A: Well, I don't really want to go yet. I haven't missed anything yet. I'm just scared.		
N: What makes you think you may be pregnant?	I am hoping she is not pregnant. This will be a hard situation for her and her family. Neither her mother nor her sister works, and she does not have the financial ability or stability to have a child.	
A: I just have that feeling. I've been getting headaches and feeling really sick and really tired. I won't be late until next week. Should I wait to take a test?		
N: If you think you're not late you can wait until next week and see if it comes. But do you feel comfortable waiting?		
A: Yeah, I want to wait b/c it might come. Maybe I can even wait longer than next week.		This is a pattern of A. She prefers to wait until a situation/problem gets too big for her to handle and she feels overwhelmed.

VERBATIM TRANSCRIPT (ENTIRE SESSION)	SWI'S (SOCIAL WORK INTERN'S) FEELINGS, THOUGHTS	ANALYSIS: INCLUDE CASE TO CAUSE ISSUES
N: That may not be such a good idea. If you still feel anxious next week and you are late let's discuss your next steps.		Again, I think about the need for more information for all of the students.
A: OK. But if I find out I am—I am going to die. I don't want to take care of no baby!		A is very immature, and her immaturity is something we have been working on.
N: If you are, can you speak to the father, or anyone at home?		
A: I am not telling him! I know this doesn't sound right, but I won't keep it.		
N: I'm not here to judge you. That's your decision to make and it will be a hard one to make but it is your decision.	Everything in me wanted to shake her and say, "Why didn't you use a condom!!!"	
A: How did this happen? We only did it once.		
N: Do you mind if I ask you who it was with?		
A: It could be one of two people. But I think I know which one.		
N: Did you guys use a condom?		Perhaps the students also need more information and skills building around condom use.
A: Yes, but it broke. You know condoms don't always work.	She didn't look me in the eye when she said that.	
N: No, they are not 100% protective and sometimes things happen, but it is important that they always be used. Do you always use a condom?	I didn't believe her that the condom broke.	
A: Not always. You know how it is, you get caught up in the moment. Like when I was with my ex we didn't always, but with C____ yes.	This is such dangerous behavior.	

(continued)

VERBATIM TRANSCRIPT (ENTIRE SESSION)	SWI'S (SOCIAL WORK INTERN'S) FEELINGS, THOUGHTS	ANALYSIS: INCLUDE CASE TO CAUSE ISSUES
N: Getting caught up in the moment happens sometimes, but you always have to protect yourself. That's important because the consequences of not using condoms could be extremely harmful.		
A: Yeah, I know, but sometimes it just doesn't work like that and the boys don't have them.	Girls need to know how to negotiate when it comes to sexual activity. They may want to use a condom but they get caught up.	This has become a common issue among many of the female clients.
N: That's true, they don't always have them. But, you know, you can always be prepared. Do you have any condoms that you keep for those "just in case moments"?	I wanted to say, "What about HIV/AIDS or other STIs?" But I did not want to over-whelm her or make her feel as though I was judging her.	
A: No.		
N: Would you like some?		
A: You have some to give me?		
N: Yes, I do. Keep them with you and if the situation comes up where you need them you will have them.	I hope she uses them!	
A: Do you think I am a bad person for not wanting to keep it if I am?		
N: No, not at all. Like I said before, this can be a hard situation to be in and you have to make the best decision for you. You can't make decisions for other people or based on what you think other people may think of you. And I know that is a hard concept to grasp, especially being 17. But you have to make the decision that is best for you and one that you can live with. It is hard. I cannot tell you not to worry and everything will be okay. I am going to tell you the truth, give you as much information as I can, and be here when you need someone to talk to no matter what decision you make.		

VERBATIM TRANSCRIPT (ENTIRE SESSION)	SWI'S (SOCIAL WORK INTERN'S) FEELINGS, THOUGHTS	ANALYSIS: INCLUDE CASE TO CAUSE ISSUES
A: OK. I guess I have a lot to think about, huh?		
N: Yes. There are things you have to definitely think about. I am not going to tell you not to worry and stress over the next week, b/c I know you are going to, but try not to let it overwhelm you. If you find yourself really stressing next week where you can't focus, come and talk to me so we can discuss next steps. How does that sound?		
A: I'm going to try, but I don't know.		
N: That's all I am asking you to do, is try.		

Impressions/Assessment

A responded well to the session. She is often abrasive and confrontational when discussing personal topics, but there has been progress. This was not our first meeting and she felt comfortable enough to come and share this with me. At first she was very tense, but by the end of the session, though still stressed, she was a bit more relaxed. I am very worried for A. I am concerned about her age and maturity level. A has a very strong personality. She is able to communicate her feelings without much probing. However, A does have challenges in establishing healthy relationships. She is extremely trusting of men in particular and at times does not use good judgment.

The session went well. The first goal was achieved. However, due to the client's objective for the session, the second was not met (but will be revisited in another session). A was responsive and engaged in the dialogue. I was understanding and non-judgmental of her situation. The questioning was non-threatening and non-critical.

Planning/Next Steps

A may go to the clinic next week to take a pregnancy test. After the appointment, A will report back to me the results of the test. From the results we will determine the next steps to take. If she is pregnant we will discuss her options, which will include the opportunity to have a meeting with her older sister. If she is not pregnant, we will discuss safe sex practices, as well as the consequences of risky behavior. We will also discuss the possibility of A joining the upcoming "safe sex" discussion group.

My Agenda

- To develop focus groups (girls, boys, coed) to discuss topics regarding safe sex, facts and myths about sex, and teenagers' knowledge and values around sex (Part of Needs Assessment)
- Create a proposal for a student-designed, -implemented, and -managed sex education program
- Collaborate with _____ Health Van personnel
- Establish training sessions for "safe sex educators"—students

Future Considerations/Questions

- Can we discuss birth control options with the clients?
- If A is pregnant and decides to have an abortion, should I discuss other options?
- Because of her relationship with her mother and her mother's beliefs, would bringing in her family/sister be beneficial or detrimental?
- The possible child's father is also a client. If it is determined she is pregnant, how should we proceed?

APPENDIX C

THE PROJECT LOG

Title: *Teens Staying Safe*
Start Date: March 15
   Description: An educational and informative class for students dealing with the ideas of safe sex and increased self-esteem.
   Goals and objectives: To establish a better sense of safe sex practices and better self-esteem among the students at the school.
   Task: The task I am working on this week is the ongoing preparation for the Sexual Education and Safety class. There have been new developments in the planning stages, and as deadlines approach and the start of the class looms, it is important to further record and understand the work that is going on. This is clearly a most relevant topic, given recent circumstances, including the admission of students to practicing unsafe sex. Up to this week, planning has been ongoing, but in the next week, the actual class should be set up, and the arrangements to enroll students should begin.
   Timeline: Within the next week, permission slips must be written, printed, and distributed. Within the next two weeks, an agency employee must be designated to run the class and space must be confirmed for the class. Within the next four weeks, materials must be purchased and the instructor must submit a curriculum for review. As they are needed, any phone calls must be made.
   Necessary Resources: STAFF, SPACE, MATERIALS, AND VISUAL AND AUDIO EQUIPMENT. This all must be further developed over the next two weeks with the instructor.
   AGPP Practice Skills: Over the course of my time working on the project, I have used a number of AGPP-related skills. First, I have used many of the skills from program development, including a literature review and

a needs assessment to make sure that the program would be well received and achieve the best results possible. Additionally, as we have talked to students, staff, and parents, I have used empathic listening and surveying skills, including how to run a focus group, which will help guide the course of our class. Finally, I have used the budgeting skills that I learned through AGPP to make a clear and concise budget for the organization, which will help to guide the program and expenditures.

Enhancements / Obstacles to Project: There are a number of potential problems for running the program. First, if the participants are under the age of 18, parents must agree to allow them to attend, and there must be a significant interest and investment on the part of the students. The instructor must be engaging, and there must be incentives to get them to come (perhaps food).

The staff of the school, including social workers and supervisors, and the Safe Sex Advocates will support the program, as will most of the parents. This will be tremendous in pushing students to attend and to learn about the practice of safe sex. Support can be enhanced, across all potential obstacles, with information dissemination and with individual discussions about what will be covered in the class, as well as the potential concerns that any students have.

Project Assessment: I believe that thus far the program is running well. The struggles have been in terms of space, staffing, and time constraints, but thus far we have overcome those concerns to build a strong program that is almost ready to begin. I know that I am a dedicated intern and that I understand the importance of the work that I am doing. This work is definitely needed, and we have worked hard to get the support of the school staff and of parents. To this point, goals cannot be measured because the program is still in the works. During this process, I have been a bit stressed, but I am also excited about the potential that lies ahead. The project is both needed and feasible, and the resources needed are attainable. In summary, the organization and I are both in the safety business, looking out for our kids and always having their best interests in mind.

Agenda for Supervision: Next Steps

- Go over the meeting time and place
- Ensure that staff and materials are all set up
- Discuss the timeline
- Discuss any barriers faced

- Talk to more parents to make sure that they are all on board with the class, encouraging their children to attend

Questions for Field Instructor:

- Does student understand his/her role?
- Does student know what his/her agenda is?
- Does student perceive where his/her actions fit as part of a programmatic goal-oriented process?
- Does student understand the possible consequences and impact of his/her actions?
- Does student anticipate the likely resistances to his/her actions?
- Does student mobilize adequate support for his/her actions?
- Does student reassess and redefine his/her objectives or agenda when new circumstances arise?
- Does student perceive growth and gain new insights as a consequence of his/her actions?
- Does student understand the function of self-reflection, and is he/she able to demonstrate this in log entries?

APPENDIX D

REFLECTIVE JOURNAL

Date of Entry: _____

Summary of Cases

Approximately 60% of my clients have a common theme of risky sexual behavior and attitudes. There is a representation of both males and females, between the ages of 17 and 22, within my client group demonstrating these behaviors. The topics range from a lack of negotiating skills to the misuse or non-use of condoms, different characterization of what constitutes sexual acts, exposure to casual sex, and multiple sex partners. Approximately 35% of my clients are parents, expecting parents, or intimately connected to pregnancies that have not been carried to term. Approximately 50% of my clients have received at least one positive result for contracting an STI [a sexually transmitted infection] and at least 2 of my clients are HIV positive. There is currently no nurse or health educator located on school premises. At present, there is no program designated on the topic of safe sex or sex education. Through my counseling of individual students, there is a desire to create such a program and/or discussion group.

Narrative of Salient Moments/Activities/Events

This week I have had sessions and held group meetings with students who share similarities in terms of their lack of safe sex education. From the information (needs assessment) I have received from my cases, I have been meeting with my supervisor as well as the agency director to discuss the possibility of creating a sex education program, sponsored by the agency and utilizing school space. I have noticed that my engagement and contracting skills with my clients have been very helpful in terms of those skills transferring over to my programmatic work. Through discussions with key staff and case sessions I can visualize how my casework/group work is influencing my programmatic work, as well as how the development of the program will affect my work with individual clients.

Next Steps

Through my work with clients I have determined that a sex education program may be beneficial to them. Clients need education regarding safe sex practices, information on STIs and how they are contracted, and ways to develop empowerment strategies. I will complete a literature review by next week on teenage sexual behaviors and attitudes, and gather evidence regarding successful programs and strategies with this population. Also, I will conduct client focus groups to assess needs in the following areas: (1) the most important sex education topics; (2) the presentation approaches most suited to the population; and (3) the person(s) to disseminate the information to whom this population would be most responsive. These groups can be held over the next three weeks during the three lunch periods. Participants will be self-selected through a referral process from agency staff. Social work interns will conduct the groups. From information gathered through process recordings and literature reviews, interns can develop focus group questions. Because we have a significant truancy rate and many students eating lunch off campus, a possible obstacle may be students not attending the focus groups. Another obstacle is students feeling uncomfortable discussing various topics concerning sexual attitudes and behaviors in groups. Also, because space is very limited in the school, finding accommodations for the focus groups may prove difficult, especially if administration and staff—both from the school and from the agency—are not vested in this program.

Agenda for Supervision (This can be adapted to your specific assignment/agency)

The skills I have utilized during this week, both programmatically and in direct practice, are negotiation, contracting, engagement, developing a needs assessment, and conducting a literature review. I saw a clear strength in my ability to connect with both clients and key staff members for my programmatic work. One area I still need to get a better handle on is identifying the barriers I may face while in the phase of program development.

6

WRITING FOR AND ABOUT CLINICAL PRACTICE

Mary Sormanti

I GREW UP BELIEVING THAT words were powerful. I'm not exactly sure where that bit of wisdom came from, but it has proven only more true as my years in clinical social work practice have accumulated. Approaching my 25th anniversary in this field, I can say without hesitation that it is the words we use—the words all social workers use, both spoken and written—that profoundly shape the lives of those with whom we work. Yes, the assessments we make and the interventions we implement are critical, but both are composed of the words we use to create and deliver them, and both take their meaning from the knowledge, values, and beliefs that underlie these words. With this intrinsic power comes a host of related responsibilities requiring us to use words thoughtfully and with care.

This chapter focuses on clinical writing. I review various types of writing associated with clinical practice and examine the purposes and principles that I believe should serve as guides for our writing. Within this framework I also highlight potential pitfalls or problems that can arise if our attention and dedication to high-quality clinical writing falter. Whether you are new to clinical practice or a seasoned veteran, the information provided here can serve as a useful overview of the central role of writing in your practice. My intention is to validate both our writing skills and our responsibilities, encourage the critical use of multiple mechanisms and venues for clinical writing, and advocate for renewed incorporation of a strengths-based perspective into all of our clinical writing endeavors and documents.

WHAT DO CLINICAL SOCIAL WORKERS WRITE?

Clinical social workers write about their clients and their work in a range of formats that vary in formality and purpose. Standard written documents include psychosocial assessments, treatment plans, letters to clients, and letters to collateral contacts (i.e., other professionals important to the client's life, such as lawyers, teachers, and health care professionals) in support of client applications or requests. Some clinical social workers write about their work in professional publications, such as newsletters and journals. Most notably, clinical social workers write "case notes," which become part of their clients' permanent records of care with a program, agency, or organization that is providing the social work services—either alone or in conjunction with another type of service, such as medical or legal services.

Case notes typically include comprehensive psychosocial assessment information, such as the reason and circumstances surrounding the referral. The notes also contain frequent updates on the therapeutic work that addresses the presenting issue, the client's adjustment to the presenting issue, and progress toward attainment or maintenance of therapeutic goals. Comments about ongoing or emerging factors affecting the clinical situation are also often included in case notes, as they serve to remind readers that the client lives in a complex network of relationships and systems that profoundly shape his or her experiences. In this way, our professional person-in-environment (i.e., ecological) perspective—which has at its core the belief that the problems of individuals, families, and communities arise from some tension or dissonance between them and the broader context within which they live and work—is continuously conveyed through our clinical writing. This is especially important given the frequency with which we work in tandem with both paraprofessional and professional colleagues from other fields and disciplines (such as education, law, religion, psychology, medicine) whose training was not grounded in this ecological perspective. Educating these service providers about the many contextual factors that figure in their clients' lives enhances their understanding of their clients and helps them to develop expectations and service plans that are more relevant and realistic.

Because agency records are public and therefore available to both the other professionals involved in clients' care and the clients themselves, clinical case notes must be written with great discretion. They should include only information that is relevant to a client's current care and should be written in such a way that all those who might read them will get a concise, clear, and accurate understanding of your work and insights about the clinical situation at hand. It is appropriate to include recommendations for ways in which other professionals' work with a mutual client might be enhanced. For example, you might suggest that a physician who is overseeing the treatment of a person with newly diagnosed Parkinson's disease provide additional clarification about an upcoming procedure that the client has already consented to undergo but that you believe neither he nor his family accurately understands. However, personal opinion or conjecture, excessive detail, and extraneous information have no place in clinical case notes. Such material would not only distract the reader from the presenting clinical issues but also undermine your credibility. Well-written case notes are concise but informative, thus increasing the likelihood that your busy colleagues will take time to read them.

Clinical social workers who work independently (i.e., in private practice) may also keep case notes, although these are not routinely read by others. Rather than being written with the primary focus of informing others about their work, private practice case notes provide a historical record of the therapeutic relationship and work that clinicians themselves refer to as a means of evaluating and, if necessary, modifying the treatment process. Social workers who practice independently are responsible for adhering to guidelines for record keeping that are established by professional organizations in their state of clinical licensure. Whether the primary purpose is to inform others or ourselves about the nature and evolution of the clinical circumstances and work, case notes should contribute to the reader's knowledge, understanding, and empathy about clients and clinical situations, in turn enhancing client care.

Treatment (or service) plans, which can be conceptualized as either a specific type of case note or a component thereof, are detailed descriptions about the work you intend to engage in with your clients to address the issues and achieve the objectives and goals that you have jointly identified. Treatment plans are developed after a comprehensive assessment of the client and her/his psychosocial circumstances, and they are reviewed routinely both to ensure that they remain relevant over time and to monitor progress. For example, if circumstances change or specific outcomes are reached (or not), the treatment plan may be updated accordingly. Although the specific format may vary from agency to agency, in general a treatment plan includes the following:

- Brief synopsis of client issue/s to be addressed, as well as client strengths, resources, and challenges that may shape this issue. For some agencies a complete *DSM-IV-TR* diagnosis may also be included.
- Theoretical orientation from which this client issue has been conceptualized (e.g., psychodynamic, cognitive behavioral)
- General goals for treatment
- Specific measurable objectives, the achievement of which will mark progress toward broader goals
- Estimated dates of achievement for objectives and suggested length of treatment (e.g., length and number of sessions)
- Planned interventions and how these are linked to the theoretical orientation
- Plans for review of progress, including specific dates and methods

Clinical writing for professional newsletters and journals is distinct from writing in case notes in a significant way. Rather than disclosing details about an individual and her particular circumstances, the social worker who intends to publish clinical writing must go to sufficient lengths to uphold client privacy. Thus, although published writing and case notes share the aim of educating readers about a particular clinical condition, situation, intervention, or relationship, the former must do so without violating any individual's right to confidentiality. Bridges (2007) pondered whether disguising clinical material, which has been a standard means of upholding this right, lessens the accuracy and utility of the clinical information conveyed and, more importantly, if it is even possible. Moreover, she raised an equally compelling question about whether seeking informed consent from clients about whom one would like to write in published format—the other standard means by which clinicians seek to uphold clients' right to confidentiality—is possible, given the power differentials inherent in the therapeutic relationship. Both approaches, Bridges and others (such as Kantrowitz, 2006) have claimed, present potential benefits and detriments to the clinical work and the therapeutic relationship. With no definitive guidelines about how best to proceed in protecting client confidentiality in published documents, clinicians must do so with extreme caution, examining these options carefully and consulting with trusted colleagues.

WHY DO CLINICAL SOCIAL WORKERS WRITE?

Clinical social workers write for myriad reasons. One of the most pressing aims is to communicate with one another and with other professionals outside the social work arena about the work we do and the people we serve. We apprise others of what we are doing and why, how our work with a particular client or client group is unfolding, whether and how contextual issues (such as agency policies or current events) are affecting our work, what our plans and recommendations are for moving forward with it, and how our work may affect the work of others. By informing colleagues about these issues, we aim to engage them in the process to the benefit of our clients.

Sometimes we want others to be more aware of the depth and breadth of our clients' lives so that their own interactions with them will be more thoughtful and caring. We want them to slow down enough in their own busy interactions and practices to remember that our clients are human beings striving to achieve, endure, and thrive in the face of often challenging and sometimes oppressive sociocultural conditions. We hope that our writing leads other professionals to recognize this common humanity as well as the unique characteristics and strengths that each client brings to it.

Given our clinical skills and the fundamental goals of clinical practice, we often come to know and understand our clients and their lives in ways that other professionals do not. While another professional (such as a physician, lawyer, or teacher) may have a solid grasp of one aspect of a client's life or personality, when you are doing your clinical work well, you will often have a more holistic appreciation of the multiple aspects of your client's identity, the multifaceted layers of her experiences, and the ways that these intersect and shape her current concerns and needs. This "big picture" view, which stems from the profession's foundational person-in-environment framework, is frequently quite valuable to other professionals. When you enlighten them with such information, often in written form, their interactions with your mutual clients are more likely to be meaningful and effective. For example, a physician who learns from a social worker's written psychosocial history and assessment in the medical chart that a newly admitted patient is a survivor of childhood physical and sexual abuse may gain a new appreciation for her "resistance" to invasive but lifesaving treatments that are more readily accepted by most of the physician's other patients. Armed with an enhanced sense of empathy for this individual, in ongoing collaboration with a clinical social worker, the physician is likely to engage with the patient in a more robust manner that takes her specific history into account. Without such critical contextual information, even the most skilled, best-intentioned physician runs the risk of either failing to engage the patient adequately (which could have serious health consequences for the patient) or moving ahead with a treatment plan that neither satisfactorily accounts for a patient's psychological and emotional health nor is founded on solid understanding and trust. In short, the patient's health care could be significantly compromised.

Sometimes we write to other professionals to elicit specific input and assistance for our clients. For example, we write to insurance companies to make a case for client eligibility for certain types of services, as well as for the duration and frequency of the services. We also write to governmental and social service organizations to influence their decisions about our clients' rights, capacities, resources, and responsibilities. In such cases our writing is used as a tool for advocacy. Even when we write to those within the very programs or organizations in which we work (hospitals, mental health clinics, schools), we are often doing so with the aim of protecting and empowering individuals and families who are coping with challenging circumstances and situations that threaten to compromise their quality of life.

A clinical social worker in a school, for example, might write a memo to the school's director of athletics sharing her assessment that the junior high student she has been working with since his recent suspension from the track team after a physical altercation with a classmate is having a difficult time coping with the recent death of his grandfather and is not likely to act out aggressively again. Understood within the context of bereavement, the social worker suggests that the student's behavior, though unacceptable, merits a different response than a lengthy suspension from the team.

With a brief written document (perhaps in conjunction with an in-person conversation if time allows), the social worker encourages the athletic director to both shorten the suspension and consider creating an opportunity for the student to work on an individual project with one of the track coaches. The social worker suggests that these changes would facilitate the student's return to a network of friends and mentors that can provide critical support at an emotionally difficult time and nurture the student's sense of competence and esteem. Additionally, she suggests that this student's full participation in school-related activities may have benefits for the wider school community. For example, using a simple list format, she points out that his reintegration will provide opportunities for his peers to: (1) develop empathy, (2) reflect on their own experiences of grief, and (3) help one another in the process.

Thus, multiple clinical social work objectives are set in motion through written clinical case feedback with an immediate advocacy aim. Moreover, in the broader professional context, even though some clinical social workers might not list advocacy as the foremost component of their practice, for most of us it is essential to our provision of solid clinical services.

In addition to sharing our professional insights and service recommendations for individual clients, we clinical social workers also write about our expertise with specific client populations, methods of practice, and practice issues. Those practitioners with extensive experience often share their practice wisdom by writing about counseling the elderly in nursing homes, providing therapy to adolescents with eating disorders, facilitating psychoeducational groups, using cognitive-behavioral techniques, or working with those who are coping with chronic illnesses. Such expertise can be invaluable to others who have less experience with these populations, practice issues, or methods, and who find themselves in a practice situation that requires (or could benefit from) such knowledge. By documenting your clinical practice experiences and knowledge in widely accessible formats (such as agency Web sites and brochures, journal articles, client handouts), you help to create an empirical knowledge base that is instructive and useful to both social work professionals and professionals in other fields. Furthermore, with some variation in the style of your writing (e.g., limited use of clinical professional jargon), such expertise also can be extremely useful to laypersons interested in your perspective, to help them navigate a clinical issue they or loved ones are facing. In this sense, as a clinical social worker, you contribute to the profession's commitment to evidence-based practice through your writing. You disseminate information about particular clinical approaches that have worked for certain populations or in specific clinical settings.

Finally, as a clinical social worker, you use writing as a means to explore the challenges, stresses, and rewards that accompany your many roles and responsibilities. Whether your work is with a young man who has just been admitted to an inpatient psychiatric unit for the first time or with an elderly woman who is grieving the death of her partner of 60 years, clinical social work requires that you open your heart and mind to issues that have loss, pain, and survival at their core. To do so in a sustained way necessitates ongoing and rigorous attention to what clinical social workers have for decades been referring to as "use of self." Transference and countertransference, self-disclosure, and physical touch are some of the mainstays in the use-of-self literature, to which social workers have contributed greatly. Candid writing about each of these topics has helped to advance clinical social work. More recently, the addition of thoughtful inquiries and reflections about compassion fatigue and vicarious traumatization has opened up new dialogues that have deepened our knowledge, skills, and commitment to clinical practice. What once may have been limited to casual conversations between stressed-out coworkers or to individual supervision sessions has now been recognized as a matter of significant concern to the entire profession. Indeed, published writings about these issues, including personal examples from experienced clinicians, have helped to minimize any stigma associated with them and have highlighted self-care as an ethical imperative for high-quality clinical care.

The following readings provide more information about compassion fatigue and vicarious traumatization:

Becvar, D. S. (2003). The impact on the family therapist of a focus on death, dying, and bereavement. *Journal of Marital and Family Therapy*, 29(4), 469–477.
Dane, B., & Chachkes, E. (2001). The cost of caring for patients with an illness: Contagion to the social worker. *Social Work in Health Care*, 33(2), 31–51.
McCann, I. L., & Pearlman, L. A. (1990). Vicarious traumatization: A framework for understanding the psychological effects of working with victims. *Journal of Traumatic Stress*, 3, 131–149.
Pearlman, L. A., & Saakvitne, K. W. (1995). *Trauma and the therapist: Countertransference and vicarious traumatization in psychotherapy with incest survivors.* New York: W. W. Norton.

WRITING AS A MANIFESTATION OF PROFESSIONAL VALUES AND ETHICS

At their best, case notes and other forms of clinical writing reflect our professional commitment to social work values and ethics as they interface with the presenting clinical issue. Although all of the profession's ethical standards are essential, one could argue that as globalization continues to accelerate and the demographics of neighborhoods, towns, and cities shift and expand, clinical social workers should pay special attention to the profession's ethical commitment to cultural competence and social diversity[1] in our writing. Unquestionably, all of our work occurs against the rich and complex background of culture—our clients', our own, and those of the systems within which we work. Consequently, strong clinical writing documents how culture shapes clients' presenting issues and draws attention to ways in which service plans might be shaped to respect and support clients' culturally influenced attitudes, beliefs, and practices.

For example, if you find yourself working with an individual who has recently emigrated from a country whose traditions and beliefs are quite distinct from those of the dominant culture (both organizational and societal) in which you are working, be sure to document these differences in a way that cultivates understanding and respect from those who will read your notes. For example, a hospital-based social worker who is writing about a recent family meeting during which a family was provided with information about their child's diagnosis, prognosis, and treatment options might write the following statement as part of a lengthier clinical note:

> Mr. and Mrs. Pho, who have lived in the U.S. for the past three years since emigrating from Vietnam, have a good basic understanding of the information that was shared with them by the medical team this afternoon. However, although they understand the team's strong belief that the suggested treatment (i.e., chemotherapy) begin immediately, they need time to discuss this information with their parents and to seek the consultation of an herbalist—all of whom represent highly valued avenues of support and guidance within their cultural heritage—before they make a treatment decision. I have made arrangements for them to call their parents in Vietnam from the hospital and know that they have made arrangements for an herbalist to meet with them here tomorrow. They agreed to participate tomorrow afternoon in another family meeting that includes the herbalist so that together we might create a treatment plan that incorporates both Western and traditional approaches, the latter of which are meaningful to them.

Unwavering recognition and support of client strengths is also evident in the best clinical writing. Strengths include all skills, qualities, capacities, and resources that are either innate or otherwise available to someone as they cope with a challenge.

> Mr. Balboa is gentle and kind.
> Tommy is engaging and funny.

> Ms. Lee has solid organizational skills and a strong motivation to learn.
>
> Shayla has loving relationships with her grandparents and younger sister.

These brief acknowledgments, which are both accurate and positive, establish a compassionate framework for all future work. Far too often, however, the very systems that are established to provide care and service to individuals, families, and communities do so in ways that are disrespectful, disempowering, and disheartening. Rather than discovering, acknowledging, and using these strengths as a foundation for ongoing growth and movement toward desired goals and outcomes, service providers may focus attention disproportionately, if not exclusively, on presenting problems; these problems are inaccurately attributed to some perceived flaw within the client rather than to a structural deficit in the client's social environment, and the proposed or imposed solutions do not match the client's views or wishes.

> Mr. Balboa's low self-esteem and passivity prevents him from sticking up for himself during disputes with other residents.
>
> Tommy is a class clown who distracts other students during class.
>
> Ms. Lee has deficits in communication and relationship-building skills.
>
> Shayla has a conflicted relationship with her mother and no relationship with her father, who has been in prison for the past four years.

Although these latter statements may have validity, they set a tone of criticism and blame that is likely to alienate clients and impede the therapeutic process, especially if strengths are not noted.

Clinical social workers should not be complicit with such organizational approaches. Rather, in sharp contrast to the many ways in which individuals and organizations fail to notice, intentionally ignore, or undermine client strengths, we must use our writing skills to highlight what others do not see. Even the briefest of case notes can lead with a description of client strengths, as clients are undoubtedly using those strengths to manage the challenging circumstances they find themselves in. This is perhaps most important for those clients with whom others have difficulty finding common ground, patience, interest, or compassion. In such cases, a written note from the clinical social worker can inform or remind colleagues that clients most often are doing their best with the resources they have, even though those resources and coping styles may be strikingly different from their own or those of others with whom they have worked. For example, a seemingly simple and benign brief clinical observation can fail to capture the client's strengths, setting up the reader to miss them as well:

> Ms. Santiago seems to be having an extremely difficult time coping with the diagnosis of her eldest son. She cries a lot, prays frequently, and is markedly withdrawn from staff.

Instead, the same clinical observation could be transformed with a subtle but purposeful rephrasing that emphasizes client and family strengths:

> Ms. Santiago seems to be drawing on her faith and family supports to adjust to the very difficult news of her eldest son's diagnosis. Although she is crying openly, this as well as prayer and brief discussions with family seem to provide her with some solace.

While the former runs the risk of almost imperceptibly leading the reader toward a slightly negative view of the client, the latter proactively guides the reader's attention toward that which is constructive about her response to an obviously difficult situation.

THE POWER OF WORDS AS LABELS

The NASW Code of Ethics requires social workers to use "accurate and respectful" language in written communications to and about clients.[2] As noted above, cultural factors and client strengths are principal components of such clinical documentation. In addition, there are multiple ways for you to ensure that your writing about clients does not violate this ethical standard. Perhaps one of the simplest ways to express respect is to use descriptors that convey the personhood of the client. Indeed it can be argued that use of the word "client" contributes to a false distance between the person seeking services and the person providing services. Variations on this term have emerged over the years—for example, "consumer," "resident," "member"—demonstrating some recognition of the power of language to shape human experience, in particular the provider-recipient relationship. Although NASW endorses use of the word "client" as a universal term to describe the many individuals, families, groups, and communities with whom we work, clinicians can replace it as often as possible to specify and humanize the particular client they are writing about. In a previous example, you learned a bit about Ms. Santiago, not simply that she was "the client." Additional written information could reveal that Ms. Santiago is a grandmother, a college professor, an avid tennis player, or an amateur cellist. Each of these descriptors contributes to readers' recognition that Ms. Santiago is three-dimensional and like them, has interests, skills, responsibilities, and commitments. Ms. Santiago is not just a "case" we follow.

Taking the above sentiment one step further, you should use diagnostic and other identifying labels and phrases with great caution. Although professionals use many such expressions as a form of shorthand to expedite communication with one another, their use can be dehumanizing. Despite long-standing controversy and debate about its utility and appropriateness, DSM-IV-TR is the prevailing classification of mental disorders used by social workers and other mental health professionals in the United States. Irrespective of where clinicians settle after a careful consideration of the arguments for and against the use of this (or another) classification system, any use of diagnostic terminology can and should be complemented with fuller details about the person being described. For example, rather than writing "I have been working with a schizophrenic," which suggests that the mental health condition is the primary, if not sole, entity of concern, it would be better to write, "I have been working with a woman who has been diagnosed with schizophrenia." The latter conveys a belief that the illness is one characteristic of the more fundamental person being described. Better still would be a slightly longer statement summarizing the key issues that relate to the diagnostic category you believe best describes the client. . . . For example, "I have been working with a woman who struggles with [insert specific issue related to diagnosis, e.g., delusions that the mayor of NY is plotting against her; disruptions in cognition and affect that have negatively affected her ability to work and maintain relationships]. Consequently, I believe she may meet the diagnostic criteria for schizophrenia." Such a statement further differentiates the person from the mental health condition, highlighting that they are not one and the same and that there is much more to the individual than the mental health condition she is living with.

Clinical social workers who practice in settings that do not focus solely or predominantly on mental health conditions (medical social workers, for example) must also be careful about the use of labels in their written documentation. Although the term "cancer patient" or "diabetic" may be apt shorthand in the medical chart, like *DSM-IV-TR* categorizations, such terms run the risks of conflating the disease with the person who has it and of blunting our and others' empathy for that person. This is particularly important in specialty areas associated with high levels of stress for both care providers and recipients. In these practice areas, you owe it to yourself and to those with whom you work—both clients and colleagues—to write about the clinical issues, relationships, and work in ways that reflect their richness and complexity. Doing so contributes to the meaningfulness, authenticity, and integrity of everyone involved and as such helps to mitigate burnout and vicarious trauma, and the negative effects on clinical work that are associated with both.

HOPE: A CRITICAL FACTOR

Hope is another related topic of importance in clinical writing. For myriad reasons—all of them shaped by cultural beliefs, values, and conditions—psychiatric and medical diagnoses, as well as psychosocial circumstances, are associated with varying levels of hope or hopelessness. Moreover, hope and hopelessness are construed distinctively by different individuals and affect coping and adjustment in similarly unique ways. While one person experiences a sense of hopelessness upon learning that she has been diagnosed with Alzheimer's disease, another feels a sense of hope that the same disease has been diagnosed early on in its trajectory. As clinicians we are respectful of each individual's perspective about his own past, present, and future and mindful of the ways that our writing (like our verbal communications with clients) might undermine, disrespect, or otherwise fail to tune in to a person's emotional state and decision-making processes. Doing so would be an affront to client self-determination and would likely have a negative affect on that person's well-being and ability to cope.

Undoubtedly some individuals and families are reluctant to engage with social workers and other health and mental health professionals, but there are often significant cultural and historical reasons for such a response (perhaps institutional racism, previous negative experiences, or trauma). Furthermore, although some individuals and families may be "untreatable" (Brydon, 2004)—that is, unable to achieve change that society deems necessary to conform to its rules and laws, and thus maintain certain rights (for example, parental rights)—such a determination may be arrived at too quickly and without sufficient recognition of systemic limitations, including professional knowledge and biases. Clinical writing has the power to contribute negatively or positively to this process.

Consider, for example, how the following clinical case note reflects the writer's hopelessness about the described person and situation, and might likewise shape future intervention by affecting the reader's sense of possibility for the client.

> Client is an uneducated 33-year-old mother of two who appears unkempt, slightly disoriented, and exhausted. She is well known to staff as she has been seen here multiple times for depression. Although numerous medications have been prescribed over the past 2½ years, client has not responded significantly well and reports that her symptoms are currently intensifying. Client has a partner who has accompanied her to clinic in the past but is not here now. Both have been resistant to therapy and support groups and have not followed up with multiple recommendations from me or other team members in the past. We could consider a referral to psychiatric day hospital, but I am doubtful that patient will follow up. Consultation with child protective services has been initiated since depression is very likely to be affecting patient's ability to care for her children properly.

There is much about this clinical note (and perhaps the clinical work it supposedly describes) that can be improved. As written, it neither reflects the profession's values nor provides the reader with useful information to thoughtfully enhance services to the client. First, nothing in the above note suggests that the woman being described has strengths and resources that have helped her to cope with her depression, although indeed she has done that for 2½ years. Moreover, it has not been noted that she has been observant enough to notice an exacerbation of symptoms and motivated enough to seek further consultation at this time, nor has she been applauded as exhibiting significant strength in the face of chronic and debilitating illness. Second, the phrase "the client has not responded significantly" subtly implies, however unintentionally, that the client is somehow responsible for the lack of significant improvement rather than the much more likely reality that the medications have failed to successfully relieve her symptoms. Such a perspective can be disempowering at best, even to the hardiest of individuals. Third, there is no indication that the writer has considered the multiple factors that may be contributing to this client and her partner's "resistance" to therapy, including, for example, the clinician's (or other professionals') inability to build trust and rapport with the couple. In this way, emphasizing a client's resistance is a form of blaming. Fourth, the writer has initiated a serious course of action (i.e., consultation with child protective services) with seemingly no evidence and in the process has planted in the reader's mind the "suggestion" that this woman may be neglectful of her children. Finally, the writer conveys an unnecessarily pessimistic tone with the conjecture that the patient would not likely follow up on a referral to a psychiatric day treatment program. Again, without noting any current evidence to support such speculation, the writer sets the reader up to assume that this is true and to approach the woman with an accordingly narrow mind-set. In contrast, consider how the following note, about the same individual in the same situation, sets a markedly different tone, one ripe with positive possibilities for both service provider and recipient.

> Ms. P is a 33-year-old woman actively seeking consultation for recurrent symptoms of depression. Because she has proactively sought treatment from this clinic over the past 2½ years, she is well known to some staff. However, no one has yet been able to establish a solid therapeutic relationship with her. Prior interventions have included numerous medications and referrals for both individual and group therapy. Although medications brought some initial reduction in symptoms, Ms. P now reports that symptoms, especially fatigue and irritability, are intensifying. To date, Ms. P has attended neither individual therapy nor support group sessions. Ms. P has a partner who has accompanied her to clinic in the past but is not here now. She also has two young children, ages 4 and 5. Ms. P has expressed concern that her depression interferes with her ability to take care of her children. Given her insight and seeming commitment to her children, we should discuss a variety of treatment options with Ms. P, including a referral to a psychiatric day hospital. All of these should be explored with specific regard to their implications for the children and their relationship with Ms. P. Also, we need to understand why Ms. P did not/was not able to follow up with prior referrals for individual and group counseling. Perhaps there are barriers (e.g., structural, cultural, knowledge) that could be addressed to make these options more appropriate or feasible for her.

Clinical notes are not a medium to voice our personal sense of hope or hopelessness about a client's clinical situation. Although such thoughts and feelings are understandable, indeed common, among helping profession-als, they should not be discussed in the context of a case note. Rather, they ought to be explored within the realm of supervision or consultation with colleagues, and could certainly be described in other formats for clinical writing, such as professional newsletters and journals. Publication in either of the latter formats would have the added benefit of stimulating reflection and dialogue among a much broader audience.

In clinical notes, you are obliged to present information that is arrived at through comprehensive assessment and that conveys your understanding of human beings as complex and dynamic. Although the past indeed may be prologue to the future in some cases, the people you work with are just as likely to surprise you with behaviors, thoughts, and feelings that you might otherwise have presumed, unwisely, they would not. As an astute and skilled clinician you recognize the strengths of your clients and impart this under-standing in everything you write about them, including their resilience, which has enabled them to cope with multiple stressors, often over long periods of time (Saleebey, 1997).

GUIDING PRINCIPLES FOR CLINICAL WRITING

Like its source, clinical practice, clinical writing is both a responsibility and a privilege. As such, it must be tended to with great skill, diligence, and care. In addition to solid writing skills, which should always be present in clinical writing, the following principles can be used as a quick reference guide for clinical writing.

- Write with the profession's values and ethics as your foundation. Your writing is an extension of your practice and as such should demonstrate your knowledge and commitment to client self-determination, strengths, empow-erment, cultural competence, and other core characteristics of the profes-sion. Remember that through your writing you are a spokesperson for the profession.
- Avoid words or phrases that could depersonalize, dehumanize, or mar-ginalize people. For example, rather than writing about the "borderline pa-tient" you are working with, consider using "woman diagnosed with borderline personality disorder" or, better still, "woman who exhibits pervasive instability in moods, interpersonal relationships, self-image, and behavior." Similarly,

avoid phrases such as "client of alternate sexual orientation," which presupposes heterosexuality as the norm and could be perceived as pejorative.

■ Infuse your writing with a solid appreciation and description of client strengths. Regardless of the format, clinical writing should do justice to an individual's narrative or to a population's shared narrative, which undoubtedly includes multiple strengths as well as challenges. Be mindful that clinical writing is often an opportunity to "give voice" to those who might not otherwise have one in public. Take full advantage. "Ms. Charpentier is a 23-year-old woman who lives in a group residence for young adults. She is hardworking and devoted to family and friends, and she displays a strong interest in the well-being of others. Recently she has experienced a series of losses that have been difficult for her to adjust to. Although she has an intellectual disability that presents challenges in some areas of daily living, including employment, she is quite capable of experiencing, processing, and discussing her grief and should be provided ample opportunity to do so in much the same way that people without disabilities are (or should be) afforded."

■ Write in ways that demonstrate your respect for clients' rights, including their rights to confidentiality and self-determination. This includes limiting your description of the client and clinical situation to only those details that are relevant to the issue at hand and to the service providers who will have access to the written material. If, for example, you are a school social worker providing parent guidance to a couple whose eighth grader is exhibiting academic and behavioral difficulties in the classroom, it is probably not necessary for you to document in the student record that the couple is actively engaged in their first round of fertility treatments. Even if you believe that this information has a direct connection to the presenting issue (the student's classroom struggles), such a detail is not required by everyone who will have access to the student record. Rather, a more general note should suffice; for example, "Manny's parents are meeting with me to discuss a variety of family issues that may be affecting his performance and behavior in school. Both Jackie and Sheila are eager to get input from me and others who know Manny, as doing so may help them to establish more effective guidelines and routines at home." Further details can be discussed verbally with specific colleagues if it is deemed essential to their work with the student or his family. Additionally, let people know when and why they are the subject of your writing, and be sure they understand and are comfortable with the process. If you would like to publish written material about your clinical work with an individual or family, be sure to consider well before publication whether heavy disguise or client consent is the appropriate way to proceed.

- Explore and adhere to agency and state guidelines pertaining to written communication about clients. For example, know whether the state in which you practice requires special protection of certain information (e.g., disability status, HIV status under the Health Information and Portability Protection Act) and share this information with your clients.

- Understand your intended audience and purpose, but also remember that your words, once on paper, may be read by unexpected eyes. In general, write as if your client will read your material. Indeed, some believe that this is likely to be an actuality for many social workers, especially those in private practice who publish articles about their clinical work. Individuals who are reading about themselves should perceive the written material to be a respectful and accurate accounting of their experiences. However, consider the possibility that your client may not understand or agree with what you intend to write; therefore, be sure to provide timely opportunities for discussion about the writing process, its uses, and potential benefits and harms.

In conclusion, although talk will always be the heart of clinical social work practice, writing is also an extremely significant, sometimes overlooked component. When done well, it has the power to facilitate connection, healing, and understanding, and it provides opportunities for social workers to teach and inform as well as to learn and grow. When done poorly, it can alienate and disempower both our clients and our profession. In addition to using the principles provided here as a guide to our clinical writing endeavors, each of us also has the opportunity to infuse the process and outcomes with the creative mind that we bring to our treasured work with those we write about. My hope is that this chapter will reinforce your commitment to clinical social work and stimulate you to use writing as a positive force to move this specialty practice area forward.

RECOMMENDED READINGS

Resources Related to Clinical Writing

http://www.socialworkers.org/practice/clinical/cswo20106.asp
http://www.socialworkers.org/pressroom/features/issue/advocacy.asp

http://www.socialworkers.org/pressroom/mediaToolkit/toolkit/MediaToolkit.pdf
http://www.abecsw.org/pub-jaffee-redmond.php

References

Bridges, N. (2007). Clinical writing about patients: Negotiating the impact on patients and their treatment. *Psychoanalytic Social Work, 14*(1), 23–41.

Brydon, K. (2004). Untreatable families? Suggestions from literature. *Australian Social Work, 57*(4), 365–373.

Kantrowitz, J. L. (2006). *Writing about patients: Responsibilities, risks, and ramifications.* New York: Other Press.

Saleebey, D. (Ed.). 1997. *The strengths perspective in social work.* New York: Longman.

7

GETTING THE POLICY MESSAGE ACROSS TO DIVERSE AUDIENCES

Shirley Gatenio Gabel and Sheila B. Kamerman

SOCIAL WORKERS MAY BE BOTH advocates and policy analysts. Social work advocates are often defined as those working to empower vulnerable groups (Jansson, 2003; Schneider & Lester, 2001). Policy analysts help to shape legislation, evaluate budgets, assess the effectiveness of programs and design new ones, and explain policy issues to a broad audience (Bardach, 2005). Policy analysts may be part of think tanks or may be working for community-based groups, and the work may be local or global (Hick & McNuit, 2002; VeneKlasen & Miller, 2002). Their work takes many forms, but the goal of policy analysis is to educate, to influence, and to shape public policies (Musso, Biller, & Myrtle, 2000; Weimer & Vining, 1999). It is likely that social workers will become involved in a social issue relevant to their clients during the course of their career and will therefore need to write a memo or explain a policy issue to a broad audience. This chapter combines the expertise of public policy analysts (Bardach, 2005; Musso et al., 2000; Weimar & Vining, 1999) and social worker policy advocates (Haynes & Mickelson, 2006; Jansson, 2003; Hick & McNuit, 2002) to provide social workers with the tools needed to help bring about changes in social policies that promote social justice both domestically and globally.

Policy analysis is no longer limited to the technical or elite offices of government agencies. Today we find policy analysts in large bureaucratic agencies, in small not-for-profit agencies, and in profit-making organizations. Like policy analysts, policy advocates use policy analysis to affect social change (Haynes & Mickelson, 2006; Jansson, 2003). The work of the policy advocate focuses on the process of change, whereas the policy analyst tends to focus on analyzing the information needed to make informed decisions. Both policy analysts and policy advocates play critical roles in bringing about social change. The tools of the social policy analyst and advocate have broadened over time, but written communication remains fundamental to the work of both. As Musso et al. (2000) noted, "Bad writing is long-winded, pointless or factless, studded with technical jargon or tongue-tied with passive construction. Good writing is decisive, compelling, and brief. If you write well and sincerely, you will get a well-deserved reputation as someone who 'speaks truth to power'" (p. 635).

The purpose of this chapter is to guide students and practitioners through the elements of good policy writing. We present an outline of generic policy writing, followed by a discussion of how structure and purpose differ for policy briefs, issue or research briefs, and policy memos. The outline consists of five steps: (1) know your audience, (2) define the problem, (3) present evidence to support the existence and extent of the problem, (4) propose and evaluate policy responses, and (5) make recommendations. This chapter presents the kinds of information needed for each step and the questions that should be answered at each step, which sometimes necessitate that the writer reevaluate earlier steps. Effective writing for both policy analysts and policy advocates is not a linear process; it requires reassessing and rewriting along the way.

The chapter will also distinguish between writing to inform readers of policy options and writing to advocate a policy position. It will briefly address the elements (purpose, structure) of policy reports, briefings, memos, legislative analysis, editorials, and letters to the editor. It presents some of the written instruments that policy analysts and advocates can use to affect social change. By no means are the options presented here exhaustive, nor do they reflect the full range of advocacy tools available.

The chapter will also discuss the mechanics of good policy writing, such as using the active voice, avoiding jargon, getting to the point, striving for clarity, and avoiding long sentences. It will use examples of do's and don'ts to illustrate good writing.

WRITING A POLICY PAPER IN FIVE STEPS

STEP 1: KNOW YOUR AUDIENCE

Before you write, you should be clear about your audience and your goal or purpose. Knowing your audience, their level of sophistication about the topic, their needs, and your goal in the process are key to writing a policy piece that will reach that audience effectively.

In this step, the questions to be considered are these:

- Who are you trying to communicate with or influence?
- What style and tone is appropriate for your audience?
- How much does your audience know about the issue?
- What do you want your audience to know from reading your report?
- What kind of knowledge would be helpful to your audience?
- What do you expect a reader to do after reading the policy report?

If you are writing to educate a community about an issue that most will know little about, the terminology used, research methodology, level of detail, and depth and extent of the information conveyed should be quite different from a policy document written primarily for academics or policy experts in an area. You want to avoid being too specific or too vague, too technical or inadequately scientific, too long or too short, and too detailed or too superficial. Most documents are not appropriate for all audiences. It is important to consider who you are writing to and for what purpose before you begin. What does your audience need to know? How can you best present the information to them (Dobel, Elmore, & Werner, 2003)?

Before you write, consider how much knowledge your readers are likely to have. Are you writing for an audience of professionals who are familiar with the issues? Is the reader likely to be new to the subject or to have considerable years of experience in the area? If you are writing to influence a decision, what kind of information is needed to make the decision? What information would be useful to have? The information must always be accurate and relevant. Decision makers value good information, and inept writers lose credibility (Musso et al., 2000). Consider, for example, the different types of knowledge that would be valued by different parties regarding the introduction of a preschool program in a local community. Parents may want to know the content of the proposed program, the expected effects on their children, and the fees they will have to pay. Taxpayers would be interested in the cost of the program against the anticipated benefits and who is likely to benefit. Researchers will be more interested in the purpose of the preschool program, what problems or issues it is intended to address, which are the key variables and measurement issues, the methodology used for assessment, and whether a rigorous evaluation of relevant outcomes will be conducted.

Think about what you would like your readers to do after they read your policy paper. Do you want them to contact public officials? Organize?

Communicate with the media? Perhaps your goal is that a social issue be understood from a different perspective and that new responses be considered. Depending on your purpose, the policy paper you write should include information on the policymaking process, recommendations, and next steps.

The better you understand your intended audience, the more accessible the paper will be to your reader. The different types of policy papers to choose from will be discussed later in this chapter.

STEP 2: DEFINE THE PROBLEM

- Why does the situation need a policy response? Why is it a social issue/problem of concern to society, and how significant is it?
- How is the issue framed and why?
- What factors have contributed to the social issue/problem identified?
- Are there other ways of defining the social issue/problem? What are the advantages and disadvantages of defining the problem in each of those ways?
- Will your audience readily understand your definition of the problem?

Students almost always think that defining the problem is much easier than it is, and they often rush through this stage, only to find incongruities in later stages. Defining the problem is crucial in policy analysis and advocacy writing; it provides direction and the reason for your work. A problem or issue may emerge from a group or a community, or from the implementation of a policy that has revealed holes in the policy, legislation, or program. Problems may also emerge from research or reviews of research.

Definitions of social problems also change over time, so they depend on contextual frameworks. For example, throughout human history there have been families and individuals without adequate food and shelter. Such family needs have generally been attributed to the lack of income or other resources, whether reflective of the inability of a family to grow their own food because they do not have the land or their inability to afford decent housing. The problem, though, has been defined differently depending on the dominant thinking of the time. In the days of the Puritans, poverty was viewed as a sign of working against the will of God—the poor were poor because their work effort was not sufficient, or they were poor because they were not strict enough about their religious practices. This conceptualization of poverty contributed to a definition of poverty as being a consequence of inadequate individual behaviors, such as acting immorally or being lazy. In current research, we see a new definition of poverty evolving, one that is based on the belief that all people have human rights, including the basic right to food and shelter. Poverty, in this framework, is defined as a denial of human rights (Reichert, 2006).

Sometimes an issue comes with its own jargon, or what Bardach (2000) called "issue rhetoric" (p. 1). The temptation is to perpetuate the jargon, but understanding an issue requires that you strip away the jargon to understand why the issue is being defined as a problem or identified as a cause for concern. A policy paper with sloppy writing, poor grammar and editing, and/or a complex structure and an overreliance on jargon will not persuade others, nor will it enhance its author's political credibility. Rather, it will deflate interest in an issue and negatively affect the author's credibility.

Jargon or issue rhetoric is often partisan or ideological by nature, functioning as shorthand for a particular position. For example, "right to life" is seemingly something we would all favor, but the term is strongly associated with those who are against abortion. Likewise, it would seem that support for values that favor the well-being of families would be noncontroversial, but today the term "family values" is a political and social concept predominantly used by right-wing and conservative political parties. When you define the issue being addressed, be cautious about using jargon—or avoid it altogether unless you know that your readers fully understand the connotations.

Another common mistake of students (and hasty writers) is that in defining the problem they present the solution. The solution should come as the result of your presentation of the facts, analysis, and exploration of alternatives, not before the hard work is done. For example, identifying the problem as "inadequate resources" for health clinics in a community automatically leads the reader to believe that the solution is to increase funding for health clinics in the community, but the problem might actually be a lack of health insurance, an inability to afford health care, inaccessibility of health care providers, or a combination of these. It would be better to define the problem as "the health care needs of a community not being addressed" and then explore the "unmet needs" and what might be the causes. Later, when you consider policy responses to the problem, you can give consideration to, for example, increasing funding to clinics and expanding health care coverage.

STEP 3: PRESENT EVIDENCE TO SUPPORT THE EXISTENCE AND EXTENT OF THE PROBLEM

- How do you know the social issue/problem exists?
- Is there evidence to support the existence and extent of the social problem as defined?
- Are there reliable data sources that support or refute your definition of the problem? If not, why hasn't this social problem been previously identified?
- If there is no direct evidence, what data sources can you use to support the existence and extent of the defined problem?
- How credible are the sources?
- What policy responses have been tried and what were the consequences?

As you develop your definition of the problem, test it out. For example, how do you know that health care needs are unmet? What proportion of the population is affected? Who in the population is affected? Children? Adults who are not working or who are working in certain sectors? Are there current related policies in place that are not addressing the needs of a certain group? Why?

Gather information that quantifies the problem, from official sources if possible and always from credible sources. In many cases, it will be necessary to "guesstimate" the magnitudes in question; however, be sure to let the reader know it is your best guesstimate and always detail how it was derived (Bardach, 2005). Guesstimates may be derived from a review of the literature, analogies of parallel situations in different fields (for example, to further develop ethical standards for social work therapists, you may look to standards for medical and legal personnel), and best practices in the field (for example, the kinds of exit interviews that social workers conduct for families leaving child welfare systems in other big cities).

You can expect to rewrite the definition of the problem in the process of analyzing it and learning more about it. *Thinking* is the most critical aspect of both a policy analysis and an advocacy process, but most of your time will likely be spent collecting data to support your conceptualization of the issue (Bardach, 2005). The data may come from statistical reports, interviews, previous research, and/or existing documents, and gathering data from such sources will be a time-consuming activity. When interviewing community members and public officials, be aware that the interviewees may be wary of speaking with you because of the potential political implications of sharing their opinions or information. From their point of view, you might possibly be the one who reveals their mistakes or recommends a policy response that will eliminate their positions or those of their staff. You will most always collect more information than you can use, and this step will take longer than budgeted. Be frugal with your time and effort—try to collect only the data that are directly relevant to your conceptualization of a problem or issue. Save the rest for a more careful academic research study. Collected data may also be useful as a counterargument to an alternative policy response presented or as a counterargument to your position with which your audience should be familiar.

Think about what your reader needs to know and why. You may find it fascinating that 100 years ago Progressive reformers fought for benefits that would allow mothers to stay at home rather than for increasing the availability of day care—but is this knowledge needed to increase funding for child care today? As Musso et al. (2000) have noted, "Do not tell your clients what you know; tell them what they need to know" (p. 637).

STEP 4: PROPOSE AND EVALUATE POLICY RESPONSES

Once you have clearly defined the problem and supported your definition with convincing evidence, you need to answer the following questions:

- What are the policy response options?
- What principles guide the policy options? What criteria will you use to assess each of the responses?
- What are the trade-offs for each of the proposed policy responses you have identified?
- Who has jurisdiction over the social problem/issue and the recommended policy responses?
- How will the policy responses identified be financed? What are the economic, social, and political risks?
- What responses have been tried and what were the consequences?

There is no one right answer to a social policy question or problem. Policy issues reflect the confluence of social, economic, and political values in a society. The better you understand your audience's guiding principles, the more likely you will be able to develop policy responses that will meet the goals of your audience. For example, in many countries childhood is considered a period during which children are protected and dependent on adults, usually their parents, to develop intellectually, socially, psychologically, and physically. In many of these countries, children attend school, and apart from small jobs, child labor is viewed as a violation of this protected period. In other countries, child labor is seen as preparation for adulthood and often as a necessary financial contribution to the family and even the community. The International Labor Organization and the International Programme on the Elimination of Child Labour (2002) have acknowledged that in some areas the economic contributions of children are essential to the well-being of children and their families and that without these contributions some children would be exposed to greater social, moral, and health risks. Depending on how child labor is framed, different policy responses come to mind. Suppose you assume that child labor is harmful to children and robs them of their rights. After reading a few research reports on this, you understand that poverty is a critical reason that children work in paid employment. Another reason is the opportunity cost of education. You may include policy responses such as subsidizing a family's income if the children are attending school, educating a community about the economic opportunities for an educated person, increasing parental wages, and establishing paid apprenticeships for older children while they are in school.

Your responsibility is to analyze and compare the strengths and weaknesses of all possible alternatives against a common set of criteria. The criteria should be derived from the guiding principles and should be applied objectively to each of the policy options. Examples of criteria used to evaluate policy options in the example of child labor are cost, political support, projected income of a child staying in school, child welfare, safety and crime reduction, and accrued health benefits. Quantify whenever possible, and if you cannot quantify, describe how the policy outcomes are likely to measure up against a selected criterion. Try to avoid scores that are ambiguous, such as "little," "some," and "a lot" or "positive/negative," as such responses do not offer enough information.

As a general rule, your policy paper should have three to four policy response alternatives. Eliminate weaker alternatives and alternatives that are subsumed under more comprehensive policy choices. No one policy option is likely to solve the whole problem. By comparing policy alternatives presented in an interesting and reader-friendly manner (matrices, charts, and tables can be helpful here), the reader can absorb large quantities of information quickly. Don't hesitate to report problems, past history, implications, as well as the positive potential of a policy. Most readers will appreciate a brief presentation of other viewpoints; in this way, they can anticipate questions and their own responses when they lobby their position.

STEP 5: MAKE RECOMMENDATIONS

On the basis of your hard thinking and analysis, you are ready to recommend a policy response.

■ How to choose a policy recommendation?

This step summarizes the defined problem, goals, and guiding principles, and how the policy alternatives measure up against the criteria. If you have been clear and thorough along the way, recommending which policy option to pursue is likely to be self-evident. For most of us, this final step reveals the shortcuts we took along the way and the flaws in our thinking or our methodology. Sometimes it reveals that although we have collected much information, we may not be answering the questions we posed. Or we may learn that the full extent of the problem is not clearly understood or delineated. Sometimes the necessary information may be there, but our organization and presentation need to be clearer and more directive.

Perhaps you arrive at this recommendation step and the solution seems too obvious. Ask yourself why you haven't done this already. Go back and reevaluate your criteria. Have you left out some critical issues related to costs? Implementation? Political risk? Public opinion? Have the positions of key stakeholders been ignored? Many readers jump immediately to this section, so be sure it covers the points you most want your reader to be clear about. Do not introduce anything new in the conclusions. If you are including a recommendations section, it should offer the best and most sound advice you can offer. Make sure the recommendations are clear, direct, and substantiated by the facts you have presented earlier.

WRITING IT UP

We have outlined the basic steps for analyzing a policy issue that applies to a variety of reports. The next step is to decide what kind of format best suits your needs and is most likely to be effective.

POLICY REPORT

Of all the policy paper options, a policy report is the longest and the most detailed. It is typically 20–30 pages, sometimes as long as 40 pages, and is written in response to a client's request. The client, in the case of a social work policy analyst, may be a social service agency, an association, a government department, or a community action group. The traditional policy report prepared for a client is organized in a reader-friendly manner, allowing the reader to easily access (skim for) information through clearly delineated sections, brief sentences and paragraphs, bulleted lists, boldface headings, and use of white space to direct the reader's attention.

The purpose of the policy report varies. A group of agencies can commission a policy report because of common problems they experience in service delivery or funding. For example, when a substantial number of homeless people were observed to experience mental health and substance abuse issues simultaneously, it became evident to many providers that the existing shelter system was not responsive to the multiple needs of their clients. In this case, a policy report would explore the policy options for developing services for these clients that combine services from several different government agencies and examine how best to house and finance such services for optimal delivery. Another example would be a public agency seeking to reevaluate and restructure its child welfare policies and system. Several years ago, national headlines were filled with stories of how New Jersey's child welfare system tragically failed the children and families who depended on the state for support and protection. Change was necessary and task forces were created to explore how policies and the system could be improved. These task forces produced policy reports that defined the problem and recommended policy responses.

The general format of a policy report includes the following:

- an executive summary
- one or two sections on defining the problem, its causes, and evidence supporting the existence and extent of the problem
- a section evaluating different policy options
- conclusions and recommendations

The executive summary is the first section of a policy report, and it is usually written last. It is a concise presentation of the report's major findings, conclusions, and recommendations. The executive summary informs the reader, usually in 500 to 750 words, of the report's substantive message. It should be written for the highest-ranking officials in your audience, with the intent of informing, educating, and influencing them. The executive summary should come directly to the point, capturing the reader's interest and making the value of the report clear. It should be able to stand alone and highlight the findings in the body of the report (Harvard Kennedy School of Government Communications Program, n.d.).

POLICY BRIEF

A policy brief is a relatively short document addressing specific people or groups for the purpose of transmitting information, updating policy or research developments, and summarizing knowledge to date. A policy brief is typically 3–6 pages. Its audience is varied and typically large—perhaps an association of those with common interests (health and mental health service providers, for instance), elected officials and their staff who have jurisdiction over a policy issue being considered (such as welfare reform, affordable housing), or a geographic community that is affected by a particular social problem. Many policy briefs are targeted to those who have interest and influence regarding an issue that they need to know a lot about in a short time. Brevity is essential; your audience is likely to include decision makers who have little time yet must assimilate information quickly and move to take fast, decisive action.

In practical terms, every aspect of a brief—its prose style, organization, appearance on the page, and content—should have a direct relationship to its purpose. Long, flowery introductions, technical jargon, and showy vocabulary all distract from the essential purpose. Here is a generic outline to follow when writing a policy brief:

- one to two paragraphs briefly defining and summarizing the problem/issue and making recommendations
- evidence of the significance of the problem/issue
- contextual information regarding actions taken to date to remedy the situation
- alternative policy responses
- recommended policy options and reasons for them

Your policy brief should be divided into sections with bold headings that make clear the type of information available in each section, such as

"History," "Community Response," "Policy Options," and "Recommendations" (Harvard Kennedy School of Government Communications Program, n. d.).

POLICY MEMO

A policy memorandum, usually two pages long, addresses specific people or groups within an association, organization, or work group for the purpose of recording an agreement, transmitting information, or enabling action. The policy memo may be sent to a group but is generally addressed to the most senior person in that group. This decision maker is likely to have little time, a wide range of responsibilities, and the least familiarity with the issue, and he or she must absorb the contents of the memo quickly. Long memos don't get read. Use headings related to the purpose of the memo so that the reader knows where to look for quick information.

The general format and content of the memo follows that of the policy brief. The memo should open with its purpose, stated as the issue, topic, or objective; it should then provide a summary of findings, including the background, relevant history leading to the current situation, previous actions, problem/issue, current situation, supporting evidence, and policy options; and it should conclude with recommendations.

LEGISLATIVE ANALYSIS

Legislative analysis is a detailed analysis of a bill considered in the legislature. It is similar to other types of policy analyses, in that it carefully examines the effects of a proposed policy change on specific populations, systems, or processes. Unlike policy analysis, a legislative analysis focuses on the effects of a particular piece of legislation. Legally trained professionals are often responsible for legislative analysis, but technology and Internet access have made legislative analysis accessible to more analysts. The length of the analysis varies according to the complexity of the legislation, but for most bills it is four or fewer pages. A legislative analysis includes: (1) a heading consisting of the bill number, the version of the bill being analyzed, and the bill's sponsors (if the same bill is being considered in both houses of the legislature, then both numbers are included); (2) a brief statement summarizing the intent of the bill; (3) the bill's legislative history; (4) a description of the bill in more detail; (5) the cost and anticipated effects of the bill on populations or sectors of interest; and (6) the entity's support or lack of support for the proposed change made by the bill. An analysis usually is easier to understand than the bill itself because it is written in narrative style and organized by topic, with the bill's key provisions described first.

Legislative offices at most levels of government provide analyses of pending laws. Information on previous legislation can be retrieved from Westlaw—Public Access (WESTPAC) and LexisNexis Academic Universe. If the executive office introduces legislation, it is accompanied by a bill summary, sometimes called a bill jacket, summarizing the need for the bill and its provisions. Bills introduced by federal or state houses of the legislature have similar bill summaries accompanying them. In New York State, for example, the legislature maintains an online service that provides a bill's text, summaries, sponsor memos, calendars, and floor votes. Other proprietary and restricted-access services are available as well.

A legislative analysis prepared by an advocacy group will be directed to the executive and the legislature in support of or opposition to a bill. The analysis of legislation written for the community's consumption may be targeted to urge concerned parties to contact their elected officials regarding their support or opposition to a bill. This type of communication would be briefer and would emphasize the bill's impact on the community. It should open with the organization's position and end with the action steps needed.

OP-ED

An op-ed is an article that appears opposite a newspaper's editorials. While op-eds can be lighthearted or satirical, most often they are timely pieces by writers who have expertise in a particular subject. The purpose of an op-ed is generally to be provocative or to highlight a particular point of view. Depending on the newspaper, an op-ed potentially has a wide audience and can introduce a new perspective, gain public support for a policy issue, and ignite debate.

The length of an op-ed will vary according to the newspaper. Publishers set word-length limits, and this information is usually available in the newspaper, appears on its Web site, or can be obtained by calling. Most op-eds are 750–800 words, though there are exceptions in either direction. Find out the prescribed limits and try to stay within them. Newspapers will typically ask for a short biography of the author, usually 25 words or less. This should appear at the end of the op-ed piece. Op-eds should be accompanied by a cover letter that includes your name, contact information, and the name of someone at your university or organization who can be contacted if you cannot be reached.

LETTERS TO THE EDITOR

Most letters to the editor are written in direct and timely response to a specific article. This is a key difference between this type of communication and other policy analyses. Effective letters to the editor have all the elements of good policy writing: They are based on an analysis of a policy issue, focused on essential issues, use convincing evidence, and present a policy response to a significant social problem. Letters to the editor can reach a large audience, are often monitored by elected officials, and can present information not previously discussed in an article.

Unlike other policy communications, a letter to the editor stresses the economical use of words and ideas. Many newspapers have strict limits on the length of letters and have limited space to publish them, generally 75–150 words. The more succinctly you make your point, the better the chance that it will be printed and remembered. Space constraints require that you stay focused on what you believe is most essential, and back it up with good evidence. Ideally you want to state your point in the first sentence. There may be details that you have issue with, but space limitations require that you address one essential point, at most two.

Avoid the common mistake in letters to the editor of summing up an article, leaving yourself space only to say you disagree. Use your knowledge and analysis of an issue, and back it up with evidence that you have gathered.

Most papers will print only letters that refer to a specific article, so it is a good idea to refer to the article you are responding to in the opening paragraph. For example, an opening sentence might be: "The NY *Times* April 18 editorial 'School Vouchers Are Right On' omitted some of the key facts in the debate." The ability to sum up a complex policy analysis in about 100 words is challenging, a skill that requires practice. The clearer you are on the purpose and recommendations, the easier the task.

DOS AND DON'TS OF EFFECTIVE POLICY WRITING

- **Do** plan on revisions. A good policy memo is the end product of re-working, rewording, rethinking, rearranging, and rereading.

■ **Do** keep your language and structure simple. Complex sentence structure and organization can be mistaken for confusion or hidden agendas. You are also likely to lose the reader's interest if your communication is more complicated than it needs to be. Each paragraph should begin with a topic sentence. Each sentence should have a subject, verb, and object that are in agreement and in that order. Two examples of problematic sentences are offered below; the problems are highlighted in brackets:

> Every policymaker would like their [should be *his* or *her*] policies to be implemented. [Singular nouns require singular pronouns.]

> Given the problems regarding job placement, and the legislation before Congress regarding funding, the task force decided to defer action until Congress made its decisions and we could assess how this was likely to affect the proposed employment program for welfare recipients. [The sentence is too long. The subject (task force) should be followed by the verb (defer) and the object (the job placement program).]

■ **Do** use words that reflect the vocabulary of your audience, not your thesaurus. Also, avoid using bureaucratic language, jargon, and slang.

> The Minimum Data Set (MDS) data are aggregated to calculate quality indicators in nursing homes by which to target the survey process, and are now available for public usage.

Unless you have expertise in this area, most readers would have difficulty understanding this.
Alternatively, the sentence could be rewritten as follows:

> Data collected regularly on patients in nursing home facilities are used to develop indicators of nursing home quality standards, and the results are available to the public.

■ **Do not** confuse nouns with other parts of speech, such as verbs or adjectives. At present, there seems to be a new trend to turn nouns into verbs. For example, people "interface" with one another and "text message" each other. Avoid such informal jargon. Similarly, avoid taking a noun or verb and placing it before a noun to make a compound adjective—for example, "programmatic decision making," or "circumvention practice" (Dobel et al.,

2003). "Circumvention practice" refers specifically to practices for avoiding anti-dumping trade measures or, more generally, to tools or strategies used to bypass restrictions. When using the phrase, it is best to explain its meaning. For example, a report using the term "programmatic decision making" explained what was meant by the term early in the report: "A framework for decision making that is 1) focused on the external context in which the foundation works and 2) includes a hypothesized causal connection between use of foundation resources and goal achievement" (Center for Effective Philanthropy, 2007).

- **Do not** use more words than necessary; doing so will obscure your message. For example, rather than saying to "afford an opportunity," why not say "allow"? Instead of "imposing a requirement," say "require."
- **Do** begin your policy paper with your recommendation, conclusion, action request, or summary. Once you have grabbed the reader's attention, you are more likely to keep that reader's interest.
- **Do** use an active voice and avoid the passive voice. Here is an example:

The proposal was considered by the task force. [Passive voice]

The task force considered the proposal. [Active voice, clearer and fewer words used]

- **Do** check for grammar, spelling, and punctuation, and when you have done that, check again. Do not rely on spell-check software. The spelling of a word determines its meaning; for example, think of "complement" and "compliment."
- **Do** use inclusive language, which is neutral and persuasive. It avoids offending others, for example, with regard to race, gender, age, ethnicity, religion, and sexual orientation.

The group invited *all* morally righteous Americans to defend the free enterprise system, the family, and Bible morality.

This statement implies that one supports these positions if one is a morally righteous American.

- **Do not** confuse Latin abbreviations such as "e.g." and "i.e." When you mean "for example," use "e.g." When you mean "that is," use "i.e." Either can be used to clarify a preceding statement, the first by example, the second by restating the idea more clearly or expanding upon it. Because these phrases are so similar, the two abbreviations may be easily confused.

- **Do** make your report skimmable. The margins should be wide enough and there should be sufficient "white space" to facilitate skimming the document. Headings and subheadings should be used as a road map for the reader to understand the organization and content of the paper. Use charts, tables, bulleted lists, and diagrams to summarize complex information, accompanied by a narrative to highlight the most important information.

CONCLUSION

This chapter presents a writing guide for policy practitioners and advocates by outlining the steps that can be followed in writing a variety of policy papers. It presents some helpful hints for writing such papers. In addition, scholars may also find herein help for preparing manuscripts for academic publications. Whereas many policy reports begin with a brief executive summary of the social issues being considered and recommendations, scholarly articles will often open with an abstract that identifies the problem addressed, the focus of the research, the methods used, and a summary of the conclusions. Policy analysis for scholarly journals will likewise include a definition of the issue or problem, but where policy analyses will focus on proposed solutions, scholarly articles are more likely to test the effectiveness of proposed policy responses and include a discussion of research methods, findings, and conclusions.

In short, the focus of this chapter is on the writing for policy analysis, policy advocacy, and policy content. The goals are to educate, influence, and shape public policy, to facilitate the identification of—and choices among—policy options, and to make recommendations. Policy analysts focus on analyzing the information available to make informed decisions, while policy advocates focus on the process of change and advancing particular options.

The chapter identifies the tools that social workers need in order to bring about changes in social policy that promote social justice domestically and globally. It is designed to guide students and practitioners through the basic elements of good policy writing by identifying the key steps, including defining the problem and its extent, proposing alternative solutions, providing evidence in support of the choices, and making recommendations. Several illustrations of different types of social policy writing are described:

reports, executive summaries, issue briefs, memos, legislative analyses, op-ed articles, and letters to the editor, as well as a brief list of "dos and don'ts" of effective policy writing.

The chapter is by no means exhaustive; rather it is intended to help policy practitioners and advocates write more effectively when communicating their policy messages. As the social work field expands, so too will the responsibilities of social workers; it is therefore essential that all social workers enhance the skills needed to communicate effectively to our diverse audiences and stakeholders.

References

Bardach, E. (2005). *A practical guide for policy analysis: The eightfold path to more effective problem solving*. Washington, DC: CQ Press.

Center for Effective Philanthropy (2008). *Beyond the rhetoric: Foundation strategy*. Cambridge, MA: Author.

Dobel, J. P., Elmore, R., & Werner, L. (2003). Memo writing. *The electronic hallway*. Seattle: University of Washington.

Harvard Kennedy School of Government Communications Program. (n.d.). *Policy analysis exercise (PAE): The writing guide*. Retrieved from http://www.hks.harvard.edu/var/ezp_site/storage/fckeditor/file/pdfs/degree-programs/oca/Communications/pae-guide.pdf

Haynes, K. S., & Mickelson, J. S. (2006). *Affecting change: Social workers in the political arena* (6th ed.). Boston: Allyn & Bacon.

Hick, S. E., & McNuit, J. G. (Eds.). (2002). *Advocacy, activism, and the Internet*. Chicago: Lyceum Books.

International Labour Organisation (ILO) & International Programme on the Elimination of Child Labour (IPEC). (2002). *Towards a national child labour action programme for South Africa*. Geneva: Author.

Jansson, B. S. (2003). *Becoming an effective policy advocate*. Pacific Grove, CA: Brooks/Cole Publishing.

Musso, J., Biller, R., & Myrtle, R. (2000). Tradecraft: Professional writing as problem solving. *Journal of Policy Analysis & Management*, 19(4), 635–646.

Reichert, E. (2006). *Understanding human rights: An exercise book*. London: Sage Publications.

Schneider, R. L., & Lester, L. (2001). *Social work advocacy: A new framework for action*. Monterey, CA: Wadsworth/Brooks Cole.

VeneKlasen, L., & Miller, V. (2002). *A new weave of power, people, and politics: The action guide for advocacy and citizen participation*. Oklahoma City: World Neighbors.

Weimer, D. L., and Vining, A. (1999). *Policy analysis, concepts, and practice* (3rd ed.). Englewood Cliffs, NJ: Prentice Hall.

APPENDIX

ORGANIZATIONS ENGAGED IN POLICY ANALYSIS AND ADVOCACY

AARP Public Policy Institute. www.aarp.org/research/ppi/

Association for Public Policy Analysis and Management. www.appam
.org/home.asp

Brookings Institution. www.brookings.edu/US.aspx

Center on Budget and Policy Priorities. www.cbpp.org/

Center for Law and Social Policy (CLASP). www.clasp.org/

The Future of Children. www.futureofchildren.org/

Henry Kaiser Foundation. www.kff.org/

Immigration Policy Center (IPC). www.ailf.org/

Moving Ideas. www.care2.com/

National Center for Policy Analysis. www.ncpa.org/

National Health Policy Forum. www.nhpf.org/

RAND Corporation. www.rand.org/research_areas/

Social Service Research Network. www.ssrn.com/index.cfm

8

WRITING IN PROGRAM AND PROPOSAL DEVELOPMENT: THE SOCIAL WORK WRITER AS TRANSLATOR

Marion Riedel

WHY WRITE A PROPOSAL?

While in New Orleans as part of an immersion course, several students and I spent two days with the founder and executive director of an organization that wanted to secure funding for a hotline and resource referral network for survivors of Katrina—those displaced from their homes still in New Orleans and those displaced outside the state. She spent hours giving us the history of the agency, telling stories about key stakeholders, and describing where people have ended up "since the storms." Sitting with this process, I became acutely aware of our propensity to rush to developing solutions. Her process of developing trust with us and her need for us to understand the complexity of her story demanded our ongoing attention and our staying with the process. It was not until the second day that she began to weave her ideas for the program into her narrative. It occurred to me that there were two essential processes taking place. One was the difference between our cultural styles—hers being that of an African American woman running a community-based organization in Louisiana and ours being that of a group of diverse students and faculty from an Ivy League university in New York City. The second part of the process was developing trust. She was not going to share her ideas with us until trust had been established, at least in some preliminary way. As she finally began to share her ideas about the network she wanted to develop, we were able to begin the translation process.

Her story was poetry, with each of her words steeped in her experiences, resilience, and belief in her community to regroup and re-create their city.

Our challenge was to translate her passion and words into proposal language that would clarify mission, goals, objectives, and outcomes without changing their intent or losing their power. With every sentence we would listen, write, clarify, rewrite, and negotiate meaning and articulation. At times the consensus language escaped us, but we found words to suffice. In the end, the proposal closely matched her vision of the program and was translated into language that enabled it to successfully pass a competitive review process. I doubt any of us will ever look at the language written in a proposal in the same way again. The proposal was funded and the project is now under way.

Writing a proposal is the key route to accessing funds for development of needed programs and activities in an agency or a community. Proposals communicate the needs of the agency or community and clarify the importance of the proposed services (Coley & Scheinberg, 2000). The proposal facilitates our movement from identifying a cause, need, or other issue to accessing the means to address the need in practice.

Writing the proposal moves us toward completion of the program development process, including program design and conceptualization. The proposal provides structure to a process of development that might otherwise seem intuitive and nonstructured, and it helps us clarify our mission, desired outcomes, and change strategies. This activity enables us to engage in meaningful dialogue with our constituencies, thereby gaining a fuller understanding of what would enhance their capacity for change and optimal functioning. Further, the ability to secure funding for such activities can provide a meaningful entrée to communities that might otherwise lack interest or trust in professional social work intervention (Fraenkel, 2006), in much the same way that providing concrete services enhances engagement in microlevel practice. The ability to write a compelling proposal for funding is a fundamental mechanism for social change (McCarthy & Zald, 1977).

Proposal writing hones our writing skills. It is an activity that requires clarity and conciseness. All components of the proposal demand acuity—from describing the history and efficacy of the organization to stating mission, goals, and intended outcomes; from clearly articulating evaluation plans that will achieve transparency and accountability to, in the end, convincing a particular funding source that this program is a better fit with its ideals than those from competitors. One of the most common reasons that proposals do not get funded is poor and/or vague writing (Porter & Tech, 2005). In an environment where competition for shrinking dollars is great, the ability to write a clear and compelling request for funding will give you the edge necessary to achieve your program plans.

UNDERSTANDING NEEDS: WRITER AS TRANSLATOR

The first step in developing a meaningful program is to determine what is needed in your agency or community—that is, the gap between the services and activities you can currently provide and those needed to foster better functioning in your community. In this capacity, the writer steps into the role of active listener and translator. Communities or agency constituents usually know what it is that they want or need, but they may not always have the skills or experience to translate these ideas into language that will motivate the funding source to allocate money. Many of the skills that social workers learn to use in the first moments of engagement and assessment in practice on the microlevel are essential tools for needs identification, the first activity of program development. A collaborative and skilled proposal writer will understand at this point how to begin the conversation through active listening, probing, and clarifying issues that will lead to a more formal and structured needs assessment (Coley & Scheinberg, 2000; Kettner, Moroney, & Martin, 2007).

A common pitfall for social workers developing programs is acting on premature ideas about solutions to needs or problems that they do not yet understand (Kettner et al., 2007). We are often moved to develop solutions prematurely in response to a request for proposals (RFP) that is issued with program targets that fall within the general rubric of our intended program. These RFPs are often time-sensitive, and the appeal of meeting the deadline can hasten program development while concomitantly abbreviating the needs assessment process. Often such haste leads to programs that are less responsive to community or agency members, do not achieve the desired outcomes, and/or are underutilized (Witkin & Altschuld, 1995). Taking the additional time to develop and implement a community needs assessment before conceptualizing program ideas and change strategies will foster more satisfying program outcomes, enhance the self- and collective efficacy of those to be served (Ohmer, 2007), and assure the best use of limited resources.

Understanding need through a thorough needs assessment process (Kettner et al., 2007) will help you to construct a proposal that is most responsive to that need and to design a program that will provide the most appropriate services to your designated service recipients. This program can be embedded in the structure and context of the agency or the community. The role of social worker as translator can continue through the development of the program, the writing of the proposal, and the implementation of services, if you are committed to continued collaboration with the service receivers.

COMMUNITY COLLABORATION AND EMPOWERMENT

If you maintain your role as translator of community needs, you will look toward community-based collaborations to inform the nature of your interactions. Community-based collaborations can range from identifying the community as the target of change to the community as a resource or agent of change (McLeroy, Norton, Kegler, Burdine, & Sumaya, 2003). Using empowerment models of developing programs will help you to identify and utilize community resources and view community members as agents, rather than targets, of change. Using empowerment models will help you identify community capacity, understand theories and models of how communities change, and demonstrate your willingness to follow the lead of the community—thus shifting power and sharing expertise (Austin, Des Camp, Flux, McClelland, & Sieppart, 2005).

Community participation builds a sense of self- and community efficacy (Ohmer, 2007; Wells, Miranda, Bruce, Alegria, & Wallerstein, 2004), and creating it is an intervention in and of itself, enhancing the power of program activities. By working with community participants, you can increase efficacy and facilitate long-term change, leaving the community healthier and with greater functioning capacity (McLeroy et al., 2003) and resources for continuing the change after you leave.

Keeping the interests of community members at the forefront of program development helps strengthen collaborative relationships and programs. The input of multiple constituents roots the ideas for change in community assets and need, increases relevance, and provides a mechanism for exploring and resolving ethical dilemmas and values (McCarthy & Zald, 1977). The use of focus groups (Trettin & Musham, 2000) and other narrative interviewing strategies (Elliot, 2005) will help you to engage with community members and guide and monitor program development. Volunteering to help agencies develop proposals in post-Katrina New Orleans forced me to revisit this reality and the notion that our guiding philosophy was that community members have primary responsibility for action and decision making (Homan, 2004).

EVIDENCE-BASED PRACTICE AND CULTURAL ADAPTATION: IN WHOSE WORDS?

Your proposal must demonstrate that you have researched the evidence and best practices that have been developed in your area of interest. The use of empirical applications of existing knowledge has been well discussed elsewhere (e.g., Gibbs & Gambrill, 2002; Neumann & Sogolow, 2000) and has become a routine part of developing defensible social work practice. There are many examples of the application of evidence-based practice in program development (Kegeles et al., 2000; Miller, 2003; Wells et al., 2004).

As writer, it is your role to locate, read, digest, and translate the empirical literature into effective programs that are adapted to the community members you hope to work with (Campbell et al., 2004). Using evidence-based work increases the likelihood that you will use effective treatment approaches and limit your need to constantly reinvent solutions that may already exist. Be careful, however, not to overgeneralize these approaches in an attempt to apply them to all people or communities without considering the fit (Paxton, Guentzel, & Trombacco, 2006; Rosen, 2003). The proposal should reflect your understanding of the impact of diversity in your practice and the ability to adapt evidence-based practices to ensure culturally relevant practices within your programs, agencies, and communities (Sue, 2006).

You can also work with community members to help expose and correct unwittingly embedded oppressive strategies related to dominance, power, and privilege in your programs (Franks & Riedel, 2008). The language used in proposal writing may be the first line of defense in combating the use of "one size fits all" programming, which is unlikely to meet the needs across communities and cultures.

Further, you can analyze institutional or community forces of oppression that might undermine empowerment efforts in the target community (Chisom & Washington, 1996; Cramer & McElveen, 2003) and use that analysis to work with community members to develop intervention strategies that expose and minimize unintentional racism (Ridley, 1995) and to identify and increase anti-oppressive forces and practices (Sakamoto & Pitner, 2005). This is particularly important while developing programs intended to correct some of the outcomes related to the impact of chronic experience with racism and oppression (Manning, Cornelius, & Okundaye, 2004).

IDENTIFY AND NOTIFY FUNDING SOURCES OF YOUR INTENT TO APPLY

Now you will want to identify funding sources that might be interested in your proposed project. Writing proposals takes much time, energy, and capital, so it is best to consider these elements wisely. The wide array of resources to be found on the Internet has greatly facilitated this research endeavor. Finding a number of appropriate matches for your proposed project will significantly enhance your success ratio (Yuen & Terao, 2003). Next, contact the potential foundation for a preliminary conversation about your intention to submit a proposal, thus beginning the relationship that could lead to a successful submission. This first contact might take the form of a letter of intent, a one- or two-page summary of your project ideas, and an approximate budget for funding them. Sometimes a phone call, e-mail, or visit can accomplish the same purpose. The initial contact is an effort to gain the support you need to work on your proposal. The letter of intent is not itself a proposal; it is a concept paper that will help you gain the attention of your audience. If your audience is uninterested in your ideas, it will likely be futile to write and submit a full proposal. A bad fit between a program idea and a funder is second only to a poorly written proposal in leading to a rejection (Porter & Tech, 2003).

You want to make it easy for the funding entity to recognize the goodness of fit. Within the limited space available, you will want to state who you are and establish your organization's credibility. Describe what you want to do, including what issue you will address, the intended recipients of service, why you think they want or need this service or project, the proposed project, and the objectives. Present your program idea early in the document to give your reader a focus. Explain why you are approaching this organization

for support and why you think this audience should be interested in what
you want to do.

The following example is a letter of intent written for a New Orleans
group to fund a one-year commemorative event. After a series of phone calls
describing the proposed project, the foundation requested a letter of intent.
The letter outlines the project, the cost, and the expertise of the writer to
implement it, and it draws on the ongoing phone relationship that had been
developed with the foundation. Here is that letter:

Dear Mr. Smith,

I am writing to follow up on our phone calls regarding our proposal for
a Post-Katrina one-year commemorative event. As you know I work with the
Public Relief Fund (PRF), and we are seeking $10,000 to support our one
year commemorative program honoring those who lost their lives through
the failure of the levees surrounding New Orleans on August 29, 2005.

PRF was founded after the storms to organize the poor and working class
community of New Orleans so that they would have a voice in the relief
and reconstruction after the storm. We noted at that time that plans were
being made about the future of our communities without our presence
and without our representation. We fully believe that a just reconstruction
must include the voices of the oppressed that make up the majority of the
population of the city.

We are seeking your support to organize a commemoration fitting the
occasion of the one-year anniversary of the hurricane. This commemoration
will be a New Orleans wide memorial and milepost to the progress/lack of
progress that has been made since the disaster one year ago and an opportunity for public grieving and closure for the friends and families of those who
perished before and after the storm. It will seek to unite widely disparate
communities to unite [sic] in a public acknowledgement of this great loss.
The program will also highlight the right of displaced people from New
Orleans, the majority of whom are still outside of the city, to return. The
program will point out the lack of progress in preparing the infrastructure
for the return of those who really desire to come back home.

We know that the Foundation shares our vision to support community
development and activities aimed at developing social justice. Therefore,
we are requesting a one-time grant of $10,000 to support the event. This
activity supports your vision and our mission to mobilize the oppressed and
displaced New Orleans community.

We thank you for your attention to this request and look forward to talking to you in the near future about the feasibility of this proposal.

Sincerely,

Mr. Jones

PRF

Foundations or other potential sources of grants want to know if the issue is important and how it fits with their interests (Porter & Tech, 2003). Some foundations have a clear agenda and seek to support issues related to it, while others invite new ideas and innovations (Dennis, 2005). Your research about which foundation you will approach should take such preferences into account. The foundation will want a well-written statement of what it is that you want to do. Be clear about the amount of money you are asking for and make the case that your agency or community is credible and capable of doing what you want to do. This initial contact can usually give you a fairly good sense of whether the grant source is interested in your ideas and whether it will be worth your effort to submit a full proposal. The source may also help you reformulate and/or strengthen the proposal. If your initial contact is with someone who is interested and knowledgeable in your area, that person can help you to further develop your ideas and thus produce a more fundable proposal.

WRITING THE PROPOSAL

Finally, you are ready to start compiling and writing the proposal. All of the preliminary work discussed above will inform and contribute to the actual proposal as well as to assuring that it is a clear representation of the needs you have identified, in collaboration with your constituents—your goals, objectives, outcomes, and evaluation plan. The format presented here is fairly generic (based on the NY/NJ area common application form, found at http://216.7.162.38/commapp.htm) and is currently accepted by more than 60 corporate and philanthropic foundations. Some funding organizations have their own form, so be sure to check that before beginning this process. This format is not the same for city, state, and/or federal funding grant applications, but some of the basic concepts will apply. It is also not an exhaustive manual, book, or course on how to write a proposal, although such resources are plentiful (e.g., Coley & Scheinberg, 2000; New & Quick, 2003;

Yuen & Terao, 2003, to name a few; also the Foundation Center has online grant-writing instruction, at http://www.foundationcenter.org). Rather, what follows here is intended to help provide structure to your proposal-writing efforts and keep your voice in the process.

The proposal is the vehicle for the clear articulation of the program you intend to develop, the community it is intended to serve, the needs it is intended to address, and the outcomes you plan to achieve (Coley & Scheinberg, 2000). The more clearly you convey this information, the more alive your proposal will be to the reader and the more likely it will be that you have a successful review. Some characteristics of proposals that draw favorable responses from reviewers include clear organization, content that is responsive to the RFP, fresh ideas about resolving the need, writing that reflects passion and enthusiasm, evidence that you know the state of the field, and evidence of program feasibility—that you can do what you propose to do with the budget you are requesting (Porter & Tech, 2005). Further, the proposal should demonstrate that you are addressing a social problem that is current and important and that you have embedded this problem in the context of your agency, community, and the larger environment (Kettner et al., 2007). The successful proposal will also be grounded in theory, show community collaboration, and be culturally relevant—all of which were discussed above.

The organization of the following sections is drawn from the NY/NJ common application form. I have taken the liberty of using this widely received format and have added suggestions on how to complete and articulate each component of the proposal. Again, you should determine the format required by the foundation you are applying to and follow that form for your final proposal submission.

COVER PAGE

The first thing a reviewer will do is glance at your cover page, so make sure it is clear, pithy, and neat. The cover page provides your first chance to make a positive impression. You will have limited space there to describe your project. Include the project name, if you have one, and a one-sentence description of the purpose of the grant. In this one sentence you are challenged to attract the attention of the reader, to convey the timeliness and importance of the project, and to produce a description that is in line with the funding priorities of the foundation you are approaching. Also include sufficient identifying information: the name of the organization, the executive director, the contact person and how to get in touch with that person, and 501(c)(3) not-for-profit status (or an explanation of other status). State the grant request amount and the total project budget (the foundation will want to know what portion of the total budget you are seeking in this proposal). It is critical here to make sure that the stated purpose and the requested amount complement each other (Geever, 2004). A key component of the decision-making process will be whether the purpose seems to justify the expenditure requested (Margolin, 2005). Finally, state the total organizational budget. This will inform the reader about how much of the organizational effort will be devoted to this project. An example is:

> **Date of application:** March 11, 2012
>
> **Name of organization to which grant would be paid:** The Brooklyn Defenders
>
> **Purpose of grant:** Advocacy for and with people involved in the criminal justice system
>
> **Address of organization:** 80 Court St, Brooklyn, NY 10221
>
> **Telephone number:** 718.628.3355
>
> **Fax:** 718.597.7980
>
> **E-mail:** mr2233@nyc.gov
>
> **Executive Director:** Joseph Strock
>
> **Contact person and title:** Mamie Wilson, project director
>
> **Is your organization an IRS 501(c)(3) not-for-profit?** Yes
>
> **Grant request:** $100,000 for project support
>
> **Total organization budget (for current year):** $5,380,908
>
> **Dates covered by this budget:** 07/01/05 . 06/30/06
>
> **Total project budget:** $200,000.00
>
> **Dates covered by project budget:** 09/01/08 . 08/31/09
>
> **Project name:** Justice Now

EXECUTIVE SUMMARY

After the proposal is completed, clearly and concisely summarize it in less than one page. This summary is your best chance to briefly convey the importance of your proposed services—and to show that you understand the context in which you wish to provide those services and that what you plan to do is feasible, with achievable outcomes (Porter & Tech, 2005). You can also demonstrate that the community has contributed to your understanding of the needs and development of services that are responsive to them, that are culturally relevant and strengths-based, and that will be well utilized in the context in which they are planned (Austin et al., 2005).

The summary should include at least one sentence from each key area of the narrative below, pulling together a blueprint of the entire proposal (Porter & Tech, 2003). An example follows.

The Undoing Racism™ Project Field Internship Steering Committee is a collaboration of the following agencies and community organizations: The People's Institute for Survival and Beyond (PISAB), the National Association of Social Workers (NASW), the Anti-Racist Alliance, the Jewish Board of Family and Children's Services, and faculty and students from the Fordham University, Hunter College, and Columbia University schools of social work. The Steering Committee was formed out of an interest from students and others who had experienced the PISAB Undoing Racism™ workshop and shared a commitment to undoing racism in social work and the United States as a whole. The Steering Committee produced the NASW 'Call to Action', a document that outlines the role of racism in social work and the United States. The 'Call to Action' charges social workers with the responsibility of working to undo structural racism (NASW, President's Initiative, 2007).

Structural racism refers to the inequitable distribution of power and resources in society (PISAB, 2007). Anti-racist social work practitioners work to undo this ongoing unequal power distribution that disadvantages people of color and benefits whites (NASW, President's Initiative, 2007). Social workers trained in community organizing, policy, and program development must embed anti-racism into the foundation of their practice to accurately reflect social work's mission of alleviating suffering and promoting human rights and social justice (NASW, 1996). Currently, social work interns from Hunter College are working on the Undoing Racism™ Project Field Internship Steering Committee. We are requesting $60,000 from the Veatch Foundation to expand these efforts into an Undoing Racism™ Intercollegiate Internship (UR™IC) that would include students from the Fordham and Columbia University schools of social work, with a long-term goal of student participation from all eight New York City schools of social work. The project will receive additional funding from the Barbara Joseph Memorial Undoing Racism™ Internship Project Fund.

NARRATIVE

The narrative is the main body of the proposal and will include all of the key elements necessary for a successful submission. The NY/NJ common application form, as most others, requests a narrative section of no more than five single-spaced pages. The following should all fit into these five pages. Please note again that this format is not the same as that for a state or federal proposal. If you are applying for one of those, you should consult sources that specifically address that format (e.g., Gerin, 2006; New & Quick, 2003).

INTRODUCTION   This is the first substantive section of your proposal. In a brief introductory statement, describe the proposal topic as well as the agency and/or community setting. In the introduction you must highlight the agency's credibility and expertise in the area covered by the proposal, or the capacity of the community to develop and provide the proposed services (Coley & Scheinberg, 2000). One way to establish this credibility is to refer to the history of the agency/community (is it the first, only, or best at providing some kind of services?). It is a truism that agencies that start to get funded are more likely to keep getting funded, as they develop a track record and establish successes in a given service area. However, a new and innovative agency or community group responding to emerging issues or supporting strengths in a population that has been without such supports can present this as an alternative approach to establishing credibility. The responsiveness of such organizations to developing issues can quickly establish credibility and gain success in fund-raising efforts. Here is an example of an introduction:

> The purpose of the Family Support Coalition (FSC) is to promote the well-being of low and no income families, especially single female heads of households. Our mission is to help families become self-sufficient and ensure that they are given all the human rights that they deserve.
>
> The FSC was organized in 1980 to support social justice for families receiving welfare and other social services. By 1985 we had raised sufficient funds and in-kind community services to become an official organization

and buy our own building. We spearheaded efforts to help shape the 1988 welfare reform bill by getting on the agenda in Washington DC to speak about welfare reform and the needs of Louisiana welfare recipients. We then organized a LA statewide meeting in which TANF recipients expressed their needs to facilitate successful transitions from welfare to work, including supports and services. The outcome of this organizing effort was to assure that recipients received educational services and job training in order to secure employment that allowed them to have productive lives upon the termination of the TANF benefits.

Subsequently, Louisiana developed one of the most humane and successful state "welfare to work" plans in 1990. This system allowed FSC and other community-based organizations to provide programs for welfare recipients that increased their understanding of the welfare system and how to negotiate it. Our program, "And Still I Rise," was a motivational readiness program that prepared participants to return to school, develop job readiness skills, write resumes and conduct practice job interviews.

Over 9 years this program served approximately 10,000 women who were able to enhance their self-esteem, learn community building skills, develop skills and experience in job search strategies, and gain exposure to university and college environments, thereby increasing their capacity to improve the quality of life for themselves and their families. Ninety percent of the women successfully graduated from the program and moved on to state employment training programs. Of these, 75% went on to end their welfare dependence, increase their self-determination, and create more independent living environments for themselves.

BACKGROUND   Start this section with a brief description of the history and mission of the agency or work of the community. Remember that the foundation will be funding not you but the agency or community group in which you work. The 501(c)(3) not-for-profit status is key to your ability to qualify for most corporate or foundation grants (Geever, 2004; New & Quick, 2003). Make sure to highlight anything remarkable that your agency/community has accomplished, prioritizing and leading with the achievements most likely to appeal to the foundation/corporation that you are applying to.

Describe in detail the population for whom the efforts are intended, including geographic location, socioeconomic status, race, ethnicity, gender, sexual orientation, age, physical ability, and language. Describe the issue(s) that you seek to address and how this particular proposed project fits into the overall mission of your group. Is this project an adjunct to current services, a gap you have identified in the match between needs and current services, or an emerging need that has grown organically out of the basic mission of the organization or community? An example of the latter might be an agency that has long served people with problematic use of drugs. In the mid-1980s the population using the programs would have begun to develop HIV/AIDS and demonstrated a need for housing, medical treatment, and a host of other related services. By the late 1990s, as a result of medical advances, this same population would be requiring long-term housing and vocational opportunities. Thus, this agency would expand and change along with the populations that use its services.

Describe the current programs and/or accomplishments of your organization or community group, emphasizing the achievements of the recent past as well as its history and long-term work. Demonstrate the formal and informal relationships your group has developed with other organizations and/or community groups to complement and expand services. Are these other groups working to address the same issues, providing similar services, or providing services that your service receivers can use, in addition to those you can provide directly? Describe how your organization is both similar to and different from these other groups. Distinguish between formal and informal linkages, including any Memoranda of Understanding (MOU) you might have with other organizations that have created a more comprehensive service system. Place the program in the context of the larger service network. Try to place it within the context of the continuum of care available to those who will use the services. In this section you might elaborate on any provider support for the program that was noted in the proposal's introduction (e.g., letter of agreement or memorandum of understanding).

Each proposal must describe how you will protect human subjects who have suffered unfortunate past abuses. Therefore, describe the Internal Review Board (IRB) for protection of the people anticipated to use your services or programs. Since the grant will require an evaluation component, it is critical that you describe how you will protect the confidentiality or anonymity of the community members who use the services. Some larger agencies or community groups will have an established IRB for this purpose. If this is the case, briefly describe the composition and operational procedures of the IRB. If not, describe how you will do this for this particular project. For example, the areas necessary for coverage and support by the Belmont Agreement (Berg, Applebaum, Parker, & Lidz, 2001)—which set protective standards for physicians and scientists using human subjects for research—include: state the purpose of project and/or evaluation; clarify that participation is voluntary and that failure to participate will not affect other services normally available; offer to clarify anything about the project that they may not understand; explain procedures, including risks and benefits; say whether participants will receive compensation for participating; and include a participant rights statement and signed consent form.

In this section describe your agency's fringe benefits (workers' compensation, health insurance, Social Security), if applicable, and your indirect-cost ratio (compensation for the organization or community group in maintaining buildings, grounds, equipment, library costs, research costs, etc.). These figures are generated by the finance department, are typically included in all funding requests, and are part of a formula already developed to assist in this part of the grant development. You can also describe the composition of your board of directors, as well as add a more inclusive list, with affiliations, to the proposal appendix. Finally, briefly state the number of paid full-time and part-time staff and volunteers (Geever, 2004).

FUNDING REQUEST
Resources Needed/Budget

Typically, the proposal instructions ask you to state and clarify your budget before describing your program components. Practically speaking, you will have already completed your program design before you do this. There is an operational link between program and budget that many social workers struggle to identify. Most social work training does not include budgetary areas, as we have more skill and comfort with programmatic areas. However, the foundation first wants to know how much funding you are seeking, to decide if it is even within its mandates to provide it. The funding entity also wants to connect the level of effort and impact that you are predicting to the cost. In other words, is what you plan to do worth the money you are seeking, and will that requested amount be sufficient to accomplish your proposed goals (Ruegg, Fraser, Howden, & Stevens, 2003)? Clarify here the resources needed to design and implement the program, and be sure to include start-up costs, separated from ongoing operating costs. Start-up costs may include items like staff recruitment and training, making a space more amenable to program activities, and developing program materials. Ongoing costs are more along the lines of staff salaries and benefits, rent, and transportation for participants, so that they may take part in the program's activities.

Outline your proposed budget and detail your resources. Note potential revenues and expenditures. The stronger proposal will usually provide evidence of multiple funding sources (Kettner et al., 2007; Ruegg et al., 2003). For two reasons, most funding sources prefer to know that the budget has diversified revenue streams. First, the money they are contributing is likely to provide more change in the given agency or community if their portion is only part of the budget. Second, they will be better assured that the program is sustainable whether or not they continue to provide funding in the future. Many foundations prefer to provide seed money to new ideas and innovations as pilot programs, and then see them flourish over time with more-traditional funding mechanisms (Dennis, 2005). Focus on the program's direct costs rather than its indirect costs, although you will need to add those at the end (Ruegg et al., 2003). A budget summary can be included in this part of the proposal with a full budget as part of the appendix. There are several good sources of style for the budget summary and the full budget (Geever, 2004; Ruegg et al., 2003; Yuen & Terao, 2003), so I will not add another. For several examples of budgeting, see the Foundation Center Web site: http://foundationcenter.org/

State how you plan to sustain the program once the grant has expired and what you will do for future funding. For example, can you fold this program into a more long-term and secure funding stream, or will the program become self-supporting from fees paid by the service users or community members, or will it be eligible for Medicaid reimbursement? If you are requesting a one-time-only grant for a particular activity (e.g., a conference) and you do not anticipate the need for future funding, state that clearly in this section.

STATEMENT OF STRENGTHS AND PROBLEM ANALYSIS   Describe why the proposed project has been identified as a target for intervention, the analysis of strengths within this community, and how the impending problem has challenged normal coping strategies (Kettner et al., 2007). This section can be informed by a strengths-based social work assessment process (Blundo, 2001), as applied to a community or other group of people desiring some service. Place the condition to which the proposal is responding in its societal context. Starting with an analysis of the existing resources within the community will help you to understand the areas challenged by this problem and the efforts already made to resolve it, in addition to framing the response as a facilitation of the coping strategies already at the disposal of the community (Wells et al., 2004). It also begins the process of supporting the community to identify the solutions that are most in sync with their preferences, values, and culture. When this analysis is missing, the way the problem is framed and the proposed solutions may not be acceptable to the people for whom they are intended.

Next you want to clarify why this condition is important for society. Social workers are charged with addressing social conditions. Convince the reader that this proposed program responds to a social condition and that the planned intervention will remove or ameliorate the factors related to the condition (Kettner et al., 2007); if you do not do so, the reader may not be inclined to continue reading. Even an exceptionally well-conceptualized program will not be developed unless you clarify why addressing the problem benefits society. What social conditions will be improved if this project is funded and successfully implemented? Describe the ideals that will be fulfilled for the public benefit. For example, how will a community be positively altered by the development of a program for building self-esteem in adolescent girls (Le Croy, 2004) or by a program that increases self-efficacy and problem-solving skills in African American custodial grandparents (Cox, 2002)? Is it of value to the community for the girls to increase their self-esteem and reduce depression or for the grandparents to improve their parenting skills? If you can show that these outcomes will increase positive participation in the community in the present and build stronger community participants in the future, then the expense of the project will be justified, the reader's interest will be stimulated, and, ultimately, the project will be more likely to attract funding (Porter & Tech, 2003).

Cite literature from the relevant field of practice in order to establish the significance of the issue you want to address. A review of the state of the situation of interest will lead you to understand the scope of the issue, what is already known about the issue, and whether technologies to resolve the issue exist that you can build upon (Gazelle, Buxbaum, & Daniels, 2001; Green, Ellis, & Lee, 2005). Sources of information that you can draw from include professional journals, government briefs, and agency reports, to name a few. It is also useful to include any available data that will stress the importance of the issue in the community and the relative need there (Kettner et al., 2007), in comparison with the situation in other communities.

NEEDS ASSESSMENT The needs assessment should start with a review of the literature that reports on the problem to be addressed and other responses to the problem. In this section you demonstrate that you have learned what others already know about this area. Here follows a brief one-paragraph example from a proposal to support an Undoing Racism™ field internship:

> Examples of the efficacy of incorporating the Undoing Racism™ framework into social work practice are emerging across the country. In Texas in 2004, African American children comprised 29% of children entering foster care, while only 12% of children in Texas were African American. Federal government studies indicate that race is not a risk factor for child abuse and neglect (Texas Health & Human Services Commission, 2006). These statistics mirror the nationwide disparate treatment of children of color. In 1999, 45% of children in out-of home care for a period of 12 months were African American (Administration for Children and Families, 2003), yet the 2000 U.S. Census Bureau (2001) reported African Americans only made up 3.9% of the population under the age of 18.

Describe here how you went from the need as learned in your literature review to learning how it is experienced by the people in your agency or community. Who are the intended recipients of the services, and what have you done to understand their needs (Witkin & Altschuld, 1995)? Indicate the multiple ways you have measured need and the implications of your assessment design. Clarify whether you used primary or secondary sources of information, triangulated between information sources, gathered qualitative and/or quantitative information, and analyzed the data you collected to develop the working hypothesis that guided your program development (Kettner et al., 2007). The needs assessment process is fairly lengthy, and you will no doubt collect much more information than you have room to describe in this section. Therefore, present this information clearly and concisely, highlighting the findings that best justify your approach to the proposed project.

STRATEGIES OR PROGRAM ACTIVITIES All the work described above has guided you to this point—the heart of your proposal. This is the narrative or functional program description that should clearly tell the funding agency what you plan to do and how. State your goals and objectives and how they respond to community needs and strengths. Think of your goals as idealized states that will exist as a result of your intervention (Kettner et al., 2007) and view your objectives as the actions (the verbs) that will achieve this anticipated endpoint. While goals are somewhat lofty notions that are long-term endeavors, your objectives should be more presently achievable. Good objectives clearly state a measurable endpoint, express the shared under-standing of both provider and receiver of services, can usually be quantified, are within reason, and have a clear time frame for completion (Coley & Scheinberg, 2000; New & Quick, 2003; Yuen & Terao, 2003). Describe the specific activities and/or strategies that will facilitate achieving the objec-tives, including who will do what and where activities will occur. Present a timeline that covers the sequencing of activities over the projected course of the funding request. Using a graphic timeline can provide a visual comple-ment to the written description of the timing of activities (Kiritz, 2004). Clarify the anticipated length of the project and state for how much of that time you are seeking funding.

Briefly describe how you propose to staff the project, and give the names and titles of the people who supervise, coordinate, and/or direct the project. Describe any consultants who will be involved in the program development and implementation and discuss their qualifications and contributions. State the anticipated length of the project, Finally, connect this program, again, to your organization's overall mission (Yuen & Terao, 2003), stating how these activities will further your mission and move your agency or com-munity forward in meeting that vision.

EMPOWERMENT EVALUATION Empowerment evaluation is a participa-tory approach that trains staff, participants, and other key stakeholders in conducting the evaluation, rather than hiring a consultant or other outside group to do so (Campbell et al., 2004). The strategies or steps of evalua-tion remain constant. First, develop a plan to evaluate the success of the services and the process in providing them (Mulroy & Lauber, 2004). This plan should be based on the clarity of goals and objectives described in the previous section, with the evaluation plan demonstrating the same clarity. Describe the types of information you will gather and what tools you will use to gather it systematically (Rossi, Lipsey, & Freeman, 2004; Royce, Thyer, Padgett, & Logan, 2006). Clarify the time table planned for your evaluation and state who will conduct the various aspects of the evaluation. If you intend to use an ongoing monitoring plan (process evaluation), describe it and include an account of how the program will assure quality and effort.

Describe the standards and criteria that will be used for evaluation (Rossi et al., 2004; Royce et al., 2006).

Identify or develop the tools you will use in your summative evaluation (Yuen & Terao, 2003)—how will you measure the impact or effectiveness of the program? Describe the instruments you will use and your plan for collecting and analyzing the data (De Poy & Gilson, 2003), and state whether they are standardized. Will you use strategies, such as event history analysis, to help you understand the differential program impact based on client or service characteristics (Unrau & Coleman, 2006)? Finally, clarify when and how the evaluation instruments will be administered (e.g., pre-test, post-test, follow-up interviews). In this section state the expected levels of goal attainment against which the program's performance and effectiveness will be measured (e.g., statements such as, "It is expected that 75% of the clients will complete training [program's product]; 50% of those who complete training will get a job within two months [outcome]"). Connect these criteria to your goals and to the evidence that supports them—back to your literature review (Kettner et al., 2007; New & Quick, 2003) and describe any cost-effectiveness or cost-benefit analysis that will be included in the evaluation plan (Kluger, 2006).

CONCLUSION What your audience reads last may be as important as what it reads first. Therefore, construct your conclusion so that it reminds the reader of the importance of the proposed program, the potential benefit to the community, and the social condition that will be improved should the program be funded and be successfully implemented. Use the conclusion, no more than a paragraph, to tie up the proposal and conclude with the goodness of fit between your organization and the reader, and the reasons that you believe this collaboration will be beneficial to all involved.

ATTACHMENTS OR APPENDIXES Appendices can be attached to your proposal to augment the information necessary for the short format expected. You can attach financial documents (i.e., your agency's most recent financial statement, a current operating expense budget, current supporters and other sources of income, other sponsors solicited for the proposed project, a line-item budget for the proposed budget, etc.) and other illustrative and supporting documents (i.e., list of board of directors, copy of IRS tax-exempt status, brief résumés of key staff, agency's most recent annual report, recent journal or newspaper articles, any proposed curriculum, letters of support, MOU, etc.). The use of appendixes can allow you to provide much-needed additional information. However, do not include anything in the appendix that is essential to the ideas in the program proposal, as your audience may not read it.

MOVING FORWARD: PROGRAM IMPLEMENTATION AND TRANSLATION

Ideally, by following the steps above you will have achieved a successful proposal and a funded program. The charge to implement your program as an empowerment-based community or an agency activity will remain in place. You will need to recruit and encourage active community participation as the program evolves (e.g., advisory boards, staff, etc.) and continue to evaluate for disempowering agency practices and community forces. The steps you took to develop a community-informed and/or -led program can be incorporated throughout the program implementation stage, straight on to the empowerment evaluation, and then to the next reincarnation of program development. If you continue to translate the voice of your service recipients, whether community members or agency participants, you will know whether the services are improving the social condition that they are intended to improve and if not, why not. Therefore, correction can occur as an ongoing process that maximizes program utilization and success. Using your writing skills to facilitate this process brings you to the vanguard of participatory social work practice and will lead to gratifying community relationships and valued programs.

Writing skills are important—foundations and other fiscal sponsors care about clear and concise proposal writing (Porter & Tech, 2003; Porter & Tech, 2005). If you need support in the particulars of the writing experience—get it. Go to an experienced colleague, a writing center, or the Foundation Center. Equally important is that you bring the voice(s) of your constituency to the program process—from needs assessment, to program development, to evaluation, and back around again. It is not a linear process but a cyclical one. If you maintain your relationships with your constituents throughout the process, your voice will be clear and the statement of importance will be embedded in your proposal. This collective voice will add weight to your enhanced writing skills and lead to a successful program with funding to operate. Good luck.

References

Austin, C. D., Des Camp, E., Flux, D., McClelland, R. W., & Sieppert, J. (2005). Community development with older adults in their neighborhoods: The elder friendly communities program. *Families in Society, 86*(3), 401–409.

Berg, J. W., Applebaum, P. S., Parker, L. S., & Lidz, C. W. (2001). *Informed consent: Legal theory and clinical practice.* New York: Oxford University Press.

Blundo, R. (2001). Learning strengths-based practice: Challenging our personal and professional frames. *Families in Society, 82*(3), 296–304.

Campbell, R., Dorey, H., Naegeli, M., Grubstein, L. K., Bennett, K. K., Bonter, F., Smith, P. K., Grywacz, J., Baker, P. K., & Davidson II, W. S. (2004). An empowerment evaluation model for sexual assault programs: Empirical evidence of effectiveness. *American Journal of Community Psychology, 34*(3–4), 251–262.

Chisom, R., & Washington, L. (1996). *Undoing racism.* New Orleans: People's Institute.

Coley, S. M., & Scheinberg, C. A. (2000). *Proposal writing* (2nd ed.). Newbury Park, CA: Sage.

Cox, C. B. (2002). Empowering African American custodial grandparents. *Social Work, 47*(1), 45–54.

Cramer, D. N., & McElveen, J. S. (2003). Undoing racism in social work practice. *Race, Gender, and Class, 10*(2), 41.

Dennis, E. E. (2005). Foundations as change agents and envoys of the status quo. *Journalism and Mass Communication Educator, 60*(1), 13–16.

De Poy, E., & Gilson, S. F. (2003). *Evaluation practice.* Pacific Grove, CA: Brooks/Cole-Thomson Learning.

Elliot, J. (2005). *Using narrative in social research.* Thousand Oaks, CA: Sage.

Fraenkel, P. (2006). Engaging families as experts: Collaborative family program development. *Family Process, 45*(2), 237–257.

Franks, C., & Riedel, M. (2008). Privilege. In E. Stannard (Ed.), *Encyclopedia of Social Work,* (20th ed.). New York: Oxford University Press.

Gazelle, G., Buxbaum, R., & Daniels, E. (2001). The development of a palliative care program for managed care patients: A case example. *JAGS, 49*, 1241–1248.

Geever, J. C. (2004). *Foundation Center's guide to proposal writing* (4th ed.). New York: Foundation Center.

Gerin, W. (2006). *Writing the NIH grant proposal.* Thousand Oaks, CA: Sage.

Gibbs, L., & Gambrill, E. (2002). Evidence-based practice: Counterarguments to objections. *Research on Social Work Practice, 12*, 252–476.

Green, R. S., Ellis, P. M., & Lee, S. S. (2005). A city initiative to improve the quality of life for urban youth: How evaluation contributed to effective social programming. *Evaluation and Program Planning, 28*, 83–94.

Homan, M. (2004). *Promoting community change: Making it happen in the real world* (3rd ed.). Pacific Grove, CA: Brooks/Cole.

Kegeles, S. M., Rebchook, G. M., Hays, R. B., Terry, M. A., et al. (2000). From science to application: The development of an intervention package. *AIDS Education and Prevention, 12*, 62–75.

Kettner, P. M., Moroney, R. M., & Martin, L. L. (2007). *Designing and managing programs* (3rd ed.). Newbury Park, CA: Sage.

Kiritz, N. J. (2004). *Program planning and proposal writing: Expanded version*. Los Angeles: The Grantsmanship Center.

Kluger, M. P. (2006). The program evaluation grid: A planning and assessment tool for non-profit organizations. *Administration in Social Work, 30*(1), 33–44.

Le Croy, C. W. (2004). Evaluation of an empowerment program for early adolescent girls. *Adolescence, 39*(155), 427–440.

Manning, M. C., Cornelius, L. J., & Okundaye, J. N. (2004). Empowering African Americans through social work practice: Integrating and Afrocentric perspective, ego-psychology, and spirituality. *Families in Society, 85*(2), 229–235.

Margolin, J. B. (Ed.). (2005). *Foundation Center's guide to winning proposals II*. New York: Foundation Center.

McCarthy, J. D., & Zald, M. N. (1977). Resource mobilization and social movements: A partial theory. *American Journal of Sociology, 82*, 1212–1241.

McLeroy, K. R., Norton, B. L., Kegler, M. C., Burdine, J. N., & Sumaya, C. V. (2003). Community-based interventions. *American Journal of Public Health, 93*(4), 529.

Miller, R. L. (2003). Adapting an evidence-based intervention: Tales of the Hustler Project. *AIDS Education and Prevention, 15*(Supplement A), 127–138.

Mulroy, E., & Lauber, H. (2004). A user-friendly approach to program evaluation and effective community interventions for families at risk of homelessness. *Social Work, 49*(4), 573–586.

Neumann, M. S., & Sogolow, E. D. (2000). Replicating effective programs: HIV/AIDS prevention technology transfer. *AIDS Education and Prevention, 12* (Supplement A), 35–48.

New, C. C., & Quick, J. A. (2003). *How to write a grant proposal*. Hoboken, NJ: Wiley.

Ohmer, M. L. (2007). Citizen participation in neighborhood organizations and its relationship to volunteers' self- and collective efficacy and sense of community. *Social Work Research, 31*(2), 109–120.

Paxton, K. C., Guentzel, H., & Trombacco, K. (2006). Lessons learned in developing a research partnership with the transgender community. *American Journal of Community Psychology, 37*, 349–356.

Porter, R., & Tech, V. (2003). Facilitating proposal development: Helping faculty avoid common pitfalls. *Journal of Research Administration, 34*(1), 28–33.

———. (2005). What do grant reviewers really want, anyway? *Journal of Research Administration, 36*(2), 5–13.

Ridley, C. R. (1995). *Overcoming unintentional racism in counseling and therapy: A practitioner's guide to intentional intervention.* Thousand Oaks, CA: Sage.

Rosen, A. (2003). Evidence-based social work practice: Challenges and promise. *Social Work Research, 27*(4), 197–208.

Rossi, P. H., Lipsey, M. W., & Freeman, H. E. (2004). *Evaluation: A systematic approach* (7th ed.). Thousand Oaks, CA: Sage.

Royce, D., Thyer, B.A., Padgett, D. K., & Logan, T. F. (2006). *Program evaluation: An introduction* (4th ed.). Belmont, CA: Thomson Brooks/Cole.

Ruegg, D. L., Fraser, T. M., Howden, A. L., & Stevens, S. K. (2003, spring). Ten steps to developing a program-based budget. *The Grantsmanship Center Magazine*, pp. 21–25.

Sakamoto, I., & Pitner, R. O. (2005). Use of critical consciousness in anti-oppressive social work practice: Disentangling power dynamics at personal and structural levels. *British Journal of Social Work, 35*, 435–452.

Sue, D. W. (2006). *Multicultural social work practice.* Hoboken, NJ: Wiley & Sons.

Trettin, L., & Musham, C. (2000). Using focus groups to design a community health program: What roles should volunteers play? *Journal of Health Care for the Poor and Underserved, 11*(4), 444–455.

Unrau, Y. A., & Coleman, H. (2006). Evaluating program outcomes as event histories. *Administration in Social Work, 30*(1), 45–65.

Wells, K., Miranda, J., Bruce, M., Alegria, M., & Wallerstein, N. (2004). Bridging community intervention and mental health services research. *American Journal of Psychiatry, 161* (6), 955–963.

Witkin, B. R., & Altschuld, J. W. (1995). *Planning and conducting needs assessments.* Thousand Oaks, CA: Sage.

Yuen, F. K.O., & Terao, K. L. (2003). *Practical grant writing and program evaluation.* Belmont, CA: Wadsworth.

9

ADVOCACY

Vicki Lens

ADVOCACY IS ABOUT PERSUADING OTHERS to adopt our ideas and proposals, and words are our most potent tool. How we speak or write about issues like health care or helping children matters as much as the content of our ideas. Across the many audiences and venues in which social workers operate, from testifying at public hearings to drafting policy briefs and op-ed pieces, to composing agency-based reports, how we communicate is as important as what we communicate.

Social workers are especially well positioned to persuade others about compelling social issues. Our daily work as professionals or students exposes us to facts, figures, and stories about social problems and the people affected by them. What is self-evident to us—for example, that child welfare workers are overworked or that welfare clients are frequently stigmatized—is often overlooked or unknown by others. The challenge is to translate our truths into other people's truths.

The spoken and written word is our vehicle for change. And our words must appeal to both reason and emotion. Westen (2007), a psychologist who studies how citizens process political messages, found that people assess political assertions with both their brain and their gut, or as he explained it, "the brain negotiates conflicts between 'data and desire'" (p. xi). Thus, this chapter begins not with suggestions for marshaling statistics and constructing rhetorical arguments (those come later), but with the place where political arguments start—on the contested turf of values and ideologies.

LOCATING THE FIGURATIVE GROUND

The first lesson is one familiar to any first-year social work student: Start where the client is. For advocacy, the client is the public and the policy-maker. For every social problem, there is what Rybacki and Rybacki (1996) called the "figurative ground" (p. 18), or in more colloquial terms, the "conventional wisdom." It's the common and prevailing understanding of a problem as represented by existing institutions, laws, customs, and ideas. It's how many, although not all, people view a particular problem and/or its solution at a particular point in time. Some examples include the notion that people on welfare should work, that the private sector performs better than government bureaucracies, and that child safety is more important than family preservation.

Identifying the figurative ground is crucial because it underlies all public discussions. Imagine traveling to a foreign country to propose that child abuse and neglect should be legally prohibited. In this country most citizens believe children are the property of their parents, corporal punishment is necessary for healthy child development, and child rearing is a private, not a public, matter. These ingrained assumptions must be addressed in order to pass a law allowing the state to regulate child abuse. In other words, advocacy starts where the client is; dominant ideologies must be identified and acknowledged before advocating change.

Discerning the figurative ground in one's own country is hard because we often take our ideas, institutions, and culture for granted, viewing them as natural rather than as socially constructed. For example, we may assume that the nuclear family or an ideology of individualism is innate. We may fail to notice that our debates about social problems are constructed around cer-tain unexamined beliefs. On the other hand, social workers often see first-hand the fault lines underlying conventional wisdom. Sometimes, though, we disagree with it without fully knowing its contours. To challenge the figurative ground, we must first fully explore the terrain. This requires listen-ing to *mainstream* chatter about a problem. Possible sources include public opinion polls, editorials, op-ed pieces in leading papers, and the experts who pop up on talk shows and news programs. I emphasize *mainstream* because it is in sources such as the *Washington Post*, the *New York Times*, and CNN where the figurative ground can be found. It is not found in less mainstream sources, whether right or left.

To be sure, mainstream experts disagree, and they hold a range of opinions. However, the prevailing wisdom can be discerned. Sometimes it is revealed in the repetitive use of certain language. For example, the oft-repeated term *personal responsibility* during the 1996 welfare reform debate reflected the conventional wisdom that people are responsible for themselves and government is not responsible for them. Sometimes journalists or others will explicitly identify the figurative ground. Reporters and experts opining on welfare reform regularly reiterated that everyone agreed the current welfare system was broken and needed reform.

Sometimes the figurative ground fortifies your position. For health care reform, the figurative ground is that private markets are suitable for providing health care. If you are proposing a private market solution to the lack of health care, building on that assumption will strengthen your position. Often, though, the figurative ground is the first hurdle advocates must overcome because it represents the inadequate status quo. Thus, advocates proposing a government-run single-payer system must explain why the private health care market is insufficient or ineffective. They must also challenge the conventional wisdom that government bureaucracies are inefficient. In short, the figurative ground may support or undermine your proposal, but either way it cannot be ignored.

CHOOSING A FRAME

Closely related to the figurative ground is the concept of frames. Frames are the lenses through which people see the world. They are the mental structures we use to process and categorize information. They are often unconscious and automatic. Frames facilitate the absorption of new information by fitting it into our existing views.

According to Lakoff (1996), a cognitive linguist scientist, the two main frames in American culture are conservative and liberal. Briefly, and perhaps a bit simplistically, conservatives emphasize the private market and small government while liberals emphasize government as part of the solution. Conservatives emphasize self-reliance and individual responsibility while liberals emphasize mutual aid and collective responsibility.

Frames, like the figurative ground, are fueled by values. *Values*, as defined by *Webster's Dictionary*, are "abstract concepts of what is right or worthwhile." They are not mere preferences, but deeply held beliefs. Hence, they cannot be ignored in public debates. No matter how many facts we marshal (more about facts later), it is people's value frames that matter most.

Thus frames are essential to advocacy; evoking them paves the way for the acceptance of specific policies. Lakoff (1996) contended that the persistent and powerful evoking of conservative themes over the last several decades has led to conservative policies. Linking the conservative frame of individual responsibility to public welfare programs gave us TANF, a temporary work-based program; linking premarital sex to family values gave us abstinence programs. In contrast, liberal frames lead to different kinds of policies and programs. A universal health care plan reflects the values of collective responsibility and protecting those who are vulnerable.

Frames should be invoked *before* making a specific proposal. Explaining the values that underlie universal health care or preventing child abuse connects people emotionally to an issue. The bureaucratic or dry jargon used to describe programs—think "Medicare Prescription Drug Benefits" or "Part D"—does little to communicate the values, or the real-life problems, underlying those programs. If your readers share your worldview, whether it be liberal or conservative, invoking shared values energizes and galvanizes support for your proposal. For people who oscillate between frames—and most people do—invoking shared values gives them a reason to support your proposal. It primes them to see the problem and the solution as you do. It is admittedly harder to persuade those with opposing worldviews. People who think that government does more harm than good will not likely agree that a government-run health care program is a good idea. However, emphasizing shared values—for example, the value of enhancing people's productivity—makes discussions about solutions less contentious and, hence, more fruitful.

Framing is often an exercise in *reframing*. Reframing is something social workers know well. We frequently do it with our clients, helping them to see a problem or situation from a different perspective. The same can be done with social problems and their solutions. Lakoff (1996) suggested how to reframe the issue of immigration (note that I did not say the *problem* of immigration; I am subtly framing). As Lakoff explained, when we use the term *immigration reform*, we are conceding that there is a problem that needs fixing. Terms like *illegal immigrants* or *illegal aliens* communicate criminality and undesirability; *alien* is a particularly offensive word that suggests a lack of humanness. Such terms trigger a cascade of negative thoughts. The popular image of aliens is one of invaders intent on destroying our way of life; this is also how the consequences of immigration have been portrayed. *Illegality* frames also suggest certain solutions. The typical response to illegality is enhanced law enforcement, which here translates into fences, increased border patrols, and criminal fines.

A better way to frame the issue, according to Lakoff (1996), is to use frames that communicate why citizens from other countries want to come here and how it benefits us (note my use of the phrase "citizens from other countries"—I am framing!). Thus we might describe such citizens as economic refugees, highlighting the effects of globalization and economic problems. Or we might emphasize that their presence in the United States allows many of us to live better, what Lakoff called the "cheap labor" or "cheap lifestyle" frame.

COMMUNICATING VALUES

Values can often be communicated in just a few words. We frequently use shorthand to describe a social problem, encapsulating our values, ideologies, and even solutions in a simple phrase. The phrasing "the war on terror" evokes the idea of a country under attack and a military solution. Describing terrorist acts as "international crimes" suggests a different response: criminal prosecutions in a court of law rather than armies on a battlefield. The catchphrases used in the abortion debate also illustrate how a few words go a long way. The phrase "right to life" frames abortion as a moral issue involving the life of a fetus, while "pro-choice" focuses on the woman and emphasizes American values of liberty and autonomy. The "Two Americas" phrase of a presidential contender in 2008 simply but powerfully communicated the idea of poverty amid affluence. Even what we name our social programs communicates our values. Compare, for example, Medi*care*, which all elderly people are eligible for, with Medic*aid*, which is only for the poor. *Care* implies concern and protection, while *aid* suggests a distant and less obligatory form of helping. Care is likely to endure, while aid can be withdrawn.

Beyond such catchphrases or names are the specific words we use when writing about social issues. Lakoff (1996) contended that conservatives and liberals actually use different vocabularies. Conservatives use words like *strong, disciplined, authority, character, virtue, competition, tough love, self-reliance, standards, authority, heritage, earn, hard work, enterprise, property rights, reward, freedom, intrusion, interference, meddling, punishment, hu-man nature, traditional, common sense, dependency, self-indulgence, elite, quotas* (Lakoff, 1996, p. 30). Liberals use words like *social forces, social responsibility, oppression, free expression, human rights, equal rights, concern, care, help, health, safety, nutrition, basic human needs, dignity diversity, de-privation, alienation, big corporations, corporate welfare, ecology, ecosystem, biodiversity,* and *pollution* (Lakoff, 1996, pp. 30–31). (You may have observed that the word *liberal* itself has undergone reframing after it became a dirty word back in the 1990s. Many people use the word *progressive* instead.)

As you can see, words communicate a particular worldview. They act as a code for fellow travelers of the same ideological stripe. But they also influence how others think. As noted above, the phrase "personal responsibility" became a mantra during the welfare reform debate, paving the way to abolish welfare as a government entitlement. Thus, when framing an issue, don't use your opponents' language. While you should be well versed in their words (see "figurative ground" above), be prepared to employ words that communicate your values.

Similarly, avoid words and phrases that carry negative associations. For example, phrases like "welfare mother" and "on the dole" (used often by journalists during the 1996 welfare reform debate) portray poor women pejoratively. *Recipient* also has a negative connotation; some advocates prefer the more active *participant*. Like other professionals, social workers have their own jargon, some of it unclear and some negative. The Depression and Bipolar Support Alliance (DBSA), an organization that helps consumers of mental health services and their families, has identified a list of "dirty words," such as "compliance," "resistant to treatment," and "front line staff in the trenches" (National Association of Social Workers [NASW], New York State Chapter, 2007). As Sue Bergeson, the president of DBSA, explained, *compliance* is a term better left to training animals, *resistance* can be an exercise of choice, and a war analogy suggests that the client is the enemy. (If you noticed DBSA's substitution of *consumer* for *patient* you detected another instance of framing.)

LIVENING UP YOUR LANGUAGE

Some of you may have noticed the blandness of academic writing, even though problems like domestic violence or child abuse are anything but bland. Advocacy writing is not academic writing. An advocacy piece should both educate and inspire. It should bring the problem to life and engage the reader. It should be well written but also lively. Compare, for example, the two halves of this opening sentence from an NASW (2003) editorial: "Poverty is a social problem that is the result of a host of complex reasons and is a problem that can not be cured with a welfare check or a scolding from the government to get a job" (para. 1). The first half of the sentence is drab and applies to virtually every social problem. The second half subtly and effectively mocks the work rules under welfare reform, using just a few words to depict them as misguided and overly paternalistic.

Illustrations, visual imagery, and literary devices can enliven your prose. People often think in analogies, metaphors, and similes (see table 9.1 for definitions and examples of these and other literary terms and devices). "All the world's a stage," a metaphor, nicely communicates the nature of social behavior. "You are as sweet as sugar," a simile, is a more engaging phrase than "you are very nice." Analogies are especially useful for decoding complex concepts in the world of policy. For example, to explain why workfare plans are unproductive, one writer, an economist, described the labor market as a "giant fast moving game of musical chairs. People who are skillful, unencumbered and highly motivated are more likely to find a seat, but it's just crazy to think these differences explain why everyone isn't sitting. The only way to make that happen is to add more chairs" (Harvey, 1994, p. A37).

Sharp-edged analogies are particularly persuasive, as when one writer described a complex funding scheme for Medicaid as being like a "loan shark exploiting a client's vulnerability" (Cohen, 2003, p. A31). Literary references that evoke distinct and colorful images are also useful. When one politician advocated a return to orphanages, critics responded by repeatedly invoking the phrase "Dickensian orphanages," triggering images of institutions staffed with sadistic caretakers and hungry children.

Keep in mind that a pithy phrase is a device, not a plan. Your argument should consist of more than a catchy phrase, some visual imagery, and a few well-chosen words. In other words, make sure there is substance behind your words.

TELLING A STORY

Your argument should also tell a story. By "story," I don't mean personal stories (although there is room for them, as I note later), but an encompassing

TABLE 9.1 Literary Devices: Definitions and Examples

LITERARY DEVICE	DEFINITION	EXAMPLES
Alliteration	Repeating two or more words that sound alike	Working women on welfare need our support.
Allusion	Using literary, classic, or popular references	The Achilles heel of welfare reform is the lack of sufficient well-paying jobs. Only a Scrooge would deny children aid.
Antithesis	Contrasting two opposing ideas	Our poorest citizens should draw from us our greatest generosity. Helping the poor can enrich us all.
Repetition/climax	Repeating words or phrases while building to a high point	The child without food, the family without a home, a nation without a heart.
Personification	Giving human characteristics to non-human things	Let us try and heal the wounds in our health care system by providing a basic level of medical care to all.
Rhetorical questions	Asking a question for effect, not for answers	Doesn't everyone deserve a home? Would you want your family to be left without health coverage?
Analogies, metaphors, and similes	Finding similarities between normally unlike things. Metaphors usually substitute one thing for another, while analogies emphasize shared characteristics.	Our welfare system is our safety net.
Dilemmas	Presenting two equally bad options to make the less bad one more palatable	We can abolish an admittedly poor system, or we can continue it so needy women and children are clothed, fed, and sheltered.

Source: Reprinted from Vicki Lens (2005). Advocacy and argumentation in the public arena: A guide for social workers. *Social Work, 50,* 231–238.

narrative with villains and victims and allegations of blame set against a backdrop of values. Narratives are essential to policy debates; they explain how the world works and how to fix it. Think, for example, of the narrative used to pass welfare reform. Poor people were the villains; they suffered from character or cultural flaws that caused them to avoid work. The government was also a villain; it created dependency by providing a way to avoid work. "Taxpayers" were the victims because their hard-earned money went to "welfare mothers." The solution was to require work and abolish or limit government aid. This narrative contained all the essential ingredients. It identified both culprits and victims, causes and cures, and set them in the context of the highly cherished American value of individualism (also known as "pull yourself up by your own bootstraps").

Imagine a different story line using an equally compelling American narrative, what Robert Reich (2005), the former labor secretary under Clinton, called "rot at the top." This narrative is about powerful elites who abuse their power and harm the common good. It surfaces periodically in American life, for example, in the robber barons of the 1890s and more recently in the Wall Street tale of greedy, corrupt, and scheming bankers and CEOs. In this narrative, welfare participants would be recast as the working poor, with big banks and exorbitantly compensated CEOs the villains who refuse to pay hardworking people a living wage.

CHOOSING YOUR EVIDENCE

At this point you may be asking, What about the empirical evidence? What about scholarly studies, statistics, and census reports? What about "best practices" and performance-based measurements? Shouldn't this information be included? The answer, of course, is yes. Good arguments rely on good evidence. Our culture values empiricism, and as Stone (1997) explained, numbers, especially, are viewed as a sign of objectivity and accuracy.

But numbers are not as neutral as they appear. Your choice of which numbers to use is itself a value choice. For example, to establish the number of homeless, do we count only those people living on the street or also those doubling up with family and friends? Do we include in the unemployment rate those who stopped seeking work or who are underemployed? As Stone (1997) explained, numbers are about "where to draw the line" (p. 167); they are not just numbers but are "political claims" (p. 167) as well. They will likely be as contested as your argument is, and may be used against you by a clever opponent. They may even determine whether a social problem is recognized at all. Thus, choose your numbers well.

As with value claims, state your empirical claims clearly and without jargon. Consider the difference between 2000 presidential contender Al Gore's descriptions of a plan to raise Medicare rates—"your premiums would go up by between 18 percent and 47 percent"—and the much simpler (and still accurate) "your premiums will go up about a third" (Westen, 2007, p. 33). The former raises more questions (Why such a spread? Where would I fall?). The latter is easier to understand and recall.

Empirical claims can also be qualitative, including personal narratives or human-interest stories. Their power is perhaps best demonstrated by the frequent use of particularly egregious stories to symbolize a social problem. Whether it is Nixmary Brown, a 7-year-old child beaten to death by her mother's boyfriend, or Kendra Webdale, who fell to her death when pushed onto subway tracks by a former psychiatric hospital patient, even a single personal story can mobilize change. Just think of the many victims memorialized in the names of laws, including Kendra's law, requiring outpatient mental health treatment, which was passed after Kendra's death; Timothy's law, prohibiting insurance companies from limiting treatment for mental illness, passed after a 12-year-old boy committed suicide when his mental health benefits were exhausted; and Megan's law, requiring law enforcement to notify the public when a sex offender moves into a neighborhood, passed after the rape and murder of a young girl.

Less sensational, and likely more typical, personal stories can be similarly persuasive. As noted above, a combination of emotion and reason persuades people, and stories tug at the former. However, stories can backfire. As Iyengar (1996) found in his study of poverty, personal stories caused viewers to empathize less, not more, with the poor. This was especially the case when the stories were about minorities. Rather than evoking a personal connection, such stories reinforced racial and ethnic stereotypes. Personal vignettes also encouraged viewers to conclude that poverty was caused by individual, not institutional, factors. In contrast, statistics and economic facts encouraged viewers to think larger and more contextually.

The best approach is to combine qualitative and quantitative information. Well-chosen qualitative stories elicit interest and make the problem real to readers. Stories also stir emotions, making it more likely that people will remember your message. Stories, more than quantitative data, rouse readers to action. Stories alone, however, are usually insufficient. Anyone can tell a story, but having the facts and figures behind it reinforces your expertise and enhances your credibility. Quantitative data also provide context, allowing the reader to locate the story within larger institutional and structural dynamics and understand the extent of the problem. Using both qualitative and quantitative data more than doubles your argument. For while stories appeal to emotion, quantitative data appeal to reason. Because people decide with their hearts and their minds, using both packs a particularly powerful punch.

BUILDING YOUR ARGUMENT

Empirical claims also have an internal logic that can be manipulated to enhance your argument. Effective arguments have three main components: claims, grounds, and warrants (Toulmin, Rieke, & Janik, 1984). A claim is the assertion being made. It can be a fact claim, which describes what is; a value claim, which judges or evaluates; or a policy claim that suggests what should be done. "Most welfare participants work" is a fact claim; "welfare participants should work" is a value claim; "welfare participants should be required to work in exchange for benefits" is a policy claim. Claims should be accompanied by grounds, which is the evidence that proves the claim. That evidence can be statistics, studies (qualitative or quantitative), or anything else of evidentiary value. Because value claims are ideological preferences, they cannot be proved by facts, but facts can strengthen them. For example, the statement "government should help its citizens" can be accompanied by factual examples of effective government programs.

The final component of an argument is a warrant, which is a form of mental reasoning that connects grounds to claims. It is often unspoken and can be based on the conventional wisdom that included values, norms, or customs. It's what makes grounds and claims believable to the reader. For example, to support the policy claim that welfare participants should be provided with educational opportunities, the grounds include labor statistics showing that many jobs require a college education and that college graduates earn more than high school graduates. The warrant that links the two is our belief in the value of education and the generalization that what is true for others in the labor market is also true for welfare participants. In contrast, readers who believe that welfare participants are different from the rest of us and are unable to benefit from educational opportunities will find this policy claim faulty. For them, additional grounds, or reference to a different set of values, are needed.

A single claim is usually insufficient to persuade. Grouping claims together can strengthen arguments. According to Rybacki and Rybacki (1996), there are two ways to group arguments: clustering and chaining. Cluster claims consist of multiple claims, but with each claim being able to stand alone. An example is McLanahan and Garfinkel's (1994) op-ed piece stating that welfare is not the major cause of single motherhood. First, they argued that single motherhood increased despite a decrease in the value of welfare benefits. Then, they noted the increase in single motherhood among educated women, who are unlikely to be on welfare. Next, they pointed out that single-mother families are more common in the United States, where welfare benefits are much lower, than in other countries. The advantage of cluster arguments is that they do not depend on one another; if one fails, the others may succeed.

Chain arguments are more linear, with one claim building on another. They are also more complex and require logical leaps. For example, consider the argument that increased educational opportunities for welfare participants will decrease welfare expenditures. The connection is not readily apparent, and several claims are needed to make the link. The first claim is that welfare participants with more education are more likely to find jobs; the second claim is that those jobs will more likely pay a living wage; the third claim is that welfare participants who earn a living wage are less likely to return to welfare; the fourth and final claim is that government expenditures will decrease because fewer people are returning to welfare. The advantage to chain arguments is that tightly strung links are more persuasive than a single loose link. Chain arguments are also useful for explaining complex issues because you build your case piece by piece. The disadvantage is that a weak link breaks the chain, leaving you with no argument at all.

CHOOSING A WRITING STYLE

Now that you have mastered the use of frames and figurative grounds, language and pithy phrases, and claims and logical leaps, the next thing to master is style. Writing styles can be formal, informal, or a combination of both. You may have noticed that I am using an informal style. This is intentional. The purpose of this chapter is to teach you. Thus I used a conversational style, which more closely mimics the classroom. This style also creates a sense of intimacy, as in a classroom, making it easier for you to absorb and recall what I have written. I chose the personal pronouns *you* and *I* instead of the more formal and distant third-person *one*, as in "you should write clearly" instead of "one should write clearly." Instead of a pedantic style filled with multisyllabic words, which characterizes much scholarly writing, my word choices are more colloquial and simple. Many of my sentences are short, another sign of informal writing (although good writing uses both short and long sentences to maintain the reader's interest).

Your style will depend on your audience. Advocacy writing encompasses everything from a letter to the editor or an op-ed piece to a policy brief or agency report to a letter to a legislator or legislative testimony. While there are no hard and fast rules, an agency report or policy brief is the most formal. In that kind of document you are not trying to establish a sense of intimacy or express your distinctive voice, and a conversational style is usually not appropriate.

Most other forms of advocacy writing, including op-ed pieces, letters to the editor or legislators, and legislative testimony, are somewhere in between. They are less generic and less structured than agency reports or policy briefs. However, because you are writing as an expert, some formality is required. This does not mean using insider jargon or obtuse arguments to establish your bona fides. It does mean using active rather than passive voice ("the research indicates," not "it was indicated by the research") and indefinite pronouns rather than personal pronouns ("one is struck by the increase in the homeless population," not "I am struck by the increase in the homeless population"). But be flexible; the use of *I* in an op-ed piece that relates a story about your experience with a client would be appropriate.

TAILORING YOUR ARGUMENTS TO CONTEXT AND PURPOSE

You may be wondering how you will ever fit in one place all the elements of a persuasive argument. The extent to which you will use these elements depends on the context and what you are writing. The figurative ground may be a single sentence in a letter to a legislator ("Virtually all citizens agree that the health care system is in need of reform"), while a policy brief may include several paragraphs on current policies and attitudes. Pithy phrases may get pride of place in an op-ed piece or letter to the editor, but not in an agency report. Narratives may be short or long; the villain or victim can be described in a single sentence or elaborated on in a paragraph. Similarly, a frame can be communicated in a few phrases or several sentences. The type of evidence you use—qualitative or quantitative, numbers or stories—and the complexity of your arguments will depend on both space and audience.

An agency report or policy brief may go heavy on statistics and light on stories, while an op-ed piece may emphasize both equally.

The different types of advocacy writing also have their own best practices. Policy briefs are designed to persuade the reader to adopt a specific policy proposal. They are typically very structured and relatively short, at 3–6 pages. Writing so few pages on a social problem that could fill volumes requires not only concise and succinct expression but also separating the wheat from the chaff. Like a short story instead of a novel, a few words or sentences must go a long way in setting a scene and building to a conclusion.

Policy briefs begin, much like stories do, with a description of the setting. The first sentence should succinctly state the problem ("Many people forced off welfare are unable to support their families"). The extent of the problem should be documented, and its defining characteristics stated ("Nearly one quarter of families who leave do not have a job; nearly a third have jobs that do not pay a living wage"). Be sure to include the causes of the problem ("Most former welfare participants jobs are in the service sector, where wages are low and benefits nonexistent") and what will happen if the problem is not addressed ("Many are unable to pay their rent or provide food for their families"). As you can see, I am setting up a narrative, depicting former welfare participants as victims, and both the business sector (whose members don't pay living wages) and the welfare system (which forces people off welfare) as the culprits. I am using primarily quantitative information, but a brief vignette about a struggling family might be helpful.

The next section details current policies (in essence, the figurative ground) and why they are not working. The problem I am writing about is complex, involving both labor markets and the welfare system. I will need to succinctly describe both what the welfare system is doing wrong and what the problems in the labor market are. It is important to include all sides of the debate (in my example, I will include why some experts think the welfare system and the labor market are just fine). This allows you to both address the figurative ground and reframe the argument (for example, I will frame the problem as one of defective institutions and labor markets rather than one of defective people). The last section of a policy brief suggests a new or amended policy, spelling out its components clearly and explaining why it will work, as well as detailing any obstacles to its adoption. An important admonition: While policy briefs suggest policy solutions, their primary purpose is not to advocate but to provide expert advice. Thus their tone should be dispassionate and formal.

In contrast, editorials (commonly referred to as op-ed pieces because they appear opposite a newspaper's editorial) and letters to the editor are where your opinion matters. It is here where you can let your cleverness rip (but not too much, or readers will be admiring your cleverness instead of your message). Most often you will be writing as an expert, so some formality is required (and if you are writing as a social worker, what you say reflects on all of us!). Editorials are short, about 750 words. The best editorials draw the reader in with a catchy first paragraph and stay focused throughout on a few points. The author's opinion is clear from the outset, and any background information is summarized quickly and concisely. Short, declarative sentences and simple, precise words are preferred. The concluding paragraph should be as catchy as the first; like the punch line of a joke, it should sound fresh but also inevitable. (For excellent examples of op-ed pieces, consult the *New York Times*, especially Paul Krugman on the left and David Brooks on the right—of the political spectrum, not the page.)

Letters to the editor should also be catchy, and many of the rules of editorial writing apply to them (short, concise writing, clearly stated opinions). But their brevity requires summarizing an entire argument in a paragraph or two. Thus, make your best point your only point. As with editorials, read several examples in the *New York Times* and other papers to get a sense of what works and what doesn't. Pick one issue you know about and one you don't. If a letter on a topic you don't know or care about captures your interest and teaches you something new, it has done its job. If a letter on an issue you do know about changes your mind (or at least makes you think), it is also a good example of a well-written letter. If a letter or an editorial causes your eyes to glaze over and you can't follow the thread of the argument, it is an example of what not to do.

Letters to legislators stand somewhere between policy briefs and letters to the editor. They must be short and to the point, but they also include more background and detail than letters to a newspaper. You must address the figurative ground, in this case the legislator's stance on the issue (and that of his or her constituents), especially if you are challenging it. Letters, like a policy brief, should demonstrate your knowledge of a problem and your expertise. They should be no more than two pages in length. In that space you should identify who you are and what your area of expertise is, what the problem is, what you want done about it and why, and why certain solutions are better than others.

The final example of advocacy writing is legislative testimony. Unlike the other examples, it combines both the written word and the spoken word.

The spoken is by nature more informal than the written. On the other hand, a written record of your testimony is preserved; thus some formality is required. Start by identifying yourself and your area of expertise. You will usually be testifying about a particular bill, so state at the outset whether you support or oppose the bill. The content of your testimony is similar to that of a policy brief or an editorial. Make sure any statistics you cite are easy on the ear; listening to statistics is sometimes harder than reading them. Thus, find ways to communicate your numbers clearly. Brief, illustrative personal stories can be especially effective and engaging.

ENDINGS

My last bit of advice is to pay as much attention to endings as beginnings. Whether writing a policy brief, editorial, or testimony, we sometimes run out of steam, exhausting our ideas in our first creative burst of energy. Sometimes it's better to leave the best for last. And remember that eureka moments, when someone suddenly and swiftly changes his or her mind, are rare. Persuading others is more like a marathon than a 100-yard dash; it requires steadiness, strategy, and staying power. It also is helpful to remember that last year's doomsayer can become this year's oracle.

Endings also sometimes require a recapitulation of your major points, especially when you have showered the reader with multiple reflections and suggestions. Your audience may be reading your piece in more than one sitting and may need to be reminded of earlier points. Some readers, especially busy legislators, may even skim your piece rather than read it thoughtfully. It is thus often helpful to include a summation, and even a bulleted list for easy reference. For those of you who could use one now, to remember this chapter, here it is:

- Pay equal attention to reason and emotion and to facts and faith.
- Start where the client is and explore and address the figurative ground.
- Use frames and language that communicate the values underlying your argument.
- Don't bore your reader; use lively and succinct prose that tells a story.
- Use qualitative evidence for interest and depth and quantitative for context and extent.
- Build your arguments logically, using chains or clusters.

- Tailor your writing style and arguments to your audience.
- Make your ending as memorable as your beginning.

Recommended Readings

Hoefer, R. (2006). *Advocacy practice for social justice*. Chicago: Lyceum Books.

Jansson, B. (1999). *Becoming an effective policy advocate*. Pacific Grove, CA: Brooks/Cole.

Lakoff, G. (2004). *Don't think of an elephant: Know your values and frame the debate*. White River Junction, VT: Chelsea Green Publishing.

Lens, V. (2005). Advocacy and argumentation in the public arena: A guide for social workers. *Social Work, 50*, 231–238.

Rockridgeinstitute.org (George Lakoff's think tank on the Web).

References

Cohen, J. (2003, March 6). How Medicaid was set adrift. *New York Times*.

Harvey, P. (1994, November 25). Plenty of jobs? Where? *New York Times*.

Iyengar, S. (1996). The media and politics: Framing responsibility for political issues. *Annals of the American Academy of Political and Social Science, 546*, 59–70.

Lakoff, G. (1996). *Moral politics: What conservatives know that liberals don't*. Chicago: University of Chicago Press.

McLanahan, S., & Garfinkel, I. (1994, July 29). Unwed mothers: The wrong target; welfare is no incentive. *New York Times*.

National Association of Social Workers. (2003). Workforce structure op-ed. *The success of welfare reform depends on good social workers*. Washington, DC: Author. http://www.naswdc.org/advocacy/welfare/toolkit/oped_workforce.asp

National Association of Social Workers, New York State Chapter. (2007). Seven dirty words that social workers should not use in their work. *Update, 31*(7), 13–14.

Reich, R. (2005). *The lost art of democratic narrative*. The *New Republic* available on line at http://www.robertreich.org/reich/20050321.asp?view=print

Rybacki, K., & Rybacki, D. (1996). *Advocacy and opposition: An introduction to argumentation* (3rd ed.). Boston: Allyn & Bacon

Stone, D. (1997). *Policy paradox: The art of political decision making*. New York: W. W. Norton.

Toulmin, S., Rieke, R., & Janik, A. (1984). *An introduction to reasoning* (2nd ed.). New York: Macmillan.

Westen, D. (2007). *The political brain: The role of emotion on deciding the fate of the nation*. Cambridge: Perseus Book Group.

10

ADMINISTRATIVE WRITING

Sue Matorin

COMMUNICATION IS THE GLUE THAT binds an organization together into an effective team that translates vision into mission (Perlmutter & Crook, 2004), and effective writing is a valuable asset for social workers who intentionally choose or shift into an administrator's leadership role in an organization. Administrators are responsible for preparing many types of written material, such as memos, policy and procedure manuals, evaluations, minutes, and agendas and reports for board presentations. What each particular administrator must produce varies depending on the particular job, organization, and responsibilities, but whatever the task, each merits a professional approach. As a clinician/administrator based in an outpatient psychiatric clinic within a teaching hospital, I view written communication as key to effective leadership. This chapter covers the content and features of sound writing that can enhance your administrative work.

CURRENT CONTEXT

Historical challenges remain a given—daunting caseloads, clients with complex problems, inadequate resources, frustrating bureaucracies, and fragmented delivery systems continue to exist at the line level. Social workers have always met these challenges, maintaining their humanistic values, and well-worded communications from organization administrators can support their efforts and boost morale. At the program management level, programs are expected to use evidenced-based methods and demonstrate measurable fiscal value in a "bottom-line," fast-paced culture shaped by multitasking skills and comfort with technology (Matorin, 1998; Murdach, 2007; Stoesen, 2008; Weinbach, 2007). As a result of the emphasis on efficiency, face-to-face time has shrunk and the written word has become the main vehicle of communication. In larger organizations, a "top down" style of management prevails (Beckham, 2008; Perlmutter & Crook, 2004). Heightened accountability and regulatory oversight have raised the bar for well-written procedures. Your job as an administrator is to motivate staff to comply, demonstrate the bottom-line value of your programs, and meet regulatory and oversight standards. Today's administrator needs to adopt a writing style that reflects an appreciation for the work environment and that highlights the relevancy and time-sensitive nature of all materials (Austin & Ezell, 2004; Hopkins & Hyde, 2002; Wimpfheimer, 2004).

BASIC PRINCIPLES

Before addressing specific content, I examine four general writing principles that should be kept in mind. First, use a clear writing style that is straightforward, brief, and focused; this enriches the value of content. Second, think about your intended audience. Third, review the tone; is it appropriate for the audience and content? Finally, use jargon-free, engaging language. As you write your content, measure it against these principles to gauge how your style supports your message.

STRAIGHTFORWARD WRITING STYLE

Verbose writing undermines the message; good writers make every word count. Edit all writing for brevity, clarity, and simplicity. Journal abstracts provide good models—an abstract summarizes key conclusions, guiding us to read further or skip and move forward. Some journals now list main conclusions before the text for additional clarity. If you are not following this principle of writing, important points can be lost on your audience. For example, one clinic defeated a potentially upbeat accomplishment— good news about client-satisfaction survey results—by posting the results in a dense, over-detailed chart better suited for an audience of sophisticated professionals than a diverse clinic population. Another organization marketed a rich offering of continuing education workshops with the goal of increasing attendance and revenue. Unfortunately, the workshop descriptions were lengthy and too detailed, and they lacked key words or bullet points to guide the reader. Professionals are barraged with written material;

therefore, recognize that flooding is a fact of current professional life and prepare material that is brief, user-friendly, and focused.

WHO IS YOUR TARGET AUDIENCE?

Our social work educational background in psychology, sociology, and cultural diversity gives us a leg up over administrators trained in other disciplines. Capitalize on this training in your writing to better communicate with and connect to individuals and groups in the agency.

Show that you understand staff pressures and begin with a clear, precise, time-sensitive title or subject line. Whether you are announcing a mandatory meeting, adding a task to the workload, or reporting results of a client-satisfaction survey, ask yourself why staff should pause now to read your message. Administrators quickly learn that staff members who feel besieged may totally ignore e-mail communications (Kallos, 2004; Song, Halsey, & Burress, 2007).

Next, apply your knowledge about differentials in social class, race, and power/privilege to your writing. In large organizations, it may not occur to even well-intended administrators and human resource personnel that these factors affect a diverse staff in different ways. To illustrate: An organization needs to issue a memo encouraging staff to get to work on time, which appears to be a simple directive. Unlike administrators in other disciplines, we have the extra knowledge to reflect on how different subgroups of the audience might respond to such a memo. Sensitized to issues of power/privilege, we can usually appreciate that staff members' status in the agency, social supports, and income influence how easily they can comply and balance work and personal demands. Quite simply, a clerk who commutes from the outer boroughs or suburbs on unreliable public transportation and must punch a time clock may be as dedicated as the professional but may experience such a memo as a stressor. Conversely, that professional, who lives near the agency, may be better able to afford a taxi or car service and have more autonomy and control over his or her time.

[MEMO TO STAFF WHO CLOCK IN: TIME KEEPING PROCEDURE]
Recently some staff have been arriving to work late. We know you appreciate the importance of getting to work on time. Please speak with your supervisor when circumstances make punching in difficult for you.

This is a good memo because it "speaks" to nonprofessional staff who are under the gun to clock in but does not threaten them by raising the specter of being financially docked. It also offers a supervisor's help if there is a personal problem.

Communicating procedural reminders to other types of staff might be more direct.

[MEMO TO NONMEDICAL CLINICAL STAFF: ATTENDING PHYSICIAN OVERSIGHT]

As you know it is a regulation that every client be seen 2 x year by the supervising attending physician. Please coordinate your schedules to meet this requirement.

This memo is written for a different audience: clinical/professional staff. It simply reminds them of a key compliance policy and assumes that the reasons for the expectation are understood.

TONE

As you think about your audience, consider the tone of your message. *Tone* refers to the latent inflection of your words. If you are an administrator, your writing carries psychological weight. A critical, negative tone can defeat the value of your content. It is safe to assume that most staff take pride in the quality of their work. They possess exacting standards and aim to do their best. Staff can "hear" the slightest intimation of a boss's disapproval as a criticism taken to heart. As many administrators replace face-to-face time with the written word, as in-person conversations shrink, and the world of work becomes more impersonal, misunderstandings and sensitivity to feeling blamed can blossom.

Too often memos are dashed off by rushed administrators who are absolutely oblivious to their disapproving tone. Staff are especially upset to receive e-mails riddled with a "why-are-things-being-done-this-way" tone and/or a dive into the problem and a demand for solutions with little acknowledgment of past efforts. Social workers are trained to understand how positive reinforcement is a tool to motivate performance, and their written communications should be a reflection of these principles. Experience has taught me that a positive writing tone defuses defensiveness and enlists co-operation (Matorin, 2008).

At the same time, good written communication can support good management techniques. Recently an administrator asked staff with high caseloads to also cover an emergency crisis service (i.e., do intakes, write up material, and make referrals). He sent a handwritten thank-you note in advance of the schedule to express appreciation of the disruption and extra work. This gesture, both unusual and fresh, dissipated any complaints, and more importantly, everyone jumped aboard to be extra-helpful!

Tone is especially important when one writes about a topic that is a "hard sell," one that predictably could evoke resistance. It takes skill to deliver unpleasant news such as an increased workload, a decision to ask staff to work on a weekend, budget cuts, or an evaluation of an underperforming individual. Competent writers do not sugarcoat unpleasant material. They do present the realities. Good writing inspires cooperation and minimizes resistance (Perlmutter & Crook, 2004).

ENGAGING LANGUAGE

Use engaging language. Our work is often painful, as we help clients reclaim lives damaged by illness, trauma, poverty, and racism, and your administrative writing should reflect the seriousness of this content, but do remember to infuse the writing with vitality and expand our collective vocabulary (Lifland, 2007; Szuchman & Thomlison, 2004). Of course, avoid computer-generated smiley symbols that detract from professionalism. Also avoid jargon; jargon strips writing of vitality (Holland, 2007). A quick scan of article titles in social work journals illustrates the dulling effect of jargon: "Situational Approaches to . . ." "Effects of Service Barriers on . . ." "Dealing with the Aftermath of . . ." "A Quantitative Analysis of . . ."

One illustration of an effort to write in a more lively manner comes from a social work conference planning committee charged with organizing and marketing a professional conference. The committee turned to media and borrowed lively phrases from a *New York Times Magazine* devoted to style. Note how this uplifting and interesting language engages the reader: "Reimagining . . . ," "Grace your mind," "Cultivate," "Sea Change," "Pathway to Possibilities." Do not substitute sizzle for substance, but I do recommend livelier language when appropriate to better engage the audience.

Having reviewed general writing principles, let's now turn to specific types of communication.

MEMOS

Memos, on paper or in e-mail form, form the basis of day-to-day interoffice communication. Memos are commonly used in business to make announcements, communicate policy changes, and otherwise inform an organization's employees. They should be informative and concise, focusing on only one topic and rarely, if ever, longer than one page.

One type of memo is an introductory memo, used to inform personnel of new staff members. Social network researchers study the importance of networking to job satisfaction, an issue that is of special concern in the current, more impersonal climate. They highlight the importance of how new hires are introduced (Haley-Lock, 2007).

> We are delighted to announce that Ms. Jones, LCSW, has joined the adolescent in-patient team. She received her Masters in social work at Columbia University, and she brings experience from internships in child welfare and the Mt. Sinai Medical Center adolescent day program to this position. We are confident she will bring this experience to our team. Thank you in advance for your help in getting her up to speed.

This memo introduces a junior social worker to an interdisciplinary team that cares for adolescents with severe psychiatric illness in an inpatient setting. Why is it effective? First, in four sentences it provides much specific information about the new hire. The content establishes her credentials and educates the interdisciplinary team about social work requirements to practice in a specialty area. (It is distressing that people in other disciplines do not always know that a social worker must possess a master's degree and a license to practice in health care.) Because this is a junior position, the description includes the fieldwork placements that have enhanced the new hire's credibility as the "new kid on the block" to join a skilled specialty team. This memo links the social worker's past experience to this new job and paves the way for her integration as a valuable addition to the work group. By spelling these details out, the administration justifies her selection for a competitive spot.

Second, the memo is honest. While in most settings the human resources department offers a formal and very general orientation, staff are
often expected to help orient the new hire. This memo wisely expresses
appreciation for the burden of this reality. Finally, the upbeat, enthusiastic
tone communicates a positive development in the organization. Contrast
this memo with a skimpy uninformative statement: "This is to inform you
that we have filled the unit social work position, and Ms. J. will start on 3/22.
Please welcome her."

Administrators write other types of positive memos, such as this one about
a staff benefit:

> Christmas Eve is not traditionally recognized as a holiday. But in recogni-
> tion of all the good work done by staff, there will be an exception to the
> policy this year. For this year only, December 24th will be recognized as a
> holiday. Individual offices may choose to remain open. If they choose to do
> so, all employees who work will be entitles to holiday pay.

This is the best type of administrative memo: It announces a specific, meaningful award to recognize staff effort. We will note but overlook the typo
("entitles"!), illustrative of failure to proofread important material in a harried climate.

Another example:

> Congratulations to all staff for our scores on the Press Ganey survey for this
> quarter. Our target goal for the year was . . . This quarter we received . . .
> Thank you for the part you played in making this quarter a success. The
> time you spent supporting the importance of the survey with each patient
> has made all the difference.

This memo to staff was followed by a note to the program from the CEO:

> Wow! What a wonderful success story . . . congratulations to you and your
> terrific and dedicated staff. I am very proud of all of you. Warm regards!
> (sent via Blackberry).

These upbeat memos certainly express appreciation to staff. The warm
tone and content underscore and communicate the premium that the administration places on such client feedback. Increasingly administrators

send information by electronic transmission rather than in person. The actual writing could have been tighter and better edited.

Some memos announce less-pleasant pieces of information, such as a mandatory repetitive task that adds to one's workload. The same principles apply: concise writing and a positive tone.

> Quarterly treatment plan updates are due on 9/23/09 (again!). We recognize this requirement disrupts your schedule. We apologize that we have not yet been able to modify the computer program to incorporate your suggestions to replace a narrative with a check list format.
>
> Not only do we appreciate your efforts but they have also been duly noted by the Department of Mental Hygiene reviewers, who consistently identify our plans as models. The "official" policy remains—we encourage you to cancel clinic patients for this task. We know, however, that most of you go beyond the call of duty and schedule your patients. Only this staff is able to set a gold standard for compliance and clinical care simultaneously.

This is a good memo, though fairly brief considering the importance of the topic—a mandated requirement. Also, it is honest. It does not sugarcoat the burden imposed on a busy staff. The memo acknowledges that schedules are disrupted. The administrator takes responsibility for failing to act on staff suggestions to replace narrative with a time-saving checklist. The material appeals to the psychology of the audience, to the spirit of high achievers who enjoy positive feedback from external auditors and who view client service as a top priority. The writer is attuned to a group of individuals who will do their best and never compromise client care because of burdensome paperwork.

Below is another example of how to constructively present potentially unpleasant news in a memo. The charge is to motivate staff to comply with a check-in procedure for clients that is fraught with difficulties. The rule seems simple: All clients must check in at reception and pay for the service before advancing to the social worker's office for their appointment. A typical memo from an administrator might read:

> It has come to my attention from reception staff that many of you see your clients before they check in at the front desk. This is a violation of clinic procedure. Any client who arrives at your door without proof they have

checked in should be sent back first to the desk before being seen. There are no exceptions. Thank you.

Let us examine why this is an ineffective memo despite such important content. First, the tone is terse, brusque, and punitive. The administrator fails to spell out why this procedure is so important. There is nothing in the material that communicates any understanding of factors that contribute to the problem. The administrator fails to engage the staff in problem solving. The material implies that professional staff would not want to be helpful or follow important procedures. The memo demands compliance but leaves no room for individual judgment. Actually the overall tone is discourteous to staff and clients.

Here is an improved version:

We need your help. Increasingly some patients skip the essential step of check-in and payment at the reception desk before they head straight to your office. We know you appreciate this procedure as necessary to our clinic's financial viability. Please help your clients comply and allow sufficient time for this step prior to their appointment. In the event that your client arrives late, has skipped this step, but must be seen, we would appreciate your escorting him/her back to the desk afterwards. We are making every effort to staff the desk adequately to decrease delays and welcome your ideas about how to improve this aspect of our clinic operation.

This memo reflects a much more courteous tone. It explains the importance of the procedures, and communicates respect for clients and an understanding that even well-intended individuals may run late in an urban setting. There is room for individual judgment. The memo sincerely solicits input to fix a problem and assures staff that administration is doing their part also.

POLICIES AND PROCEDURES

Agency policy and procedure manuals communicate the bedrock of how an agency organizes goals and services. These materials serve internal and external purposes. Internally, manuals orient a new hire to get him/her up to speed about agency operating rules; externally, they serve as benchmarks against which regulators or auditors measure how an agency meets its own established written standards and complies with city, state, and federal mandates. For example, an auditor may review a procedure for recording requirements and then select a case, read an actual chart entry, and match this to the policy. Polices are often located in large binders or, increasingly, on the agency computer system. Hard copies must be accessible, but in reality they are rarely consulted in day-to-day practice.

Organizing your time at the outset saves actual writing time. Start by preparing several lists. Your policy manual may need to include, for example, agency and program mission/value statements, a statement of agency priorities, and specific policies dealing with high-risk areas of practice. Mission statements are more global, so that list will be short. Lists regarding priorities and high-risk areas are more specific.

In general, when writing a policy manual, be comprehensive but recognize that it will be impossible to include every issue. Identify what is reasonable, what to prioritize, and which policies cover risk. Be proactive: anticipate and cover the agency for unintended errors. There will always be instances when, even with the best of intentions, your agency cannot reach goals or comply with standards. Allow margins for error as you write policies and include corrective action plans. Check for consistency to be sure that one policy is not countermanded by another.

Support the content with a straightforward writing style. Avoid the pitfalls of long-winded, formulaic language. Use headings, bullet points, and other such tools to break up the material into manageable sections that will help the reader quickly locate a specific policy.

MISSION STATEMENTS

A mission statement is a tool to tell your organization's staff, constituency, funders, and the general public about your agency's focus. It often includes what an organization values, along with what it aims to do. Mission statements are used on signs, stationery, brochures, Web sites, and in other media to keep all interested parties aware of an organization's mind-set and goals. "Mission" is what the agency does; "value" is the principle that shapes how the agency does it.

Mission statements are best when written with the input of staff across the organization, which also increases staff buy-in, or commitment, to the result. The process itself can be quite involved, and there are many management books devoted to the subject. Generally, crafting a mission statement involves identifying the core reasons why your organization exists and what unique characteristics or principles differentiate your organization from others. Below are two examples:

The mission of [Agency A] is to support, with dignity and respect, people of all ages in order to enhance lives and affect positive change in communities.

The mission of [Agency B] is to provide comprehensive services for those suffering with serious mental illness, and to provide compassionate services with a goal of enabling people to live independently in the community.

Agency A offers a wide range of services to different populations, and its mission statement reflects a general overview of the agency's philosophy. In large organizations, each program may have its own mission statement to reflect the specialized work its does. Both mission statements reflect actions ('nurture and support . . . affect positive change," "enabling people to live independently") along with values ("dignity," "respect," "compassion").

Make sure that agency or program mission and value statements are reflected in, supported by, and agree with agency policies. For example, one agency *mission* might be to serve a diverse underprivileged population while endorsing the *value* of consumer input. How would you actually operationalize that? Your list of what to include in the manual to demonstrate how the agency aims to achieve this mission-based goal might include "access to translator services" and "formation of a consumer advisory committee." Another *mission* statement might express the *value* of providing "exceptional" care to build a loyal client base. Again, this is a laudable *value*, but how would one translate that general *value* into a tangible measurable agency policy? A procedure for quarterly satisfaction surveys could be a tool for making the value tangible.

AGENCY PRIORITIES

Your agency priority list is much more specific and might include items like timeliness of appointments, expectations regarding interagency collaboration and contacts with collaterals, and documentation requirements. Ask yourself how you would operationalize these goals. Such thinking, along with your list, will guide you in spelling out the procedures to minimize waits for service; specifics to involving the family in the assessment/treatment process or linkages with other health and social service providers; and requirements to comply with external mandates and to obtain reimbursement.

Agency priorities are one area that administrators may wish to recognize as having goals that may not be uniformly achieved. For example, an audit revealed that clients who called for service experienced a two-week delay before receiving an appointment. The written policy stated that all clients would be seen within a week of their initial call, an agency goal. The administrator was now in a tight spot, as he or she had to explain to an auditor the disparity between a written policy and the audit findings. This illustrates the value of including a simple phrase that gives a bit of breathing space for exceptions. Perhaps this particular agency's good intentions to provide immediate service were defeated by unexpected staff turnover or absenteeism. Simply rewording the policy by using a phrase such as "will make every reasonable effort to schedule an appointment within one week" can cover the reality that even the best of agencies cannot always live up to stated goals.

HIGH-RISK AREAS OF PRACTICE

External reviewers will scrutinize risk management policies. Therefore, pay particular attention to your list of *high-risk* areas—for example, management of emergencies in the agency, evening and weekend coverage for client emergencies, client safety (e.g., infection control, fire safety), and child- and elder-abuse reporting requirements. Your list should reflect attention to detail, as the margin for error with regard to safety issues is much smaller than that for some other areas, such as a paper task like completion of a closing summary.

One illustration involves staff licensing. An agency's manual mandates that staff provide proof of license renewals, a non-debatable standard for consumer protection. Agencies have been known to halt practice on the spot and contact state education department registers for licensure proof if, in the course of an external audit, paper proof is missing; absence of proof can even result in suspension. The policy should also include a corrective action plan, to be undertaken if a staff member should fail to comply. An agency might also mandate that staff participate in continuing education, a requirement that is important but far less urgent. A few suggestions about how staff could fulfill this obligation will suffice, and at a much lower level of specificity/urgency.

On occasion an agency may need to make a policy change regarding a high-risk activity, and it may need to communicate this to staff immediately rather than waiting for the next scheduled policy manual revision.

[*FOR YOUR IMMEDIATE ATTENTION*]

We want to thank you for your hard work and support during the mock survey, a time consuming but constructive process. Overall, charts are exemplary. However, surveyors identified one key area of vulnerability we need to immediately correct.

In assessment of suicidal risk, we failed to meet a national patient safety standard at a sufficient level of detail. We cannot await recommendations from the committee to address this. Therefore, we ask that you immediately adjust your chart notes to include the following:

* Document that you have checked client access to a weapon and taken safety measures if necessary.

* Rate severity of risk from mild to severe. This rating is based on a client's past history of attempts, family history, and other factors, such as social isolation, alcohol/drug abuse, and treatment compliance.

This policy is urgent. We know we can count on each of you to prepare notes that reflect this information, and we thank you in advance for your help. We will keep you updated on committee recommendations, and we welcome your input/ideas at our next staff meeting.

This is a well-prepared policy. It labels the issue as urgent. It credits the staff with good work and enlists their immediate help to better document a high-risk issue. It provides very specific guidance on how to correct the problem in the short term. Staff can appreciate that immediate action is required and cannot await the work of a committee. Administration invites staff input for the lengthier revision process.

EVALUATIONS

In contrast to policy materials, which tend to be more formulaic, evaluations allow room for creativity. The writer can describe the uniqueness of an individual social worker and qualities that he/she possesses that add value to an organization. Writers can use language that has some spark. Evaluations serve to: (a) identify performance goals that have been met and that are clearly linked to the agency's mission, (b) outline steps to correct any problems, and (c) motivate an individual to perform better and/or encourage career advancement.

First, some general principles: Be cognizant that an evaluation can evoke some anxiety in the recipient (Weinbach, 2007). Apply psychological savvy to this function. Some people may have previously received unfair evaluations focused on irrelevant personality traits rather than on job-related performance behaviors, and it is quite common for anyone receiving a performance review to focus more on one negative "need for improvement" item, even when many positives are acknowledged! Good administrators identify problems as they occur so that nothing is sprung in writing that has not been discussed in person (Villano, 2008). There should be no surprises.

Most individuals want to do a good job and take written feedback to heart; however, issues appear more ominous when spelled out in black and white. Professionals recognize evaluations as a necessity but would prefer that competence be assumed as a given. Emphasize this tool as a growth opportunity.

As you apply psychological attunement, monitor the writing for tone. Stay positive and acknowledge strengths, not just problem areas. Many administrators quickly identify problems but are quite stingy with well-deserved praise. It is important to focus on the work and avoid character comments unless a glaring personality issue intrudes on the actual work.

Specifically, the evaluation should include: (a) a brief job description; (b) knowledge base and skills; (c) specific examples of how the individual does or does not fill the role and contribute to the agency's mission; (d) strengths and areas for improvement; (e) next steps for professional growth; and (f) external feedback, if available (e.g., grateful client letters, professional awards, publications). The evaluation should comment on all aspects of performance. Therefore it is important to comment constructively on behaviors that may undermine performance, including specific examples and suggestions for growth. A social worker's capacity to tolerate feedback nondefensively and use it to improve job performance is actually an indicator of professionalism.

Here are examples of how to address uneven performance, acknowledge strengths, note problem areas, identify expectations for improvement, and avoid jargon:

Mr. S. has strong clinical skills with couples and families, which enables us to assign him some of our more complex cases. He has received numerous accolades from appreciative clients; thus, he is a real asset to our setting.

However, over the past year we have discussed the importance of timely documentation. Less attention to this aspect of his role undermines his otherwise stellar abilities. We now need him to bring this aspect of professionalism up to speed in the coming year.

~~~~~~~~~~~~

Ms. S approaches her practice in a methodical manner, an important asset in the current climate of risk management. At times, however, she has struggled with pacing herself, causing her to get easily flustered with the unexpected, despite her experience. In such a fast-paced setting, new demands on staff to take on multiple roles call for more flexibility; as a result, Ms S will need to pitch in on short notice and may have to step outside her comfort zone.

Notice that in the last example the statement implies rigidity but avoids commenting on the person's character. In both examples, the evaluator focuses on agency needs, avoids jargon, and tailors comments to the individual.

In many settings knowledge-based competencies for specific populations have been identified at the initial hiring. In the absence of sit-in observation or videotaped interviews, it is not always easy to evaluate a skill. Agencies increasingly rely on client-satisfaction surveys for feedback. In these surveys clients often identify or single out a social worker who has been especially helpful. Others may actually take the time to write a letter to the agency director. This type of feedback should be included in the evaluation, as should positive comments from other staff members, especially in interdisciplinary settings where teamwork is highly prized.

To set the stage for constructive critical feedback, always acknowledge positives first, such as handling multiple competing responsibilities, working with a collaborative spirit, and providing humanistic care of clients. From this foundation one can home in on tough problem areas and offer steps for growth.

Last, and of much importance, is the evaluation conference. The staff member should be encouraged to add comments, not just asked to read and sign the material. Harried administrators rushing to meet their own deadlines may skip this conference, thereby devaluing and undermining professionalism.

MINUTES

The preparation of minutes poses special problems. As a member of a number of organizations and boards, I have received numerous minutes, and I still struggle with preparing minutes for meetings I attend or chair. Wordiness must be avoided, and the tone should be geared to the seriousness of the topics and the professional roles of the participants. For example, minutes of a meeting of volunteers for a client advisory group might be a bit warmer in tone than the more formal and precise record of a meeting about a new clinical skills center at an academic medical center.

One key goal of minutes is that they provide a record of decisions made. Proofreading is also important, since the material can be an official record.

Here is an example of poorly prepared minutes that are too detailed and lack a decision.

> The group discussed honorariums and a lively debate ensued. SF noted it would be tough to get a speaker on a Saturday to offer a free lecture; JS disagreed, noting that some might feel honored to present at such an important event; GF added that many speakers are not allowed to accept a fee; PM suggested some fees are elevated.

These minutes fail to (a) identify a key issue—whether or not the group has a budget to support an important alumni event, (b) summarize the discussion, and (c) report on a decision or action.

Here is a suggested improvement:

> Honorariums: The conference committee debated honorariums for potential workshop speakers. Issues included the difficulty of inviting well known professionals who expect compensation for their time / expertise; the absence of a budget to cover the cost; the prestige of the sponsoring institution as a sufficient reward.

Action Plan: Chairs will approach the Dean with a cost/risk benefit, i.e., the risk of losing potential speakers of prominence who could draw a larger audience without a compensation offer, and report back at the next meeting.

These minutes are an improvement. They are more formally written, in keeping with the importance of the issue. They identify a problem, present both sides, and offer a next-step action plan. The attachment of participants' names to specific points lengthens the material. You will have to weigh the added value of identifying particular speakers.

EXECUTIVE SUMMARIES TO BOARDS

As an administrator you may have to periodically present to the agency board. You are expected to deliver a progress report that describes how the agency as a whole is meeting its goals, and if not, why not. Such presentations are formal, require thorough preparation, and are often preceded by a written report that allows board members the opportunity to prepare informed, appropriate questions. It is customary to deliver the report to the board in advance of the actual meeting. The efficiency with which an agency accomplishes this first step often reflects how well organized the agency is. Your goal is to write clear, succinct, formal material. Accompanying graphs and charts should not require a degree in statistics to comprehend.

First, it is important to know your board's composition. Some boards include only social workers; therefore, all the board members speak the same professional language. Others may include people such as senior lawyers, business professionals with considerable financial savvy, and laypersons who may share the agency's values but are largely unschooled in its mission. A mixed board is a tough audience. You can expect that a lawyer will be attuned to risk and liability, a financial wizard will home in on any budget deficits, and a layperson, well intentioned and humanistic, may raise questions that are naive and reveal a failure to appreciate how difficult it can be to deliver cost-effective complex services. The report must satisfy all subgroups of this audience.

A good report will include (a) a statement of mission, (b) data to document how the agency is meeting its service goals (e.g., number of clients served, types of services, new programs), (c) a transparent budget to demonstrate accountability and explain how money is being allocated, (d) if needed, an explanation for why the agency has fallen short of reaching a target, and (e) a future direction. For an example of dealing with an unmet target, consider how a transit strike can lead to a drop in clinic visits, or how the departure of a key staff member could lead to the closing of a program. A quality report includes explanations for why certain goals were not met, and it offers a corrective action plan.

Last, the report should be oriented toward the future, with a focus on specific requests for assistance. Board members are expected to give both a donation and their time and ideas. Additionally a board member may provide access to an invaluable resource that could benefit the agency—for example, a media contact to publicize the agency's work, or even a graphic arts student who could design a brochure on a pro bono basis. A report should provide a wish list for agency needs and growth, and it should be written concisely, with bullet points to break up the material.

It is a good idea to include a client vignette that illustrates a positive outcome. A quote from a grateful client who benefited from the agency's service brings outcome data to life. As noted, agencies focus considerably on "client satisfaction" and want satisfied clients to refer others, or to return themselves if they need more care. For example, here is an introduction followed by a quote from one such grateful client:

> Nicole (a pseudonym), an African American young woman, was briefly hospitalized as a teenager for suicidal depression, and revealed rape by a relative. With brief outpatient counseling, she achieved marriage, motherhood (two children), and her goal—a career in teaching. Ten years later, about to embark on a master's program, she returned to the same emergency room following an abortion. Conflicted about her decision to have an abortion, she was again seriously depressed, but adamantly refused admission or medication. She did agree to brief counseling by the same social worker she had worked with years back.

> I know you are all terribly busy, but I just wanted to let you know that overall I had a good first year teaching. I believe I learned a lot about myself with that year and have matured as a woman. I can't believe I have known all of you for almost 10 years. I will always attribute much of my success to you. Thank you!

This quote validates the outcome of treatment at two different crisis points in this young woman's life, and it is a tribute to the quality of the agency and staff that cared for her. The feedback speaks volumes and amplifies the data in an annual report.

CONCLUSION

In this chapter I've provided a road map for administrative writing. I am very optimistic that we can adopt a writing style—a feature of leadership—that enables staff to embrace challenges. Social work administrators compete with managers who have administrative training from business and public health backgrounds (Nesoff, 2007; Packard, 2004; Patti, 2003; Vickers, 2007). We know how to motivate individuals, groups, and organizations to embrace tough missions, demonstrate appreciation for fiscal pressures, and show our professional colors. I encourage you to tap into this unique expertise and meld it with sound writing skills. Those who do so offer added value to any agency. The art and science of effective administrative writing is a priceless credential.

References

Austin, M., & Ezell, M. (2004). Educating future social work administrators. *Administration in Social Work, 28*(1), 1–3.

Beckham, D. (2008). Tough love. *Hospitals and Health Networks Online, 82*(3).

Haley-Lock, A. (2007). Up close and personal: Employee networks human service context. *Social Service Review.* http://www.journals.uchicago.edu/doi/full/10.1086/522218

Holland, K. (2007, September 23). In mission statements, bizspeak and bromides. *New York Times*, p. 17. Retrieved August 21, 2010, from http://www.nytimes.com

Hopkins, K., & Hyde, C. (2002). The human service managerial dilemma: New expectations, chronic challenges, and old solutions. *Administration in Social Work, 26*(3), 1–15.

Kallos, J. (2004). *Because netiquette matters! Your comprehensive reference guide to e-mail etiquette and proper technology use.* Bloomington, IN: Xlibris.

Lifland, S. (2007). An interview with a "recovering CEO dad." Tom Stern. *E-Newsletter, 2*(6). Retrieved October 20, 2007, from http://www.amanet.org/lifland.html

Matorin, S. (1998). The corporatization of mental health services: The impact on service, training, and values. In G. Schamess & A. Lightburn (Eds.), *Humane managed care?* (pp. 159–170). Washington, DC: NASW Press.

———. (2008). Strive to inspire (Letter to the Editor.). *Hospitals and Health Networks, 82*(4), 8.

Murdach, A. (2007). Living in the trenches: Managerial skills for practitioners. *Social Work, 52*(4), 375–377.

Nesoff, I. (2007). The importance of revitalizing management education for social workers. *Social Work, 52,* 283–285.

Packard, T. (2004). Issues in designing and adapting an administration concentration. *Administration in Social Work, 28*(1), 5–20.

Patti, R. (2003). Reflections on the state of management in social work. *Administration in Social Work, 27*(2), 1–11.

Perlmutter, F., & Crook, W. (2004). *The administrator's use of communication in changing hats while managing change.* Washington, DC: NASW Press.

Song, M., Halsey, V., & Burress, T. (2007). How to stop spinning your wheels and start managing your e-mail. *E-Newsletter, 2*(2). Retrieved October 20, 2007, from http://www.amanet.orgsong/html

Stoesen, L. (2008, April). Report explores social worker stress. *NASW News,* 9.

Szuchman, L., & Thomlison, B. (2004). *Writing with style.* Belmont, CA: Brooks/Cole.

Vickers, M. (2007). The long goodbye to literacy. *E-newsletter* 2, #4. Retrieved October 20, 2007, from http://www.amanet.org/vickers.html

Villano, M. (2008, November 30). Your performance has come up short. *New York Times,* Money and Business, p. 9.

Weinbach, R. (2007). *The social worker as manager: A practical guide to success.* Upper Saddle River, NJ: Pearson Press.

Wimpfheimer, S. (2004). Leadership and management competencies defined by practicing social work managers: An overview of standards developed by the national network for social work managers. *Administration in Social Work, 28*(1), 45–56.

PART THREE

WRITING IN DISTINCT FIELDS OF PRACTICE

11

WRITING IN FAMILY AND CHILD WELFARE

Brenda G. McGowan and Elaine M. Walsh

THE FAMILY AND CHILD WELFARE field has traditionally been focused on providing services for children whose parents are unable to fulfill normal parental roles and responsibilities. In the 19th century, "child saving" was the focus of early reformers and social workers. Child savers sought to remove children and adolescents from all contact with their families of origin and offer institutional, adoptive, or foster care instead. In the 21st century, protective and substitute care for children and teenagers continues to be an important child welfare measure, as are strategies to keep children safe and well at home through preventive and developmental services that aim to strength parents' capacities to nurture and protect their own children. Consequently, unlike many other social work fields of practice, family and child welfare is heavily defined by federal and state laws and regulations. This legislative framework has a direct influence on the types of writing required in this field, especially in those components that involve any type of direct or implied state intervention in family life.

This chapter will review the recording requirements in protective and foster care services and the range of writing expectations and options for preventive and developmental services for families and youth at risk. The former core services, which are legislatively mandated and governed by state statute, require very careful, fact-based reports that will hold up when subjected to court scrutiny. Also, perhaps as a result of the enormous public investment in these services, they tend to have extensive accountability demands that emphasize facts and numbers and are often reduced to standardized computer reports. Because of variations in state statutes and accountability demands, the precise nature of these reports can vary from one location to another, but the basic principles are similar across jurisdictions.

In contrast, child and family services geared toward early intervention and prevention of child maltreatment and/or foster placement are usually not governed by law and consequently can be more flexible in their recording requirements. They ordinarily require the traditional sorts of competent professional writing, such as that done for intake summaries, psychosocial assessments, referral letters, and position statements on public policy issues relevant to the agency.

CHILD PROTECTIVE SERVICES

An important obligation of social workers in family and child welfare, like social workers and other mandated reporters in other fields of practice, is to report a suspicion of child abuse or maltreatment to the responsible state authority. This is commonly done first by telephone or e-mail and then by a written report. The written report must present the known demographic information about the child or children involved and other persons in the household, the precise nature of the alleged abuse or maltreatment, and the specific reasons for the worker's suspicion—that is, time and date of alleged incident(s), nature and extent of child's injuries, and evidence or suspicion of parental behavior that may have led to the problem. In addition, the reporter is asked to provide his or her name, address, and role in relation to the case. All information about the reporter is confidential and cannot be reported to the family. (A copy of the 221A reporting form mandated by New York State, as well as copies of all other related forms, can be obtained from the Web site of the New York State Office of Children & Family Services: www.ocfs.state.ny.us.)

Once the State Central Registry accepts a report, a worker from the local child protective services office must investigate the allegation. This may take one or several visits, but ultimately the worker must write a very thorough report describing the fact patterns in each case in detail. This includes a description of the condition of the house or apartment, with attention to the amount of space, sleeping arrangements, and cleanliness; a summary of the interview(s) with the parents and any other adult member of the household, with specific attention to the family's financial situation; whether there is any substance use or domestic violence in the home; parent's description of the children and any special concerns regarding the children; and summaries of interviews with, or depending on age, observations of, each child.

Most important, the worker must also describe each family member's response to or thinking about the specific concerns raised in the allegation of abuse or maltreatment. As this is an investigation, the child protective services worker's report must provide explicit, factual data.

In addition to conducting the investigation in the family home, the worker may also want to interview, by telephone or in person, the mandated reporter who filed the complaint—for example, a teacher, physician, social worker, or day-care worker. It is important that the facts derived from these interviews also be recorded in careful detail.

Ultimately, the worker will have to make a recommendation as to the services required to help this family. If the recommendation is to make a finding of child abuse or maltreatment and perhaps to remove the child to foster care, the worker must be prepared to make this recommendation in court and must have data available to support the recommendation. If the recommendation is for in-home services, the details must be spelled out clearly to assist the next person who assumes responsibility for the case. If the worker concludes that the allegation of abuse or maltreatment is not justified, or is "unfounded," as it is sometimes termed, then that finding must be clearly recorded. And throughout the record, the worker must document that the parents have been informed of their rights.

FOSTER CARE SERVICES

When a child enters foster care, either voluntarily or through court order, the state assumes temporary custody and is obligated to protect the child's welfare. This is an enormous responsibility because the state is essentially assuming parental responsibilities. Consequently, many state statutes and regulations have been adopted to ensure that the state fulfills its responsibilities to the child. There are two primary roles for social workers in foster care: recruiting, studying, and certifying potential foster and adoptive homes, and working with the foster children, their biological families, and their foster families.

HOME STUDIES

Because the state is selecting parents for children who enter foster care through the decisions of workers in licensed child welfare agencies, many policies and procedures have been adopted to ensure the wisdom of these decisions. These policies are often embodied in state forms that must be completed to authorize foster care and adoption actions. To illustrate, New York State currently has 8 forms that must be completed to permit various actions for children in foster care and 16 that must be completed to authorize various actions for children entering adoption. Given the prevalence of these standardized forms, one of the first challenges for workers in foster care is to learn how to write the information required in a succinct, factual manner that will enable the agency to take whatever action seems most desirable for the child in question.

When conducting a home study of either foster or adoptive parents, the worker must explore many aspects of family life, including the parents' motivations for caring for children who are not their biological children, who may be different from them in many ways, and who may be very difficult to care for. Approval of new families for children is never left to an individual worker. A supervisor and an administrator responsible for home finding usually share responsibility for this decision. Therefore, the worker conducting a home study must write a full assessment of the family's strengths, limitations, and motivations. If the study is conducted on behalf of a specific child, then the worker must also describe the potential fit between the family and the child. If the family is applying for a child or children in an open-ended way, then the worker must carefully consider and describe the number, gender, and age(s), as well as the types of children (e.g., a child with a physical disability or a mental illness), that this family potentially could or could not handle.

One of the difficulties that beginning workers often encounter in writing up home studies is assessing in writing the potential limitations of a family that has volunteered to assume responsibility for a child in need. That part of the process may make a new worker feel that he or she is violating the family's privacy. Yet honesty in writing a home study is essential because a child's life and well-being depend on it. It sometimes helps for new young workers to be reminded that they are not writing about their own parents and should not compare other families to their family of origin.

PROVISION OF FAMILY SERVICES

Although caseload arrangements vary from agency to agency, usually a single worker carries responsibility for work with the biological parents, the foster parents, and the foster child. In some settings, these distinct responsibilities may be assigned to different service units, and the primary worker must coordinate the activities of the other workers. Such coordination demands careful written and verbal communication among the different departments. Because the state essentially places the welfare of each foster child in the hands of strangers, the foster care workers must monitor the well-being of each child and the quality of the care that he or she is receiving. At the same time they must try to help the birth parents address the range of problems they may be experiencing that contributed to the need for placement—for example, substance abuse, poverty, unemployment, serious mental and/or physical illness, or lack of adequate parenting skills.

RATIONALE FOR EXTENSIVE CASE RECORDING

For many years little state attention was given to record keeping in foster care. Different agencies each had different requirements regarding progress notes, process recording, case summaries, and so forth. Children placed in foster homes were often allowed to grow up in these homes with little ongoing monitoring by the state or the child placement agency. Consequently, foster children were frequently lost in care or left in what Maas and Engler (1959) called a foster care limbo. There was no clear plan for them to return home or to move into a permanent adoptive home.

In an effort to address this problem, Congress passed a law titled the Adoption Assistance and Child Welfare Act of 1980 (P.L. 96–272), which introduced the concept of permanency planning, the requirement that foster care workers engage in a range of goal-directed activities designed to give children a sense of permanency and belonging. This can be accomplished by returning them to their own families in a timely manner or by placing them in a legally permanent alternative (adoption or legal guardianship) as soon as possible. The legislation had a number of provisions related to funding for preventive and foster care programs, placement in the least detrimental setting, and establishment of a regular case review mechanism for each child in care. In addition, the law mandated that each state develop a statewide information system identifying the status, demographic characteristics, location, and goals for placement of each child currently in care and all who were in care during the preceding twelve months (Allen & Knitzer, 1983). The objective of the requirement was to permit the collection and analysis of aggregate data at the federal and state levels. In response to this law, all the states developed elaborate information systems that have evolved over time in accord with changes in computer technology.

Compounding the requirements related to implementation of the law, in 2001, in response to a Congressional mandate, the U.S. Department of Health and Human Services implemented a new system, called Child and Family Service Reviews. The department uses state-provided data, as well as interviews and an on-site case review, to assess performance on 14 outcome measures, such as length of children's stay in foster care and level of services provided, to meet children's health and educational needs. The reviews require states to track their progress in program implementation plans or face financial penalties. This federal requirement places an additional burden on front-line workers to ensure the accuracy of their records. All foster care workers are now required to maintain detailed factual records regarding the placement of each child, service objectives, the child's progress in care, contact with the biological parents, and permanency plan.

COMPUTERIZED INFORMATION SYSTEMS

All states have their own computer information systems; though each one is unique, they are all geared to provide the required information on each foster child in that particular state. For purposes of illustration, this chapter will highlight the information system Connections, used in New York State. This system combines a number of narrative sections with many others that instruct the worker to select one of the precoded options. It is a complex system designed to cover each case, from intake, assessment, and service planning for each family member to recording of case activities, objectives and outcomes, progress notes, and a final case summary. Social workers using this system or a comparable one in other states will have to draw on everything they know about exploration of relevant case data, case assessment, and service planning to complete this record in a meaningful way.[1] To illustrate: Connections requires that intake workers write a brief narrative describing why the case is being opened now, and it specifies that this entry will be frozen as soon as it is saved, so no changes can be entered later. The intake workers must then identify all behavioral issues and family concerns from a precoded list—for example, "food, shelter or clothing needs unmet," "family crisis: death, fire, or other catastrophic event"—and then identify which, if any, of these issues are critical and require emergency services. In addition, the intake workers must list all the requested services as described on a precoded list and provide basic demographic information about the family and the decision made about opening the case.

Once a case is opened, the assigned worker must prepare a Family Assessment and Service Plan (FASP), combining both narrative and standardized data entries, and this information must be updated regularly. As part of the service plan, the worker completes a checklist for family caretakers and children, indicating how each family member rates on a number of predefined scales measuring needs and risks. The service plan summary, which must be completed every six months, indexes all desired outcomes, as specified in the initial assessment, and asks the worker to record achievements, needed changes, and ongoing plans. There is also room for all workers involved in the case to record progress notes. These notes may be kept in "draft" status for 15 days, but most of the other recording cannot be changed once it is saved. That most of the information cannot be changed after the worker has made an entry highlights how important and prudent it is for the worker to take the time needed to think through every issue and perhaps write a first draft before entering the actual data.

This computerized system of recording has significant advantages and disadvantages for the foster care worker. The intake, case assessment, and service plan sections are so carefully laid out that it would be difficult for a worker to neglect any major factor that should be remembered in service planning. The computerized lists also save a good deal of recording time. However, there is a real risk that workers who are in a hurry, perhaps overwhelmed with too many cases, will simply check boxes in a somewhat thoughtless manner. Also, computerization permits easy copying of text from one case or worker to another without careful attention to the need for individualization. Not only is this practice unfair to the client but it also places the agency at risk of losing credit at the time of an accountability review, and perhaps even losing funding, if errors are detected through the state monitoring system.

Although the computerized family assessment forms may not seem as elaborate as the psychosocial assessments of the past, they require just as much careful thinking and separation of facts from diagnostic hypotheses. Therefore, it would be wise for the worker to think through what needs to be said and write notes or a draft before starting to fill in boxes on a computerized form. The computerized data are used to justify service funding and assessment of agency functioning, and so from an organizational perspective it is essential that the information and impressions recorded be accurate and open to scrutiny. Moreover, these records can be stored permanently in state computer files until the youngest child in the family turns 21. Since errors or omissions in the record could have negative consequences for children while they are in placement or later, workers have a strong ethical and legal obligation to report accurately, and their supervisors have an equally strong responsibility to ascertain the veracity of these records.

A recent case illustrates the harm that can accrue from inaccurate recording. A large, venerable child welfare agency had all of its foster care contracts with the New York City Administration for Children's Services (ACS) canceled when city investigators discovered that agency workers "had doctored case files for children in its care—forging signatures and inserting made up notations about whether foster homes had been inspected for safety, or whether children were receiving things as basic as clothing" (Kaufman, 2007, A16).

OTHER WRITING EXPECTATIONS

In addition to completing the computerized information forms on each foster child case, workers are ordinarily expected to write a number of other types of reports, which may be used for communication between workers, different departments, or different agencies. To illustrate, before transferring the case to a permanent worker, the intake worker may want to write a brief description of the encounter, specifying what type of help the client is requesting, the family's availability to attend meetings, and, if the case is mandated, how the client is responding to this requirement. Foster care workers often have to write referrals to specialized treatment programs, and they regularly need to communicate with the foster children's schools. In addition, some agencies may ask workers to write progress notes and/or case summaries separate from those included in the information system. Since the writing in these types of reports is ordinarily the same as in those written in early-intervention/preventive service programs, it will not be discussed separately here.

Workers involved in different capacities with the foster care system may also be asked to write a report to the court with recommendations about the most desirable action in a specific case situation, for example, termination of parental rights, adoptive placement, or movement to a different agency or foster home. Such reports rest on the basis of the worker's professional knowledge and experience, and they should include the worker's opinion as to what would be in the "best interest" of the child. In the report, the worker must specify all his or her sources of information, contacts with the client(s), what is known about the facts of the situation, the views of the child and other involved parties, the worker's psychosocial assessment, and the worker's professional recommendation. The appendix to this chapter presents a copy of the report of a social worker employed at a legal rights organization regarding the potential adoption of two children in foster care. Note that the author describes in detail what she learned through her interviews with the foster parent and children, in addition to her review of records and her home visit. She presents her assessment of the quality of care the children are currently receiving and the meaning of adoption to them. She concludes with a paragraph that summarizes and presents a rationale for her recommendation.

Finally, foster care workers, as well as those in other types of family and child welfare programs, sometimes want to write a process recording of a particularly difficult or sensitive client contact or meeting to reflect for themselves or with supervision about what happened and how to move forward. Reports written to communicate with others, as well as those written for the formal record, such as case closing summaries, are ordinarily maintained in the client's official case file. However, workers' process recordings or other types of informal notes or memos to themselves should be maintained separately from the client record, with no identifying information. This procedure ensures that a worker's thinking and notes are not subject to review if a client's case records are subpoenaed for any reason. In all types of record keeping, the worker must be certain to protect client confidentiality to the full extent permitted by law.

EARLY-INTERVENTION SERVICES

The heading "Early-Intervention Services" is used here to frame a wide range of programs—such as parenting education, preschool and after-school child care, parent-child and marital counseling, youth development, and family preservation and preventive services—that are geared toward supporting children and families in their own homes. Some of these programs are available to all children; others are targeted to specific groups, usually low-income families, where there may be risks to healthy child development. Although there is public funding for many of these programs, they are all voluntary, so there are many fewer recording requirements. The one exception is family preservation services, called Preventive Services in New York State; these services are directed toward families in which there is risk of child maltreatment and/or foster placement. Some of the cases are voluntary, but most are mandated by child protective services. Consequently, family preservation workers may have to use the computerized information forms required for foster care cases. Most other early-intervention programs have much looser recording requirements, which vary according to agency policy and funding source requirements.

In such settings, workers ordinarily have responsibility for writing intake summaries, case assessments and service plans, referral letters, and closing summaries. They may also be engaged in different types of advocacy and public relations efforts, and writing letters and other documents related to these efforts. What is important in all kinds of professional writing is that it be clear, grammatically correct, and as succinct as possible. The writer should keep the reader and the purpose of the communication in mind at all times.

INTAKE REPORTS

Although intake procedures vary from one setting to another, a worker conducting an intake will always want to obtain basic family demographic data, including why the family is seeking assistance now, the views of different family members regarding the presenting problem, their expectations of service, and their interest in and availability for future appointments. The intake described in Box A provides a clear example of a thoughtful, succinct report of an intake prepared so that the case can be referred to a worker. (Basic case data regarding address, family composition, ages and schools of children, and parent employment were recorded on a separate intake sheet.)

Note that this report conveys a flavor of how both mother and daughter presented themselves, the mother's strong motivation to receive help, and the daughter's relatively passive response. It also describes precisely what the clients were told about the availability of service and the potential for delay, as well as the clients' availability. The worker writes freely, in the first person,

---

BOX A

SAMPLE INTAKE REPORT

Ms. R.S. came to apply for counseling services out of concern that her daughter Diane has been cutting classes recurrently, even though she had promised to stop this. She leaves home, but sometimes does not get to school, or she leaves classes. When mother and daughter came for the first intake session on 6/10, Diane's only explanation was that she cuts when her best friend does so that she can be with her. Diane was polite yet very constricted, so I could not obtain a clear picture of what this friend meant to her. I did not think it advisable to press her on this issue. Her mother expressed great worry about the consequences of her behavior. Diane is entering 12th grade in September, and her chances of getting into college may be in jeopardy. Ms. R.S. expresses determination to solve the problem through receiving help here, but she is also thinking of sending Diane to her parents' country, Jamaica, or enrolling her in a Catholic high school for her senior year, although the family is not Catholic. She would not stop because of the expense.

In response to my question to Diane about either of these steps, she did not show any objection. When I asked if she thought she could resolve the problem, she said, "I do need counseling."

As the agency was then confronting a waiting list problem, I explained I would need to explore whether we could enroll the family soon enough so there would be enough time before a planned 3 week visit with relatives in Jamaica in August. I said I would call to let them know on 6/13. When I called on that date to say we could begin counseling and asked if they still wanted to enroll, Ms. R.S. affirmed this, and we set a date for 6/15. They came promptly, and Ms. R.S. said she had begun to explore Catholic high school. Diane's response seemed positive at that point.

---

which is appropriate in a report summarizing one's contact with others. It is unnecessarily awkward and distancing to refer to oneself as "the worker."

CASE ASSESSMENT AND SERVICE PLANNING

Case assessment and service planning are ongoing processes, but it is customary in many agencies to have workers write case assessments and service plans at a specific time in the life of a case. Case assessment involves making inferences from the psychosocial data that have been gathered about the interaction of different variables, possible contributing factors to the current client situation, and strengths and resources in the client situation. Service planning asks that the worker identify the problem(s) for work, the proposed time frame, and the modality of practice (Meyer, 1993). In such reports the worker is expected to capture the basic facts of the situation, the bio-psychosocial characteristics of the relevant family members, the relationships and interactions among different family members, and the transactions between family members and their environments. Since multiple interactions and transactions can be difficult to express in words, many workers find a visual tool, the eco-map (Hartman, 1995), useful in conveying the totality of the situation. At the same time, it is important for the worker to assess the specific strengths and needs of each family member. And in the context of child welfare services, special attention must be given to the adequacy of provisions for the safety, permanence, and well-being of the children in the family.

Although such a case assessment may need to be lengthy to capture all the case dynamics, it should be phrased tentatively, since it is essentially the worker's hypothesis about the dynamics of the case situation, and it may need to be revised over time. Moreover, since the purpose of a case assessment is to lead to a service plan, it is important that it highlight the most significant and pressing issues in the case situation. On the basis of this identification of case needs, the worker should be able to lay out a service plan that describes the overall strategy, objectives, and time line, as well as the specific tasks that should be carried out and by whom.

Since clients have a right to see what is written in their case records, it is also important that the case assessment, as well as all other reports, avoid use of diagnostic labels and professional jargon. It should be written in a clear, straightforward manner, incorporating the clients' views and setting realistic service objectives.

REFERRALS

Although referrals are frequently made by telephone, many agencies expect to receive written referrals, the use of which eliminates unnecessary miscommunications and misunderstandings. Before releasing any client information to an outside source, the worker must obtain the client's written consent on a simple client consent form. In a referral summary, the worker needs to convey truthfully the basic facts of the case situation and describe just what service is being requested from the other agency and why.

Although it can be tempting to neglect to mention certain case features that might prevent the referral from being accepted, such a practice is unethical, and in the long run it may cause difficulties for the client and potential legal problems for the worker. For example, it is dangerous to omit the fact that a child being referred to a group home has a history of fire setting.

ADVOCACY INITIATIVES

Child welfare workers, like all social workers, have an ethical responsibility to advocate on behalf of their clients on both case and class levels, to pursue social justice and ensure meaningful participation of all in public decision

---

BOX B

SAMPLE ADVOCACY LETTER

Letter Head
Date
Commissioner
Dear Commissioner_____:
I write to ask for your review of the issues posed in the enclosed May 10th article in the *New York Times* relating to psychiatrists' prescriptions of medications not approved for children. While the article focuses partly on the complicity of the drug companies in promoting their products, I am more concerned about the five medications listed:

　　Risperdal, Seroquel, Zyprexa, Abilify and Geodon

These drugs are being prescribed for children commonly enough so that, as one clinical director of a child welfare agency has stated to me, the practice is "rampant". I encountered the use of Risperdal in a case some four years ago, but it has clearly grown more common, as has the use of the others listed.
I am greatly worried about the risks, especially since I find that in some mental health clinics psychotropic medications are provided to children with only a once-monthly office visit, with no other individual or family counseling. In addition, the boundary between a diagnosis of mental illness and behavior problems is sometimes in question, making criteria for selected drugs more uncertain.
Where in the Office of Mental Health or elsewhere is the responsibility for oversight and accountability when psychotropic drugs are prescribed for a child either in a mental health clinic or a child welfare agency? Does the Office of Mental Health have guidelines, conditions for funding or reimbursement, or other controls? An early reply would be greatly appreciated.
Sincerely,
Director of Clinical Services

making. The types of writing required for different advocacy initiatives vary in relation to the issue being addressed and the objective. For example, at times it may be important for a worker to write to an administrative official or a legislator or to present testimony before a legislative body. Other times it may be important to write a letter to the editor of a newspaper or to create a petition that clients or colleagues can sign. Or a worker may wish to testify as an expert witness in a legal case brought by a children's rights organization. Alternatively, a worker may want to write a newsletter story or bulletin to inform clients about their rights and encourage them to take action in the political arena.

Box B presents a copy of a letter written to the commissioner of mental health by the director of clinical services in a child welfare agency. Note that the writer is attempting to bring to the commissioner's attention a practice that he believes violates clear professional standards. Although the letter ends with a series of questions about current policy and procedures rather than with specific recommendations, the intent clearly is to prod the commissioner to take action. Such an approach can be a subtle but effective way to challenge public authority without sounding confrontational. Writing appropriately for advocacy purposes requires both political and writing skills!

ETHICS OF RECORD KEEPING

As discussed above, most of the writing and recording requirements in family and child welfare services derive from various federal and state laws and regulations, as well as the guidelines and accountability demands of different funding sources. These multiple reporting demands can leave workers with the impression that priority must be given to filling out forms and that clinical and advocacy work on behalf of clients is secondary. On the contrary, these recording policies are designed to protect children who may be at risk because their parents are unable or unwilling to provide the care they need. And it is the worker's ability to gather the necessary data and write an insightful assessment and service plan that will determine the quality of the services the child and family receive. Many decisions about a child's life may depend on the accuracy of his or her case record. Therefore, it is essential that the worker write clearly and truthfully.

Unfortunately, the regulations and requirements designed to benefit most child welfare clients may not meet the needs of individual children or families. Social workers should assess every writing request or requirement to determine if it is beneficial to the individual case, or at least poses no risk to the individual child or family. If it does involve a risk, the social worker has a professional responsibility to challenge the requirement. For example, when what was called the Uniform Case Record—the recording system preceding Connections—was introduced in New York State, the state required that the recording on preventive services cases be parallel to that required for foster care cases. This requirement made for a coherent information management system but ignored the fact that there was no reason to store at the state level potentially harmful information about voluntary clients. Since the commissioner of social services technically serves as guardian for all children in foster care, there is good reason for information about children in foster care to be stored centrally, but parents of children receiving preventive services have not given up their parental rights, even temporarily. To counter this requirement, 18 preventive service agencies brought suit in 1981 against the city and state Departments of Social Services to stop enforcement of the regulations promulgated under the Child Welfare Reform Act of 1979 insofar as they would require the plaintiff agencies to turn over to the city or state client-identifiable case records on preventive service clients. The city and state entered into a court-ordered settlement outlining their ethical obligation in 1982, which became permanent in 1984. This settlement, known as the Advocates Agreement, prohibits the departments from compelling private preventive agencies to transmit case records except in narrowly defined cases of child abuse or foster placement. It was courageous of these private agency administrators to file a lawsuit challenging public authority, since they could have thus risked losing their service contracts. However, their actions were totally consistent with their ethical obligation as social workers to respect client privacy and protect the confidentiality of all the information received in the course of professional service.

The Advocates Agreement has protected the interests of the many thousands of preventive service clients over the years since the settlement was reached. However, there are many other child welfare clients in New York and elsewhere who are not protected by this settlement. Therefore, when writing about clients in family and children's services, social workers must be careful to get informed consent from clients before divulging any information, for accountability purposes or other reasons, to any funding or regulatory body. Finally, workers must be vigilant about protecting client confidentiality at all times.

CONCLUSION

Writing in family and child welfare, as in all other types of social work practice, should be as purposeful, clear, grammatically correct, and concise as possible. It is impossible to predict with any certainty how writing expectations in this field may change over time, but it seems likely that the demand for computerized recording will only expand to meet public demands for increased accountability. Such computerized records do make it much easier for case and program monitors to track factual case data. However, standardized recording forms have two big disadvantages for social work practitioners. First, they make it difficult to portray critical details about context, although careful assessment of the context of clients' lives and problems is an essential component of professional practice. Second, such forms essentially eliminate information about client-worker interaction, although understanding of this interaction is often key to skillful case intervention and planning.

There is no clear answer to this dilemma. Recording requirements in the family and child field tend to be dictated by government funding and regulatory agencies, not by local direct-service programs. Practitioners can advocate for change if the required recordings do not facilitate their work; otherwise, they have little control over the matter. What they can do instead is use the computerized forms as fully as possible, and then write brief notes to themselves about client context and interaction that may impede progress if not addressed. All social work graduate students suffer having to write process recordings, but they have also learned their value. Although these are not required in agency practice, social workers can demonstrate their professional competency by taking the time to write process recordings for themselves or to discuss in supervision those case elements that must be remembered to enhance their practice with clients.

References

Allen, M. L., & Knitzer, J. K. (1983). Examining the policy framework. In B. G. Mc-Gowan & W. Meezan (Eds.), *Child welfare: Current dilemmas, future directions* (pp. 93–141). Itasca, IL: Peacock Publishers.

Hartman, A. (1995). Diagrammatic assessment of family relationships. *Families in Society, 76*(2), 111–122.

Kaufman, L. (2007, November 5). Foster children at risk and an opportunity lost. *New York Times*, pp. A1, A16–17.

Maas, H. S., & Engler, R. E. (1959). *Children in need of parents*. New York: Columbia University Press.

Meyer, C. H. (1993). *Assessment in social work practice*. New York: Columbia University Press.

APPENDIX

ADOPTION REPORT

To: The Honorable Judge X
Bronx Family Court
From: Staff Social Worker
Date:
Re: *In the Matter of Peter and John Stewart*

This report is being submitted at the request of the court. _Ms. Joyce Evans was assigned as law guardian for Peter & John after the court learned their prospective adoptive father, Mr. Vincent Smith, had prior criminal convictions. The law guardian was asked to assess whether finalization of the adoption is in the children's best interests.

Sources of Information:

1. Review of "Petition for Adoption" for Peter and John- dated April 24, 2007.
2. Review of "Investigation and Report"—dated June 10, 2007.
3. Review of "Affidavit Concerning Criminal History Review"- dated April 14, 2007.
4. Review of "ASFA Safety Assessment of Foster/Adoptive Home"-dated October 23, 2004.
5. Home visit/interview with Shirley Chisholm Smith and John Stewart on August 5, 2007.
6. Office interview of Vincent Smith and Peter Stewart on August 12, 2007

Assessment:

Peter and John Stewart have lived with Shirley and Vincent Smith for almost eight years. The family lives in a two-family house in Brighton Beach, a residential section of Brooklyn, New York. During my home visit of August 5th, I interviewed the foster mother, Ms. Smith, separately in a private room. I spoke with the foster mother about her husband's past convictions, her care of the children and future plans for Peter and John. I found Ms. Smith to be mature, well-spoken and sincere. Her husband was arrested in 1991, before they were married. He was accused of armed robbery, went to jail for four years and is currently on parole. Ms. Smith explained that Mr. Smith has consistently denied committing the crime. Furthermore, she does not think that his past conviction has any bearing on his suitability as an adoptive father for Peter and John. He is very committed to all of children in their home. He interacts appropriately with them and has developed a strong relationship with both Peter and John. Ms. Smith and Mr. Smith share childcare responsibilities. Ms. Smith works from 8AM to 5PM weekdays at NF retail store. Mr. Smith has a rotating schedule and works for CB manufacturing plant. In the summer, Mr. Smith cares for the children during the day, and Ms. Smith cares for them in the evening. During the school year the children attend an after-school program. If necessary they are taken care of by Ms. Smiths' adult biological brother, James Chisholm, who resides in the basement.

> During my conversation with Ms. Smith we discussed the academic performance and service needs of both children. John was promoted to the 6th grade and in September will attend IS 414. He is in regular education and is not receiving any school-based services. He attends therapy weekly with Mr. Wilson Keene, LCSW. John was diagnosed with Oppositional Defiance Disorder and recommended a trial of medication. Ms. Smith opted to continue weekly therapy and work with John on behavioral modification techniques. She is open to re-evaluating his need for medication in the future, if necessary.

Peter was promoted to 7th grade at IS 414. He is in regular education, doing well and does not receive any school-based services. He is well behaved in school, at home and in the community. Peter is not currently in therapy. He was in therapy following his placement with the foster mother because he demonstrated behavioral problems and depression. After a period of time it was discovered that Peter desperately missed his initial foster family, with whom he had developed a significant bond. The previous foster family located Peter, re-connected with him and his behavior has been fine since.

Peter continues to visit the former foster family on the weekends and during school vacations. According to the foster mother, Peter still expresses some anger surrounding the abuse he received from his biological mother, however he is better able to discuss his feelings. Peter does not want to participate in therapy and the foster mother is comfortable that he is not presently in need of psychological services. If a need for therapy develops in the future, she is open to having him attend.

Throughout our conversation Ms. Smith expressed appropriate concern for the health and well-being of both children. She stated that she "wants what is best for them." She believes that she provides them with a stable, loving home where they are flourishing. She encourages them to get a good education so they can go to college and become successful adults. She feels that the children are benefiting from living in a kinship home because they are able to maintain important relationships with immediate and extended family members.

On August 12, 2007, I met with Vincent Smith in a private room at the offices of The Legal Aid Society. He told me that in 1991 he was accused of robbing a race track. He served four years in jail and was released early on a work release. He worked for Oxford Plumbing Company and for the past three years has had a stable job working for CB manufacturing plant. He has been on parole since 2004. He meets weekly with his parole officer, Mr. London, and he should be completing parole this month. Mr. Smith understands why the court is concerned about his conviction however he states that he "did not commit the crime." He recognizes that the court will make the final decision regarding the adoption, but he does not believe that his conviction has a negative impact on his ability to parent. He describes himself as a strict, but fair parent. He believes that he has a good relationship with Peter and John. He provides them with a stable, comfortable and supportive home. He stated that the boys are doing well in the home, they are a part of the family and he is concerned that if they are moved to another home it will be "a big step backwards."

As part of my assessment I individually interviewed Peter, age twelve and John age eleven in a private room. Both boys possess a developmentally appropriate understanding of adoption and expressed a desire to be adopted by Vincent and Shirley Smith. Peter understands adoption to mean "living with his aunt and uncle until he is an adult." John stated that adoption means "when someone takes a child and cares for them until they get their own house." Both boys appeared happy living in the foster home. They felt well taken care of and had everything they needed such as food, clothing, games, books and toys. I asked both of the children about the rules and discipline in the home. Peter stated that the rules are to "be quiet, don't run and don't fight." If he breaks a rule his punishment is "no TV and he can't go outside." He is usually punished by his aunt, but sometimes his uncle screams at him. John stated that the rules in the home are "no fighting, do your chores and complete your homework." He described punishment as "no TV or play station." The children appeared well bonded with the foster parents and the other children in the home, Paul Allen (12/22/96) and Steven Smith 2/8/05). Both children expressed a strong desire to remain in the home and did not want to live anywhere else.

Based on a careful review of the court records, a home visit on August 5, 2007, and conversations with Vincent Smith, Shirley Chisolm Smith, Peter and John Stewart, it is my professional opinion that it is in the children's best interest to be adopted by the petitioners. Peter and John have been living with their maternal aunt and foster mother, Ms. Smith continuously for approximately eight years and her husband, Mr. Smith for approximately three years. During that period of time they have developed a psychological bond to the petitioners and the other children residing in the home. Both children possess a developmentally appropriate understanding of adoption and clearly stated that they wish to be adopted. When the issue of the criminal background of the foster father was addressed, Mr. and Ms. Smith acknowledged the court's concern however, they did not think that his past conviction had an impact on his current ability to parent. They feel that they are meeting the emotional and physical needs of the children and are committed to providing a stable and loving home where both children will have the opportunity to flourish.

Respectfully Submitted,

_____, LCSW
Staff Social Worker

12

WRITING STRATEGIES FOR SCHOOL SOCIAL WORKERS

Alida Bouris and Vincent Guilamo-Ramos

SCHOOL-BASED SOCIAL WORKERS PLAY AN invaluable role in promoting and maintaining the well-being of children, youth, and their families. Through professional writing associated with their employment, these social workers can have a significant impact on the lives of students and their families.

The purpose of this chapter is to provide examples of the different types of writing that school-based social workers engage in as part of their professional positions. We begin with a brief overview of the field of practice known as "school-based and school-linked services." At different grade levels, elementary, middle school, and high school social workers encounter different roles and writing responsibilities. We seek to define the nature of the work that social workers perform in different school contexts and to review the relevant writing opportunities directly associated with each role.

Our approach is to offer social work students and social workers who are interested in or are currently working in schools a broad perspective on writing in the school context. The examples are not intended to be an exhaustive list. Rather, we hope to identify key writing opportunities associated with a particular developmental age or school type. Drawing on our own experiences in developing written materials for students and their parents, we also offer suggestions that we feel are important to consider, and we encourage readers to apply them to their own school-based writing projects.

OVERVIEW OF SCHOOL-BASED SOCIAL WORK

School-based social workers have a long history of addressing the psychosocial needs of children, youth, and their families (Franklin, 2005). For more than 100 years, social workers have been working in a professional capacity in American schools. In general, schools are charged with serving as the primary academic socializing agent in our society. It is through participating in school that children and youth develop the requisite knowledge and skills to become productive members of society. In this regard, the educational mission of schools cannot be overstated.

School-based social workers bring a unique knowledge base and skill set to further enhance the core mission of schools (Allen-Meares, 2004). The academic trajectory and emphasis on preparation for adult roles and careers are of primary concern to school-based professionals. It is from this vantage point that the role of the school-based or school-linked social work practitioner is best understood. Unfortunately, many children and youth face a range of biological, psychological, and social problems that interfere with their learning and hamper their ability to succeed. The interface between the educational goals of schools and the psychosocial challenges encountered by many children and youth provides a rich context for the practicing school social worker.

Throughout the United States, school-based social workers provide children, youth, and their families with a diverse array of services. Often, the nature and extent of services delivered to students and other constituents in the school system depend on school and community contexts, the characteristics and needs of the student population, and the resources and funding available to support school-based social work. Despite this diversity, a set of common services offered by school-based social workers has been identified: (1) consulting with other school-based professionals as part of an interdisciplinary team; (2) providing direct intervention and practice with students and their families in different practice modalities, including individual, family, and group; (3) assisting with and leading program development efforts in schools to support students and their families; and (4) conducting assessments in order to identify unmet needs and deliver appropriate services (Constable, Kuzmickaite, Harrison, & Volkmann, 1999). In the subsequent sections, we provide examples of the different types of writing opportunities in each of these service areas.

INTRODUCING SOCIAL WORK TO STUDENTS AND FAMILIES: WRITING A LETTER OF INTRODUCTION

Regardless of the school setting, one of the most common types of writing encountered by school-based social workers is the formal letter, designed to be sent home to the parents and primary caregivers of students. Such letters can vary in purpose and scope. We describe here a letter of introduction, intended to introduce students and their families to the social work team and to the services based at, or linked to, the school. Most often, letters of introduction are sent to students' homes at the beginning of the academic year. The letter provides the families of enrolled students with information about the availability and nature of the social work services offered at their child's school. At a minimum, the letter should address the following key points: (1) an introduction of the school social worker(s); (2) a clear delineation of the roles of the social worker; (3) a description of the types of services offered by the social worker; (4) the availability of services; and (5) the procedure(s) for obtaining services.

Letters of introduction should be formal in tone. For many families, this letter will be their first introduction to social work at the school, and the school-based professional will want to make a good impression. Careful attention should be paid to important social, cultural, and linguistic differences among families served by the school. Increasingly, the demographic profile of families in the United States is changing, and the demography of any given school district can be highly diverse. In some instances, schools will serve immigrant families who may be recent arrivals to this country. Other families may have resided in the country for many years. The use of English in a letter of introduction may not be the most effective form of communication for all families, and school-based social workers need to consider carefully the language needs of their families to ensure that materials are written in a language that families served by the school can access. The good news is that many schools recognize the diverse linguistic needs of their population and may already have translation services available for communicating with families.

The second point we want to highlight has to do with the overall tone of the letter. Too often, parents perceive the school as not being responsive to their needs. It is therefore critical that the writing style employed in the letter conveys openness to supporting students and their families. When writing a letter of introduction (and other materials for students and their parents), school social workers need to consider how to address the diverse cultural, contextual, economic, and social differences among distinct families attending one common school. Strategies for achieving this include: (1) knowing the primary languages of the parents of the children attending your school; (2) avoiding emotion-laden terms that could convey that parents are "doing something wrong" or are not parenting correctly; and (3) familiarizing yourself with the cultural differences and worldviews of families whose children attend your school. Attention to these areas will ensure that the letter of introduction is clear, concise, and effective in alerting parents to the available supportive services at their child's school. All of these issues are illustrated in the sample letter of introduction below.

[EXAMPLE 1: LETTER OF INTRODUCTION]

Dear Parents,

The Social Work Department at [*School Name*] would like to take this opportunity to welcome you and to introduce you to the social work services available to you and your child.

Here at [*School Name*], a team of three full-time social workers are available to provide supportive services to students and their families in addressing a range of issues. Services offered by the social work department include assessments, individual, family and group counseling, case management, skills training, crisis intervention, and assistance with Individualized Education Programs for students who may be in need of special education services. In addition, we are able to refer students and families to more specialized services within the community, including psychological or psychiatric assessment, testing and treatment.

During the academic year, services offered at the school are provided free of charge to all enrolled students. Services are available in English and in Spanish. To reach a social worker, please call us during regular school hours at XXX-XXX-XXX.

If we do not answer your call, please leave a message on the answering machine, and we will return your call within 24 hours. Please be sure to leave your phone number or the best way to reach you.

We look forward to meeting you and to ensuring that all of the students at [*School Name*] have a safe, productive and healthy academic year.

Sincerely,

Social Worker

Phone #

Note that the letter is straightforward and informs parents of the following key points: (1) the nature and extent of available services; (2) how to contact the social worker; (3) the cost of services; and (4) the availability of services in English and other languages. In addition, the letter adopts a formal tone and seeks to establish a partnership with parents that is focused on the health and well-being of their children.

EARLY SCHOOL YEARS: KINDERGARTEN AND ELEMENTARY SCHOOL

School-based social workers often address issues of child abuse and neglect. In addition to their role as mandated reporters and providers of services for abused and neglected youth, they may be tasked with developing school-based programs to help prevent reportable instances of abuse and neglect. Typically, such preventive programs are offered as either workshops or curricula. Whereas workshops are offered for a shorter period of time (perhaps for one hour during a regularly scheduled class), a curriculum can span several sessions. School-based social workers should consult with teachers and administrators to identify which program is most appropriate and how best to design the program so that it is integrated with existing classroom protocols. This consultation is especially important given that an increasing amount of class time may be spent on preparing students for mandated tests.

Preparation for either workshops or curricula requires strong writing skills. Each presents the challenge of developing materials that can be effectively used by students in kindergarten and elementary school. Written materials developed specifically for children of this age need to take into account the developmental needs of these new learners. Materials that incorporate visual aids, such as pictures and colorful images, along with limited text, are considered best practices for children this age. Effective written materials will use words that are easily understandable and draw upon the emerging vocabularies and comprehension levels of young children. Content for the curricula should be based on existing empirical evidence. If school-based social workers lack access to such evidence (which is commonly available in professional journals), we recommend consulting with child protection workers or researchers working in the specific area of interest in order to identify appropriate and effective content for their student population.

MIDDLE SCHOOL AND THE EMERGING ADOLESCENT: PREVENTING ADOLESCENT RISK BEHAVIOR

Middle school presents yet another opportunity for the development of written materials. In early to middle adolescence, a small percentage of youth may begin to use alcohol, tobacco, and/or drugs, and to engage in risky sexual behavior and/or delinquency. As part of an effort to help youth stay healthy and focused on school, school-based social workers may choose to develop prevention programs that incorporate written materials targeting a specific problem behavior. These materials may be directed toward adolescents directly or may seek to enlist parents in helping to prevent or reduce the risky behavior.

Increasingly, schools have become interested in fostering greater linkages between themselves and the parents of enrolled students (Oulette & Wilkerson, 2008). The increased effort in enhancing parent involvement stems from a general concern about how best to involve parents in school-based initiatives. Schools and families, being the primary contexts in which children and adolescents develop, share a similar goal: fostering the well-being and preparation of children and youth for transition into adult life. Although teenagers begin to experience more independence during adolescence, studies consistently show that the vast majority of youth maintain strong relationships with their parents and view their parents as one of the most important and trusted sources of advice and information. Social workers are in a unique position to support strong linkages among parents, communities, and school, and the importance of writing relevant, engaging, and helpful materials for parents cannot be overstated.

In writing for parents, school-based social workers need to consider several issues. First, are the materials written at a comprehension level that is understandable and accessible to parents? The writer must consider the reading proficiency of the audience. Many of the families who participate in American school systems today may have resided in this country for only a short time. Written materials designed by school social workers for ethnically diverse families should take care to address the unique worldviews, values, beliefs, and customs of different types of families.

School-based social workers also need to consider whether families in their school system are more comfortable receiving written documents in a language other than English. If this is the case, the written materials must be carefully translated so that the result is equivalent in meaning to the English version (rather than a literal translation). In documents that are translated for "meaning equivalence," the translator seeks to ensure that the core message is comparable or equivalent, though specific word choices may vary. This approach is ideal for school-based social workers and will ensure that materials are accessible and appropriate for families. A number of resources are available for guidance to appropriate translation of written documents, among them work by Baker (1992) and Larsen (1997).

On a practical level, the school-based social worker also needs to consider how best to reach parents and what topics parents are most interested in. School-based parent organizations provide an ideal venue to reach a large number of parents. Many schools have a parent-teacher association or other similar group. We recommend that school-based social workers establish formal linkages with these organizations as they move forward with developing materials for parents. There are two main reasons for creating such linkages. First, this relationship provides a mechanism for disseminating written materials to parents. Second, by partnering with a parent organization at the outset, school-based social workers will ensure that parents' needs and preferences are reflected in the final product. This latter point cannot be stressed enough. When writing for parents about topics like preventing adolescent risk behavior, it is important to elicit parents' perspectives on what type of information they would find helpful; otherwise, one may create a document that is not relevant for its intended audience. This same principle applies to writing materials for adolescents. The social worker should elicit involvement from both students and parents.

One example of parental and youth involvement in the development of a school-based prevention program using written materials is the Linking Lives Health Education Program in New York City. Funded in 2001, Linking Lives was a six-year parent-based program to enhance parent-adolescent communication and other important parenting processes for parents and adolescents. The program was developed by Drs. Vincent Guilamo-Ramos, James Jaccard, and Patricia Dittus, and a cohort of parents and adolescents who lived in the communities where the project took place.

Linking Lives was designed to be cost-effective and to reach a large number of parents and their adolescent children. One of the unique aspects of the program was that it relied heavily on social workers in its development and implementation. In order to reach parents, the developers decided to use written materials because parental input suggested that too often, face-to-face sessions were not ideal. As many school-based social workers know, families are busy, and making too many demands on parents' time can mean that only a limited number of families can participate in a program. Because the developers wanted to reach large numbers of parents, written materials seemed to be the ideal means of communication.

The materials for the Linking Lives program featured a number of booklets or "modules," designed especially for ethnically diverse urban families. The modules provided parents with core information about how to best support their adolescents' health and well-being. The written materials were accompanied by a set of parent and youth activities that fostered skill acquisition and role play. Although the program included a limited number of face-to-face group activities, the core component was the set of written materials.

As our next example, we include two excerpts from the Linking Lives materials (Guilamo-Ramos, Jaccard, & Dittus, 2003; Guilamo-Ramos, Jaccard, Dittus, Bouris, Gonzalez, Casillas, & Banspach, 2011; Guilamo-Ramos, Jaccard, Dittus, Gonzalez, Bouris, & Banspach, 2010). The materials were designed for parents *and* for adolescents to promote parent-adolescent communication about why middle-school youths should abstain from sexual activity. The first excerpt addresses the issue of teen pregnancy and describes a group of adolescents who are dating and struggling with the decision of whether to have sex or not. The story was developed as an interactive activity for parents to read to adolescents, with the idea that they would discuss key themes with each other.

[EXAMPLE 2: PARENT-ADOLESCENT ACTIVITY]

Everyone always tells Anthony how much he looks like his father because they both have green eyes. Anthony doesn't really know what his father looks like. Since he moved out of state, they don't see each other very often. Anthony's older brother is in the tenth grade and works part-time selling sneakers. Even though he bosses Anthony around too much, Anthony still respects him because of the hard work and help he gives to their mother. Next year, his older sister Christina will graduate from high school and will be the first one in the family to go to college. Everyone is very proud of her.

Anthony's older cousin, Victor, is his best friend. Victor is only one year older, but he is about five inches taller. He always sticks up for Anthony, even when Anthony is in the wrong. Victor never bosses Anthony around like his older brother and sister do. They have been best friends their whole lives.

On the weekends, Anthony and Victor usually hang out at the movies or at the arcade.

One Friday night, at the movies, they met Elizabeth and Maria. Immediately Anthony liked Elizabeth. She was small with long brown hair and big brown eyes. What he liked about her most was her spirit—she always had a smile and made people laugh. He felt lucky to have her as his girlfriend. Last week he brought her home for the first time to meet his mother. After being together for four months, the relationship between Anthony and Elizabeth was serious.

More and more, Anthony and Victor were getting pressure from their "crew" to have sex with their girlfriends. Someone was always telling a story about a girl they had sex with. Anthony is very curious about sex, but he knows that there are a lot of risks, like pregnancy and infections. His good friend, James, got an infection the first time he had sex, which the other guys don't know about. He wonders how many of his other friends have infections or have gotten girls pregnant. Anthony does not want either of those things to happen to him.

A few weeks ago he and Elizabeth spoke about their future together. They decided to wait to have sex until they were older, until they could better handle the responsibilities of sex. Besides, they always had so much fun together, they didn't need to have sex. One Saturday afternoon, Anthony was hanging out at Victor's house. Victor wanted to invite his girlfriend Maria over and thought it would be a good idea if Anthony invited Elizabeth. That way, they both could have "some fun." Anthony was shocked. He knew that Victor wanted Maria to be his first, but both boys had agreed to wait until they were older. Anthony was uncomfortable and didn't know what to say.

When the girls arrived, Anthony put on a movie and sat next to Elizabeth. He relaxed. Elizabeth was making him laugh by pretending to be the lead actor. A few minutes later, Victor and Maria got up and left the room. Anthony knew what was going to happen, that Victor and Maria were going to have sex. Even though Anthony was curious about sex, Anthony was having fun without it.

After Victor's mom came home from work, the boys walked the girls home. Anthony knew Elizabeth was mad. He wanted to make sure that she knew how he felt. Anthony said, "Elizabeth, please listen, I did not invite you over to have sex. I really like you, and I respect the decision we made together, the decision to wait." Anthony was also curious about sex, but felt that because there were so many other ways to express their feelings towards each other, it was not necessary to have sex now.

A month later, Victor told Anthony that Maria was pregnant. Anthony had to swear to keep it a secret because they didn't want anyone to know. Victor did not know what to do. He was thinking of quitting school to get a job so he could support Maria and the baby. But he did not know what kind of job he could get that would pay enough without a high school degree. Anthony felt terrible. He did not know how to help. But, at the same time, he was glad that he and Elizabeth were not in the same situation. He was happy they did not have to face these choices or responsibilities.

In both example 2 and example 3 (below), the materials are written in an engaging, straightforward, and non-complex manner. In particular, they reflect a *non-technical discussion* of the topic at hand. This is especially important in example 3, which uses content that is based on scientific studies on sexually transmitted infections, teenage pregnancy, peer pressure, and adolescent sexual behavior. Despite being evidence-based, however, the text avoids technical jargon and communicates ideas in a simple and straightforward way. Example 3 was written with adolescents as the target audience and covers seven key points that youths of middle school age should know about the important social and health issues associated with adolescent sexual behavior.

[EXAMPLE 3: SEVEN THINGS ADOLESCENTS SHOULD KNOW ABOUT SEXUAL BEHAVIOR]

1. *Sexually Transmitted Infections (STIs) are far more common than teens realize.* Most teens know about the risk of pregnancy and AIDS that go with having sex. Many teens do not think these things will happen to them, but they have to happen to somebody! The fact is that they can happen just as easily to you as anybody else. But pregnancy and AIDS are only part of the story. Most teens do not know that there are other sexually transmitted infections (STIs) out there. That is, infections you can get from having sex with someone who is infected. Have you ever heard of Chlamydia? How about Human Papilloma Virus (also called HPV; one type is commonly known as genital warts). How about herpes? Gonorrhea? About

15% of teens in high school have Chlamydia. That's 3 out of every 20 kids! Rates are even higher in African American and Latino teens. In some areas, almost 40% of teens are infected with Chlamydia. The problem is that most teens do not even know they have it. Chlamydia often shows no symptoms. But it is there and it is hurting the infected person. If untreated, it can lead to infertility, making it so you can't have kids when you get older. HPV can lead to long lasting and painful pelvic infection and even cancer. These are not things to mess around with. STIs can be caused by bacteria or by viruses. If an STI is caused by bacteria, it can be treated and cured (if the person knows they have it!). Most STIs caused by viruses have no cure. You are stuck with them for life. Herpes is like this. When you have sex, you are putting yourself at risk for an STI. This is something that is best left to later, when you know for a fact that you have an HIV-negative partner who has been tested, who is in love with you and who is faithful to you. Not now.

2. *Everybody is not doing it.* Most teens your age have not had sex. Over 90% of teens your age have never had sexual intercourse. If you hear that "everyone is doing it," this is simply not true. And the fact is that most teens disapprove of their friends having sex. They think it is a bad idea.

3. *Having sex does not make you more mature and grown up.* Some teens think that having sex will make them seem more mature and grown up. After all, don't most grown ups do it? Being mature means making the right choices for you given where you are at. For a teenager in middle school, being mature means staying focused on school, on friends, and on family. Having sex can take away from these things and if you got pregnant or got someone pregnant, or got an infection, it could throw a wrench in everything. Having sex now is a sign of less maturity, not more.

4. *Sex does not make you more attractive as a partner.* Some teens think if they have sex, others will like them more and find them more attractive. It usually does not work this way. Many kids who have sex at a young age get a bad reputation. Other kids see them as easy or immoral, caring about nothing but themselves, or not interested in a real relationship. This can lead to others only being interested in them for sex, not for a relationship, or for who they are. You want your partner to like you and love you for who you are as a person. Having sex is not the way to get this. If your partner cares for you (looks out for you) and respects you, he or she will not be pushing for sex.

5. *When you are down, you are at risk.* We all have times when we get down on ourselves. We get sad or depressed or we do not feel good about ourselves. When this happens, we are vulnerable. We might do things we normally would not do just to gain the approval of others or to try to feel better. Highs and lows are a natural part of life. But be careful when you are in a low. You are at greater risk of doing things you normally would not do. This includes having sex.

6. *Even if you think you will like it, it is better to wait.* Some teens are curious about sex. Some think that they will like it a lot, that it will feel good. The fact is that sex does feel good for most people. And there are positive emotions that go with it. But just because it feels good does not mean that you should do it now. Many people want to save the special bond and feeling that comes with sex for when they are in love and married to another person. At your young age, having sex comes with a lot of risks and social consequences. These risks can have a big effect on you and even if you think you will enjoy sex, it is better not to chance it. Most teens your age do not take the chance. They do the mature thing and wait.

7. *A girl can get pregnant the first time.* Many teens think they really want to try sex just once, that one time won't matter and after they know what it's like, they will go back to not having sex. Some believe that a girl can't get pregnant the first time she has sex, but they are wrong. A girl *can* get pregnant the very first time she has sex, so just once may matter a lot!

PROFESSIONAL WRITING FOR YOUTH AND FAMILIES IN NEED OF SPECIAL SERVICES

In many settings, school-based social workers may need to assist with the evaluation of students in need of special education services. In the United States, the Individuals with Disabilities Act mandates that students with special education needs receive an Individualized Education Program (IEP). An IEP is a formal evaluation of a specific student and is designed to systematically address core areas of a student's academic functioning. In addition, the IEP identifies areas where a student may need additional services in order to optimize academic performance.

Effective IEPs require a writing style that integrates distinct components of the assessment. This is because IEPs are usually completed in consultation with other school-based professionals. For example, school psychologists may be asked to conduct psychological testing or to assess the student for specific learning disabilities. Similarly, a speech pathologist may assess a student's speech difficulties and identify specific speech areas where a student is struggling. Each of the distinct types of professional involvement associated with the IEP evaluation process must be summarized, using a writing style that is accessible to (1) the parents and/or caregivers of the student being evaluated; (2) other members of the interdisciplinary team evaluating the student; and (3) the professionals who will provide services to the student. In their own writing, school-based social workers must synthesize distinct areas of expertise to produce one cohesive report that can be used to help guide the allocation and provision of student support services.

Key components of an IEP that a school-based social worker may be called upon to address include the student's social and emotional development, psychosocial and behavioral functioning, and areas related to health and mental health. In addition, as part of an interdisciplinary team, school-based social workers may be required to produce supplemental materials, such as team meeting reports summarizing a student's progress on his or her IEP or writing that advocates for necessary services on behalf of a student. Through careful attention to assessment and consultation, school-based social workers are in a key position to help support students who need special education services.

GRANT PROPOSALS FOR SCHOOL-BASED OR SCHOOL-LINKED PROJECTS

Thus far, we have focused on writing and developing materials that target key stakeholders in the school system—students, parents/caregivers, teachers, administrators, and other service professionals. However, there are also constituents outside of the immediate school system with whom school-based social workers need to communicate in writing, most notably grant administrators and funding agencies. In the next section, we highlight key aspects of preparing proposals for submission to funding agencies.

Part of the professional role of the school-based social worker is to develop and assist with grant proposals. Typically, such proposals will be programmatic in nature, usually soliciting funds to support school-based or school-linked activities. Examples of ideas that have been routinely funded

TABLE 12.1 Written Components of a Program Proposal

PROPOSAL COMPONENT	PURPOSE
1. Letter of Intent / Cover Letter	Introduces the school and proposed project to the funding agency.
2. Executive Summary or Abstract	Provides a brief summary of the proposal.
3. Needs Statement / Statement of the Problem	States the nature, severity, context of the problem, and the affected population.
4. Project Narrative / Description	Describes program goals, measurable objectives, and the implementation plan.
5. Evaluation Plan	Describes how the program goals and objectives will be evaluated.
6. Applicant Capability	Describes applicant's ability to complete the proposal as described. Discusses previous performance and the availability of resources to complete the proposal.
7. Timeline of Project Activities	Clearly states when activities designed to meet project goals and objectives will be completed.
8. Budget Request and Justification	Itemizes proposed expenditures and provides a justification for the requested funds.
9. Plans for Sustainability	Describes plans for future funding and how the project will be sustainable beyond the requested funding period.
10. Letters of Support	Letters from partners and key stakeholders stating their commitment and support for the project.
11. Appendix Materials	Other documentation requested by the funding agency or key supplementary materials provided by the applicant to support the proposal.

include programs that foster youth mentoring, programs designed to prevent student involvement in problem behavior, and programs that foster educational performance. Most proposals follow a specific format that is required by the funding agency. Although formats may vary from agency to agency, there are some common components of program proposals. These components and their respective purposes are presented in table 12.1.

To be clear, the components described in the table are not a definitive list of what may be required when submitting a proposal. The majority of funding agencies provide their own detailed guidelines of required elements, and school-based social workers should defer to these instructions. In the next sections, we focus on two additional aspects of proposal writing: (1) the letter of intent and (2) the problem statement.

WRITING A LETTER OF INTENT

Many funding agencies request that applicants provide a letter of intent, which is designed to tell the funding agency about the proposed project. It is usually a one-page, single-spaced, typed letter addressed to the director or other designated person at the funding agency. A good letter of intent provides basic information about the proposal and should be concise and formal in tone. When writing the letter, remember that funding agencies are most often interested in: (1) the nature, extent, and importance of the problem that is being addressed by the proposal; (2) whether the proposal is consistent with the agency's mission and funding priorities; (3) the clarity of the proposed program and its feasibility; (4) the nature of support requested by the applicant; and (5) the credibility and capability of the agency to complete the proposed program.

Given these points of interest, a letter of intent should accomplish the following objectives: (1) introduce the school to the funding agency and establish that the school is competent and credible; (2) state the problem or need that the proposal is seeking to ameliorate, who is most affected by the problem within the school, and why the problem is worthy of a funding commitment from the agency; (3) describe the proposed program, the key goals and the broad objectives, and say how the proposal intends to ameliorate the problem; (4) explain why the funding agency should be interested in the school and the proposed program, highlighting how the proposal fits with the funding agency's mission; and (5) summarize the strengths of the proposal and enumerate the benefits of a partnership between the school and the funding agency.

Ultimately, the letter of intent is an opportunity to generate agency awareness of, and interest in, the school's need, the student population, and the proposed solution. Like a letter of introduction, it is often the funding agency's first encounter with the school and its student body. As such, it should be informative, clear, and engaging. A poor letter of intent can harm a school's chances of securing funding, while a well-executed letter of intent can generate excitement on the part of the funding agency and raise the profile of the proposal that is going to be submitted.

WRITING A PROBLEM STATEMENT

A good letter of intent should be followed by a well-written proposal. Competitive grant proposals require a strong rationale for why the funds should be awarded to a particular school or school district. In part, this rationale will be based on how well the proposal describes the specific problem that is going to be addressed and alleviated. Thus the school-based social worker is charged with the critical task of convincing the funding agency that the problem in his or her school is more deserving than the problems being addressed by competing applicants. Typically, school-based social workers will conduct a needs assessment to document a given problem or unmet need in their school. A school-based needs assessment is important because the most persuasive arguments will be highly contextual.

A problem statement should cover four key points: (1) the nature of the problem; (2) the number of people affected by the problem; (3) the severity of the problem; and (4) the context in which the problem is occurring (Kettner, Moroney, & Martin, 1998). These points are illustrated in example 4.

[EXAMPLE 4: PROBLEM STATEMENT FOR A HIGH SCHOOL LITERACY PROGRAM]

Public School 47 (P.S. 47) is a senior high school in the Bronx, NY, for youth in grades 9 through 12. As of July 2007, there were approximately 1,157 students enrolled at Gonzalez High School, making it one of city's largest public high schools. Academic performance and achievement among P.S. 47 students are a pressing concern. Although scores on city achievement tests in Math and English have improved in recent years, only 32% of students met English Language Arts standards in 2007. In addition, approximately 30% of the student body performed below the standards. In contrast, 60% of students in city schools met existing standards and only 13% performed below the minimum acceptable standards. In the 2006–2007 academic year, 58% of the school's population identified as Latino and the remaining 42% as African American/Black. School-wide, an estimated 23% of the student body is in special education and 18% are classified as English Language

Learners. In addition, 73% of the school's population is eligible for free school lunch. All of these figures are higher than the averages observed in other city schools. As these data show, improving literacy outcomes among P.S. 47 students is a critical educational priority. A recent quality review of the school found numerous strengths, including excellent leadership by Principal Smith, a high level of commitment by teachers to the diverse learning needs of students, strong relationships between school staff and students and their families, and a history of administering after-school programs designed to support students' academic achievement. In the present proposal, we are requesting funding to design and evaluate an innovative in-school program designed to improve literacy outcomes among P.S. 47 students.

As illustrated by the example, it is important to be as specific and descriptive as possible. The problem statement clearly shows that there is a literacy problem in the high school. This is demonstrated by the inclusion of school- and citywide test scores, and the severity is demonstrated by showing how many students are affected. The demographic characteristics of the student population provide the funding agency with a description of who is being affected by the problem. Finally, the problem statement also highlights the capability of the school leadership to address the problem, and briefly describes how the problem will be ameliorated.

Remember, the grant writer is charged with highlighting why the resources are needed and why the plan for their use is likely to result in a significant positive outcome in the school. A number of texts have been developed on conducting needs assessments and writing competitive grant proposals (e.g., Coley & Scheinberg, 2007; Rossi, Lipsey, & Freeman, 2004; Yuen & Terao, 2003). School-based social workers who want additional information on sources of funding should visit the Web sites of the Department of Education (http://www.ed.gov/index.jhtml), as well as the Foundation Center (http://www.foundationcenter.org/). Both organizations can provide the school-based social worker with a wealth of funding options and assistance with preparing a proposal for a school-based program or activity.

CONCLUSION

In this chapter, we have provided a number of practical writing strategies and examples for school-based social workers. Whether writing for students, parents, other school-based professionals, or organizations outside of the immediate school system, school-based social workers are in a unique position to use professional writing as a way to improve the services offered to students and their families. Although the examples presented do not represent all types of professional writing encountered by social workers, the writing styles, strategies, and issues discussed will undoubtedly be useful in addressing the diverse types of professional writing required of them.

References

Allen-Meares, P. (2007). School social work: Historical development, influences, and practices. In P. Allen-Meares (Ed.), *Social work services in schools* (5th ed., pp. 26–59). New York: Pearson Education.

Baker, M. (1992). *In other words: A coursebook on translation.* London: Routledge.

Coley, S. M., & Scheinberg, C. A. (2007). *Proposal writing* (3rd ed.). Newbury Park, CA: Sage.

Constable, R., Kuzmickaite, D., Harrison, W. D., & Volkmann, L. (1999). The emergent role of the school social worker in Indiana. *School Social Work Journal, 24,* 1–14.

Franklin, C. (2005). The future of school social work practice: Current trends and opportunities. *Advances in Social Work, 6*(1), 167–181.

Guilamo-Ramos, V., Jaccard, J., & Dittus, P. (2003). *The Linking Lives / Uniendo Vidas health education program: Families talking together.* Authors.

Guilamo-Ramos, V., Jaccard, J., Dittus, P., Bouris, A., Gonzalez, B., Casillas, E., & Banspach, S. (2011). A comparative study of interventions for delaying the initiation of sexual intercourse in Latino and Black youth. *Perspectives on Sexual and Reproductive Health.*

Guilamo-Ramos, V., Jaccard, J., Dittus, P., Gonzalez, B., Bouris, A., & Banspach, S. (2010). The Linking Lives Health Education Program: A randomized clinical trial of a parent-based tobacco use prevention program for African American and Latino youths. *American Journal of Public Health, 100*(9), 1641–1647.

Kettner, P. M., Moroney, R. M., & Martin, L. L. (1998). *Designing and managing programs* (2nd ed.). Newbury Park, CA: Sage.

Larsen, M. (1997). *Meaning-based translation: A guide to cross-language equivalence* (2nd ed.). Lanham, MD: University Press of America.

Oulette, P. M., & Wilkerson, D. (2008). "They won't come": Increasing parent involvement in parent management training programs for at-risk youths in schools. *School Social Work Journal, 32,* 39–53.

Rossi, P. H., Lipsey, M. W., & Freeman, H. E. (2004). *Evaluation: A systematic approach* (7th ed.). Thousand Oaks, CA: Sage.

Yuen, F. K. O., & Terao, K. L. (2003). *Practical grant writing and program evaluation.* Belmont, CA: Wadsworth.

13

WRITING ABOUT CONTEMPORARY SOCIAL ISSUES: LESSONS LEARNED FROM WORKING WITH STREET-BASED SEX WORKERS

Susan Witte

AS A CENTRAL COMPONENT OF our professional practice, writing is as challenging, messy, and sometimes unpredictable (in terms of result) as the art and science of direct social work practice with clients. We are lifelong students of writing, constantly evolving and improving. Reflecting on what I wrote then, I think now about how I could have said it more clearly, efficiently, effectively. In fact, I do it as I write and reread this sentence: reflection in action (Schon, 1983).

When writing for practice in contemporary social issues (CSI), where issues of social justice, power, and privilege are so pervasive, we need to be especially mindful that our writing represents us in our absence and that it holds power as a memorialized version of what we perceive to have taken place in the past. Consider the excellent example we often discuss in the classroom: the impact of entering a diagnosis for a client into a chart. A simple act for the clinician, yet the power exercised is enormous. The impact for the client is lifelong, complex, and unknown. Beyond the immediate impact we have in our person-to-person interactions, it is through our writing that our work becomes established and introduced into "the literature." Just as we use ourselves intentionally in our clinical practice, writing for CSI requires you to consider who you are, where you are, what you believe, who your audience is, where they are, what they believe, who you are writing about, who they are, what they need from you as writer, and more, as they each and all will affect decisions about your writing.

This chapter will first define "contemporary social issues" (CSI) and then describe lessons learned and recommendations about writing in CSI practice, illustrated with examples specific to working with women engaged in sex work.

WHAT IS "CONTEMPORARY SOCIAL ISSUES"?

Just as social work may have "the most complicated assignment of any profession" (El-Bassel, Yoshioka, & Moultrie, 2001, p. 324), I would argue that CSI has the most complicated assignment as a field of practice within social work. CSI was originally introduced as a field of practice, in 1995, as "contemporary social problems" (CSP), in an evolution of the social work curriculum by faculty at the Columbia University School of Social Work. It was specifically designed to equip students with the skills and knowledge needed to respond to changing and emergent social problems, pressing issues with which our cities and communities struggle. CSP evolved in response to observations by faculty, field instructors, and students that there were several severe social problems that warranted particular attention because of their seriousness, recency, and multi-morbidity, but that were not getting adequate attention in existing fields of practice. These issues included family and community violence, alcohol and substance abuse, homelessness, HIV/AIDS, and the mental health problems (e.g., trauma) related to the occurrence or co-occurrence of these issues. Because the criminal justice system cuts across each of these social problems, there is also an emphasis on the role of the justice system and forensic social work practice. Since the inception of this field of practice, demand for it has grown steadily, suggesting both its timeliness and its utility. The name *CSI* came about more recently, in 2006, in response to requests from target audiences working within CSP—faculty, students, administrators and agency staff, clients, and others—to remedy the stigmatizing effect connoted by the term *problems* and to place the origins for these issues in a social context, away from the individual.

CSI is distinguished from other fields of practice in a number of ways. First, CSI clients are often the "undeserving" poor, and are very often involuntary clients. The issues affecting these clients are highly stigmatized due to their involvement in (or merely intersection with) the criminal justice system. Many CSI clients, individuals most directly and frequently affected by homelessness, violence, substance abuse, and HIV/STI infection, are already historically on the margin—often people of color and the poor, and most often living in urban centers. Individuals, families, groups, and communities targeted in CSI practice are traumatized populations, including those who have experienced child sexual abuse, who perpetrate sexual violence, who are prostitutes or sex workers, or who are substance-using individuals who perpetrate violence. Because of their intersection with the criminal justice system, populations and agencies targeted by CSI are easily sensationalized and often politically volatile, meaning that writing about them takes a level of care and consideration of the ramifications of the writing for the writer, the subject, and the target audience. Some behaviors in which our clients engage are referred to as "illegal" or "criminal," indicating "morally wrong" and "deviant," though often it is the macro structures— for example, power, privilege, and social injustice—that need to be targeted for change, not the individual. There is the danger for us as social workers, and as social work writers, to lose the perspective of social justice and resort to using deficit-based language.

Second, CSI practice addresses social issues that often occur at the same time: the homeless substance abuser; the alcohol-dependent survivor of domestic violence; the violent, drug-dependent, HIV-positive father. These are social work populations that challenge us in practice because of the lack of service integration, leaving us unable to address all of the issues involved. In terms of writing, the challenges presented have to do with what issues to focus on and the tendency to go to deficit-perspective language, forgetting strengths, an error that can lead us to perpetuate social injustices and retraumatize our clients or the communities we serve.

WRITING ABOUT SEX WORKERS

As a social worker I have been privileged to work with, learn from, and write about women engaged in sex work. Sex work, as I define it here, is the engagement in a broad spectrum of behaviors and activities within the sex industry that includes, but is not limited to, exchanging sex for money, drugs, alcohol, or other commodities. The choice of this language, *sex work* or *sex worker*, rather than *prostitution* or *prostitute*, is preferred by many advocates because it recognizes a sexual exchange not as deviant or a deficit, but as a strength and a form of work that should be made legal to enhance the health and safety of the worker. The shift in terminology used moves the label from deficit-based to strengths-based.

Sex workers are a marginalized group of individuals in almost every culture around the world. Most of the sex workers that I have met are poor women with concerns about survival and subsistence income. For these women, there are a number of "secondary" concerns that would be highly traumatic and primary for others, including concerns about sexually transmitted infections such as human immunodeficiency virus (HIV) and others, alcohol dependence or substance dependence, frequent exposure to interpersonal or community violence, and homelessness. There is also the added disadvantage of gender disempowerment they face as women in the context of a patriarchal culture.

My perspective on sex work and on prostitution was first influenced as a women's studies major in college, when I was introduced to radical feminist theory. Over the years my experiences and exposure, dialogue, and readings have provided opportunities to examine the multiple feminist perspectives on sex work, and more specifically on "prostitution" (for a complete discussion, see Overall, 1992). As my perspective shifted, so did my language. Illustrations will follow. Sometimes my perspective shifted first, and then the language followed much later. In preparation for CSI writing, I would ask you to consider your own position on contemporary social issues. How will your position influence your writing and the language you choose? What is your position on substance use and abuse, on a harm-reduction approach versus an abstinence approach to treatment, on the causes and consequences of homelessness, on intimate partner violence? What will you do to prepare yourself to write intentionally, with an understanding of your own biases and with openness to issues about which you hold strong opinions? You will need to address these issues through professional use of self to be the best writer in CSI practice.

DEVELOPING SELF-AWARENESS AS A WRITER AND STARTING WHERE THE READER IS

An early experience writing for CSI illustrates my initiation into the field of social work and writing for social work. I came to contemporary social issues freshly degreed with a BA from Duke University in public policy and women's studies, as the only research assistant on a modestly funded study of sexual crimes against children in the state of North Carolina. Using mixed methods, the study, funded by the Office of Juvenile Justice and Delinquency Prevention for one year in 1986, quantified the prevalence of sexual crimes against children (e.g., child pornography, molestation, incest, prostitution, and other related crimes) and collected narratives from victims/survivors, perpetrators, and forensic and social work professionals working with survivors and perpetrators. I believed that the purpose of the study was to identify the scope of the problem and to identify recommendations for prevention, treatment, and clinical and policy-related approaches that might ameliorate the problem.

As a white, privileged young adult establishing myself as a professional, the sudden immersion in a very dark and disturbing side of human behavior was traumatic. The experience was isolating and stigmatizing. Throughout the process I felt as disenfranchised as I perceived the study participants to be. There was a parallel process between researcher/writer (future social work clinician) and the participants (clients) targeted in the research. I was asked by a friend to write about my experience for a local weekly college newspaper. Two excerpted paragraphs follow:

> "I'm sorry, you do what?" friends ask me, squinting at me as if I'd answered in a foreign language. "I'm working on a research project. It examines the crimes of the sexual trafficking of children." I reply clearly and with a slower, more deliberate tone. I know it is difficult to understand what I mean initially, but I've learned to expect a somewhat puzzled and disinterested reply: "Oh, well, that's very interesting." My reluctance to offer additional information right away is what probably puts most people off, but after all, this is a difficult issue to discuss with acquaintances. Those persons who show interest often leave our conversation intrigued, disgusted and feeling somewhat alienated when they discover that they have no frame of reference with which they can assimilate such an unusual and offensive a subject.
>
> Perhaps, after 10 months of research, my attitudes have become jaundiced. It seems that too many judicial and social service officers have many reasons why nothing can be done to aid the victim, and few constructive solutions. There are ample solutions at hand. The molested child, juvenile prostitute, underage victim of pornography needs effective advocates within the state (Witte, 1987).

It was only through the process of writing that I became aware of the stigma and disenfranchisement engendered by my work. I realized that when people would ask me what I did, and I began to describe it, I could watch their disposition shift from morbid fascination to revulsion, upon hearing even the term "sexual crimes against children," and, with more detail, they would shrink away, distancing, making an excuse to end the discussion. Given the experience of feeling alienated or distanced by others with whom I spoke, I began to understand that because of the nature of the content, I needed to make a choice about how I filtered oral and written communications. Should I speak candidly in vivid detail, or should I summarize and edit to reduce the impact of potentially painful or difficult material? To what end was the communication that I intended dedicated? Did I have any responsibility in this writing process? Did I have a responsibility to the audience?

The study ended with a summary report and conference presentation directed at political and community leaders in the field, with the hope of seeing immediate systemic changes and media coverage to bring the problem to public attention. The document highlighted the widespread occurrence of such crimes, as well as significant flaws in the existing systems (Campagna & Witte, 1987). Naive about politics, I was enraged to learn that the document would not be printed or distributed beyond conference attendees. Instead the recommendations document was whisked away to a back shelf with lofty promises of some "future task force to be formed to look more closely at how best to address these issues moving forward." No such task force emerged.

Here are some sample excerpts from an early section of the summary report:

> The sexual trafficking in children is an extensive, habitual, and frequent event in North Carolina. As a result, a substantial number of minors are sexually victimized every year throughout the state. Their adult offenders, moreover, represent virtually all ethnic groups, socioeconomic classes, and occupational types. In short, a segment of the juvenile population of North Carolina can expect to be subjected to some form of sexual mistreatment by adults.

> . . . It is of necessity to reconsider the role and obligation of the state to underage victims of sexual trafficking. Such issues have typically remained dormant in popular discussion of exploitation as a manifestation of intra-familial sexual abuse. . . .

> . . . What follows, therefore, is not an indictment of the state's judicial system but rather a critical overview of the reasons why the sexual trafficking of minors continues to flourish despite the efforts of many concerned and talented agency practitioners.

Had the document been more carefully crafted from a position of strengths and challenges, not pointing so directly to the fact that it was a state problem, it may have been better received and led to more immediate efforts for change. Were I to write it today, it might sound more like this:

> This study and the recommendations for change generated by it suggest strong and courageous leadership in the State of North Carolina and a commitment to the health and welfare of its children. Sexual crimes against children have occurred for a very long time and in many cultures. They remain challenging to address due to their taboo nature. The U.S. is not immune. To keep children safe and to prevent sexual trafficking of children, states must take the initiative to study the problem, identifying the mechanisms, strategies, and resources enacted in committing these crimes, as well as in understanding what is needed to help survivors and perpetrators of such crimes. With these findings, North Carolina is uniquely positioned to reduce the incidence of sexual trafficking and improve the health and well-being of all affected by it.

Distinguished from adult prostitution, child prostitution is regarded globally as a serious social issue requiring prevention, intervention, and treatment support services for survivors and perpetrators. However, to engage change and have impact, writers in CSI need to use great discretion in the tone of their written communication. Consistent with best clinical practice, to engage a system in change we may need to consider using a generative approach and not necessarily one that provokes conflict or defensiveness. Who is the target audience? How motivated are they to solve the problem or maintain the status quo? What is the most effective writing strategy to appeal to their sensibilities in a way that is consistent with our intention and concern as author? In the case of this study on child trafficking, the principal investigator and I were so focused as advocates for immediate action on the issue that we may have missed an opportunity to more effectively appeal to the needs of the audience.

Finally, as noted earlier, my orientation toward some participants in the study was extreme and polarized: I found it nearly impossible to hold empathy for perpetrators of sexual crimes. I saw the human services and law enforcement personnel working with survivors and perpetrators as people serving the public good and fighting against the bad, and I saw survivors as damaged people who would suffer lifetime trauma. How do we account for our biases toward the players (clients, helpers, others) we are writing about while maintaining objectivity in our reporting and writing for CSI practice, research, and policy? My perspective on issues of sex work and prostitution, right out of an undergraduate program in the late 1980s, was informed by the perspective of dominance theory and Marxist theory (Mackinnon, 1983), and having worked predominantly with children involved in prostitution (taboo in most cultures and raising more complex questions about trafficking and choice). I found my perceptions limited to a deficit-based perspective: "It's my job to highlight the 'problem' and fix it." I believed that sex workers were "victims" and that those who solicited sex workers were deviant "criminals" and "abusive." Sex workers were "prostitutes." They had no choice; their behaviors and rationale were "trauma-induced"; they were "re-enacting their trauma" through their choices; they were "abused," "acting out," "misguided," and in need of professional intervention to get out of "the life." I learned from this experience that writing for CSI can be very personal—that is, your work will certainly require you to reflect on your feelings and opinions about issues. In order to prepare for successful writing, you must engage in self-awareness preparation, applying the same social work skills we use to ground ourselves for clinical practice.

FROM DEFICIT TO GENERATIVE PERSPECTIVE

More exposure to adult sex work and readings from liberal feminist theory (e.g., Jolin, 1994) shifted my perspective on sex work. Ten years after my first exposure to prostitution I moved to a polar opposite stance of perceiving female sex workers as needing to be empowered and to have their choices viewed from a generative perspective. I believed it was my job to stand aside and allow women to make their own decisions with regard to if and when they would engage in sex work. I believed that one's personal choices, moment by moment, needed to be honored. Sex work is not unlike all other forms of work, and it deserves the same recognition and establishment of policies and procedures to safely regulate the industry (see, e.g., New Zealand Occupational Safety and Health Service, 2004).

In 1997, employed as an HIV/STI prevention intervention researcher in New York City, I was invited to collaborate with a local physician who ran a community-based agency providing health care and preventive services to street-based sex workers. The agency's mission and staff orientation were strengths-based, and I was exposed to the legalization movement and strong advocates for both decriminalization and legalization of sex work. Readings from women involved in the sex workers' rights movement taught me that many sex workers felt that oppression comes from some feminist thinking. Sex workers often did not want others to speak authoritatively about their lives; they resented the assumption that their work was necessarily demeaning and never freely chosen. Instead they defended their "right" to be prostitutes and the value, dignity, and liberty of the work, which many of them took to be a "profession" (Overall, 1992). While I was aware at this time that my personal perspective with regard to human rights and autonomy had shifted, it took me much longer to write in a manner consistent with this perspective, as illustrated in the next section.

TWO SIDES OF SCIENTIFIC WRITING FOR SOCIAL WORKERS: OUR VOICES OR THEIRS?

The purpose of the collaboration with the physician treating sex workers in 1997 was to introduce the female condom, a new contraceptive barrier, to sex workers in an effort to reduce their risk for HIV and other STIs. My staff and I rode with social workers from the agency in a mobile van unit around New York City, meeting sex workers, teaching them how to use female condoms, asking them questions about contraceptive use and STI risk behaviors, providing female condoms, and then asking them to return in two weeks' time to answer the same questions again and to share with us their impressions of the device for reducing their risk of HIV infection and other STIs while working. During these interviews I witnessed the strengths of street-based sex workers and learned about the lack of adequate services available to these women and how challenging it was for them to access any care. Below, I will look at two passages from this work to deconstruct what the writings communicate.

Both excerpts are about study outcomes with sex workers. They tell very different stories and use very different language, targeting sometimes different audiences, sometimes the same audiences. Literature on social work in CSI is often found in quantitative reports from peer-reviewed journals. These reports represent summaries of data collected during research studies. Such articles on study outcomes follow a formalized template typically requiring an abstract, background/purpose, methods, results, and discussion sections (e.g., see Moxley, 1992).

The first example is a study published in a medically related journal. The audience is both human service professionals and social service professionals, as well as medical and education professionals. This paper reports on a quantitative study testing the acceptability of the female condom among 100 women engaged in street-based sex work (Witte, El-Bassel, Wada, Gray, & Wallace, 1999).

> Despite inexperience with the device, the majority of study participants used the female condom with regular partners, customers, or both partner types. The finding that sex workers used female condoms more often with customers than with their regular partners is consistent with findings of studies on male condom use acceptability. The results in this study are promising and suggest that the device is a feasible and acceptable alternative barrier method for STD and HIV prevention among drug-using commercial sex workers living in poor inner-city neighbourhoods.

> As with any relatively new product on the market, familiarity with the female condom, including having heard of it and discussing it within their social networks, contributed significantly to the use of the device. Social norms regarding sexual attitudes and behaviors, including those involving adoption of safe sexual practices, such as female condom use, are confirmed and reinforced when shared with network members.

> The majority of sex workers felt that this device would offer them protection from STDs, including HIV.

The purpose of this article was to quantify the acceptability of the female condom among sex workers in New York. My intention, based on the findings of the study, was to highlight the message that greater access to alternative female-initiated barriers, such as the female condom, is needed among this vulnerable and at-risk population. The findings provide evidence that if the device were made accessible, the women would use it, strengthening the public health imperative to make the device affordable and accessible.

In this article I treat sex workers as participants or "subjects" of the study, but I do not go so far as to describe them as "vectors" of transmission. The women in the paper are treated monolithically (but not as deviants); I use aggregated data to demonstrate evidence of significant findings, but the voices of the sex workers themselves do not come through. As the first author, I recognize that I speak on their behalf and make summary statements and recommendations, based on the evidence, that I believe will respond to their needs. Yet the women are absent and represented more as targets of needed prevention. They are women we need to "help." Were I to write this piece over again, I would include some voice or narrative or interpretation in the discussion section that gives voice to the participants, such that the reader ultimately understands just how capable this group of women is and how ready they are to engage with the support of clinicians or researchers in their own empowerment.

> The environment in which street sex work takes place is extremely dangerous. Most of these sex workers also describe having "no choice," or feeling that their work may be their only means of "survival." The fact that—in this environment and context—the women who participated in this study indicate that they are willing to use the female condom indicates that despite the extreme circumstances in which they find themselves, they have the presence of mind to engage in protective behaviors on behalf of themselves and their paying partners. These findings demonstrate resilience and creativity in adapting to their environments and innovation in problem solving how to achieve immediate needs but purposefully enacting behaviors for protection. A number of women indicated that the device was especially useful when used with paying partners who are using drugs or alcohol, as they are unaware that the woman would insert the female condom ahead of time. The woman was protected and the partner did not have to put on a male condom.

In comparison to the quantitative data analysis described in the above text, the next writing is an important complement to quantitative or more traditional research writings. It is a case-based writing, and more accessible to clinicians in the field. When written well, such a paper provides an authentic voice of a client. In this "commentary" piece on how to target HIV prevention to street-based sex workers, the first author and I used our experience conducting in-depth interviews with sex workers in New York City to illustrate the dichotomy of what "worked" and what "did not work," to help them reduce their risk for HIV infection. Below is an excerpt from the paper, including a brief transition paragraph and some verbatim from the data analysis from the participant for whom HIV prevention worked and why:

> Consistent safer sex practices may not be achieved until street sex workers have a reason to stay healthy. According to her [sex worker], this requires that sex workers have an opportunity to "feel like human beings" again. Multiple traumas, psychological distress, and stigmatization due to drug use, poverty, and prostitution leave these women with no sense of themselves and little self-worth. She reflects on her own experience in a rehabilitation center and describes what she believes is an important element to supporting health and sobriety first, and HIV prevention second:
>
> And as soon as I got there, they said to me, "would you like to have your hair done?" And I said, "Yeah!" I mean, I hadn't had my hair done in years, and they had a little beauty parlor right there. And I got a pedicure and a manicure. And you know how I felt? Like, yeah, wow! Then, they gave me a key to my own room. And then, it was like being in college, we went to the mess hall and got food. In one day's time I was a whole different person. The next day I woke up, I put that business suit on. I'll never forget that moment. These women [street sex workers] need that. They will become human again, too. If I were in charge [of an HIV prevention program], I would focus my attention on how getting myself fixed up made me feel like a person again. It was like, I mean, you think, "Don't look back!" I think that's a very important first step. Then you ready for the next step. (El-Bassel & Witte, 1998)

The writing is a simple presentation and interpretation of statements from the women participants themselves, who clearly articulated that in order to improve approaches for prevention, and as a prelude to any other potential intervention, including HIV prevention, there needed to be a broader lens that enabled one to see the women as human beings in search of dignity and respect, able again to become autonomous beings in the world. Communicating this message could not have been done with quantitative summaries of data; however, using a first-person individualized, contextualized perspective worked.

Writing that paper, I began to recognize how easily we as writers, practitioners, researchers, and community stakeholders overlook the strengths and resiliencies of our "clients" or those with whom we work. We so easily take the position of power away. We hold authority, perhaps especially as writers.

Yet our clients are often well able to negotiate the "system" and have done so in our absence to date. Don't we have a professional responsibility to see that our writings empower? In the piece above, one of the barriers to the women's willingness to access care is a sense of dehumanization, of not belonging, of not having value or being worthy of the services to which many of us feel entitled. Many women feel that they are subhuman and should not have access to care. Others are unable to care for themselves because their drug or alcohol dependence rules their lives, and they have become so disenfranchised that each day is simply about survival and chasing their next drink or drug episode. How can we be sure that our professional writing about or on behalf of CSI clients highlights this narrative of stigma and loss in a way that reflects strengths and resiliencies and also acknowledges or questions whether issues for individual client work are also issues of social injustice?

My current perspective on sex work and prostitution is no longer polarized to one extreme or the other. Twenty years into my social work career, I would describe my perspective as consistent with the recommendations of Sloan and Wahab (2000), who acknowledged the diverging ideological and theoretical positions on sex work but nonetheless articulated positions for best social work practice (and writing, I would argue) with sex workers. Environmental and ecological issues influence individuals and their histories, and our role as social workers is to provide empathy, understanding, resources, and support best matched to the needs of each individual client at whatever degree of readiness to make changes she happens to find herself. Our role as social workers with women engaged in street-based sex work is to provide the best possible information to help them be safe and whole, to advocate for decreasing danger and increasing safe contexts for those who choose to engage in sex work, and to provide best evidence for treating their psychological and physical needs.

The following is an excerpt from an article in progress that reports the findings of a qualitative study to inform the development of HIV/STI prevention and other health care services for street-based sex workers in New York City:

> We asked the women directly if they were to plan and implement a program to best reach and assist street-based sex workers in need, what would it look like. The women were clear, articulate, and did not hesitate in response. They described a safe, stable, accessible, confidential, nonjudgmental ser-

vices location as a point of entry that would feed into a broader, open-access service system. By offering a single point of entry that would include sensitivity to the needs of women with a history of sex work, the women indicated a greater likelihood of successful engagement, leading to more likely follow through, attendance, acceptability of services. There were several components of this single point of entry agency the women highlighted: 1) that the services would be "gender specific", meaning provided by women; 2) that the location and staff be safe, confidential, respectful, accessible; 3) that service provision be flexible, allowing for individual consumers to choose their level of engagement and intensity; 4) that there be a component of peer support, so that some of the staff had "been there" and had some firsthand experience; 5) that psycho educational components would be integrated; and 6) that services take advantage of transient motivation, recognizing that not all consumers are ready to engage right away, but may need to come and go from the service location and have the experience of their choice being respected, prior to officially becoming a client or committing to any long term services attendance.

WRITING IN CSI CLINICAL PRACTICE: THE LANGUAGE OF SOCIAL JUSTICE

Compared with other fields of practice, CSI social workers engage with more "involuntary" clients, that is, clients mandated by the criminal justice system (e.g., for having sold or used substances) or society (e.g., for living on the streets). With a professional mandate to support our clients, how best do we then represent them in writing? We conduct intake assessments and record ongoing case notes, and very often, if we are not conscious and critical, we may contribute to their oppression instead of providing support. Much of what I learned about best practices in writing for CSI practice in the field comes from teaching MSW students in a second-year clinical practice class on CSI. I have observed that in the first weeks of each semester, second-year CSI students will often describe their clients from a distant stance:

Jean is a 45 year old, Caucasian woman with two children who presents as anxious, irritable, and unkempt. She comes to the agency seeking shelter due to having been battered by her spouse. She was reluctant to discuss with this worker any details regarding violence in her relationship. . . .

Contrast this first description with one below from another student, writing later in the semester, also about a women coming to a shelter setting:

> One of my clients, Shirley, is the proud mother of two girls. She came to the shelter because she recognized that she "needed to get help to keep herself and her family safe." She demonstrates courage, is able to articulate her needs, and despite significant stressors, has been willing to open up to me about how I may best support her through this process.

I encourage students—as I would ask myself—to consider why they write from such a distant stance. Is it in the writing alone or is this a reflection of their engagement or disposition toward their client? Do they know their client? Do they have empathy for their client? Do they see the strengths and resiliencies or only the deficits? I will ask them to resubmit sections like the first above and to reconsider and highlight resiliencies as well as deficits.

In more recent years I have taken this exercise a step further, speaking with students about what Swartz (2006) described as the Third Voice: our need to be aware of the power, privilege, and authority that we carry as writers of case notes. We speak for our clients in our own voices—not in theirs. What power! We must be aware that written case notes, when done well, allow the voice of the client to come through, integrated in a positive way with the clinician's interpretation and advice-sharing. To prepare students for doing this better in the field, I use a popular introductory exercise for classes where we break into dyads and interview each other, then report back to the larger group on our partner. The exercise may be introductory, or a role play on engagement around a specific issue. After everyone has been introduced by their partner, we debrief by discussing how it feels to have and to hear another person represent you, including the vulnerability and strengths of the experience. How attuned are we to our clients and what level of responsibility do we feel for that individual so that we would be sure to get it right? Another helpful exercise for students is to ask them to imagine the most difficult client they would have to work with, one with whom they would be most challenged to connect, one whose life story they would have difficulty understanding or for whom they would have difficulty feeling empathy. I do this in order to begin to bridge the distance between "us" and "them," between self and other. In the CSI field of practice, the added issues of stigma, deviance, and criminality often serve to distance us even more from our target populations, and yet our work is to bridge the distances and build supports.

BALANCING BEST PRACTICE REPORTING, CONFIDENTIALITY, AND CLIENT SAFETY

When writing about or recording information about clients, we need to be concerned with issues of confidentiality. We also have an imperative to put a client's self-interest above our own. In CSI, social workers are challenged by how much and what information is best written down in case files. Barker and Branson (2000) highlighted two important considerations for writing case notes in CSI practice settings: to avoid questions of malpractice and, perhaps more important, to accurately reflect client experience without endangering clients further by putting them at risk of having your words used against them in the criminal justice system. Consider the woman engaged in sex work who may have been raped by a paying customer or the woman who is severely beaten by her intimate partner. If I were to describe the first woman as engaged in sex work or the second woman as someone who has a violent history, those descriptions might carry weight in court should the files be subpoenaed. In the case where client records may be subpoenaed for use in a legal proceeding, some agencies and supervisors will offer specific direction as to when you should incorporate more- or less-detailed comments about what has been shared between client and clinician.

Consider the following example from a case involving a woman (who engaged in sex work to support her children) presenting at a domestic violence program:

> Janet is 40-year-old African American woman who presented at the agency after her husband was arrested. She is the victim of severe abuse and is seeking legal assistance as well as counseling for herself and her two children — Damon and Dana. Damon is seven and Dana is four.

The intake worker learned a little bit about her case in order to create a safety plan (the batterer was in prison and not likely to make bail, so Janet was not requesting shelter).

The intake worker is trained not to ask more questions than necessary to create a safety plan so that victims do not end up being questioned by multiple people. The intake worker is also trained to take only the required notes, as many victims of domestic violence end up in family court, where their files might be subpoenaed and notations about depression or other symptoms can be used against them. Another concern when working with female survivors of intimate partner violence is that sometimes their insurance is through the batterer, or the insurance requires that there be a diagnosis to justify treatment, which could subsequently become part of the record subpoenaed for court.

The assigned therapist linked Janet with the agency's child therapists and an attorney, and conducted advocacy with the police and district attorney's office to ensure that the case would receive proper attention. Counseling began, and all three members of the family were actively engaged; they bonded with their therapist and began to make good progress.

As Janet began to trust her therapist she revealed that she feared her children had also been abused, but she had never witnessed the abuse. She said it was just her instinct that something was wrong in her household. Her batterer physically and sexually abused her, but perhaps more damaging, he controlled every aspect of her life. He forced her to take part in sexual acts that left her with a profound sense of shame.

She feared the worst—that her children had also been sexually abused. She said that her four-year-old daughter was masturbating in public. The therapists noted that this can be normal for that age, but they were also concerned, since the masturbation seemed somewhat compulsive rather than exploratory, as is typical for that age of development. Three weeks later, Damon reported specifics of sexual abuse to his own therapist, as the mother had feared.

Therapists unaccustomed to working with CSI clients who end up in court might have written the following about this case:

> Janet Note: Mother noted she believes that her children were also abused by the batterer. Though she was unable to describe details, she noted trying to protect her children. Mother presents with signs of depression caused by trauma. Mother was weepy throughout session. Rule out major depressive episode.

> Dana Note: Mother reports child is compulsively masturbating, potentially indicating sexual abuse. Mother was compliant with therapist's suggestions on behavioral ways to work on the issue. Rule out sexual disorder in child.

Damon Note: Child reports being sexually abused by father. Mother and sister were in the house at the time. Mother interrupted abuse and child reports. Mother was later beaten, which made him feel scared.

Social workers coming from a child-focused, mental health perspective could have written this set of notes without realizing the ramifications in a forensic setting. Unfortunately this set of notes might create more difficult situations for the clients, including accusations of a failure to protect one's children, inability to parent due to mental disorder, or actual loss of child custody.

Instead, the therapists in this particular case received training consistent with that of many forensic agencies protecting victims in court. This case is taken from the caseload of a social worker at a New York State county district attorney's office. Notes of the events described above were written as follows:

Janet Note: Mother discussed concerns about the impact of her abuse on her two children. Mother noted fearing for their safety but also noted that she attempted to control the abuse so that it occurred when the children were asleep or out of the house. She also tried to ensure that the children were never in the house alone with the batterer, so she would be there to protect them. Mother shows active concern for her children's well being. Despite her own severe victimization, she worked to protect her children, and therapist has witnessed her warm, thoughtful, and consistent parenting style. Child therapists also note positive parenting by mother and serious concerns about father's treatment of children.

Dana Note: Mother reports child is masturbating in public, which is concerning to mother. Therapist has not seen behavior in session. Therapist worked with mother to have positive conversations about public versus private behavior. Mother was very receptive to support and guidance and followed up by phone to report that conversation went well. Therapist to follow up to see if behavior changes.

Damon Note: Child was discussing playing in the bath tub and revealed that he had been sexually abused by his father [using details from case or client's own words would threaten confidentiality]. Child noted that he cried out once for help and that his mother, who was always with him, began banging on the door, which was locked, demanding to be let in by his father. This interrupted the father's behavior, and the father became very angry. The child reports that later he heard his mother crying in her room and saw a broken plate on the floor of the kitchen. Child noted many incidents of abuse by the father toward the mother. Child feels strongly attached to his mother, to whom he says, "keep me safe," and that's what "makes her a good Mommy."

All three therapists took required action to report suspected abuse. When talking with child protective services, they requested that notes be added to the report record about the mother's cooperation with the report and the actions she took to protect her children, that the father be arrested despite the risk to her, and that the family be provided with therapeutic support. There is no mention of sex work in the notes. In some forensic settings, including some district attorney's offices, for example, social workers will explain that they do not keep additional notes, but rather will work only with those notes already available through the court system, to ensure that none of what they record may be used against the client.

Many women engaged in sex work are reluctant to share their work experience with clinicians. They fear rejection and judgment, loss of child custody, and the criminal implications of disclosure. At the same time, knowledge of a woman's engagement in sex work could help a clinician better understand specific needs related to a best course of treatment or assistance (Wahab, 2004; Weiner, 1996). Some sex workers have experienced severe early trauma, including childhood sexual abuse. A trauma-focused intervention could be used to address broader coping issues. Some others may, in more immediate circumstances, be forced into sex work to earn income or to support their drug or alcohol dependence. A focus on alternatives to employment (when the client requests it) or drug or alcohol treatment would be more appropriate considerations in that case. Why does she engage in sex work and what assistance does she need to obtain alternative employment or economic support? Does she need a referral to alcohol or drug treatment (in the case that her sex work supports her ability to obtain substances), referral for housing or shelter (where sex work is in exchange for housing), or referral to a safe house or shelter because of intimate partner violence (she engages in sex work under duress from a partner in exchange for drugs or in order to support herself so that she may leave an abusive relationship)?

CONCLUSION

The social work writer holds power and has a responsibility to use that power with care, empathy, and in the service of client empowerment and the promotion of social justice. Writing in CSI practice requires attention to personal preparation and a commitment to be responsible for the consequences of the written word. We need to be aware of our own issues and those we bring to practice, preparing for our writing just as we do for our face-to-face clinical encounters.

As clinicians in CSI we can enhance our writing by reading and understanding the political and philosophical positions relevant to our field of practice, as they also influence our writing. There is a place in our writing for theory, as well as for our own voice, experience, and opinion. But we also have an obligation to represent the voice, experience, and opinion of our clients, and to understand their experience in historical and cultural contexts. Best writing in CSI practice, I believe, grows out of an awareness of these elements, allowing us as writers to make responsible decisions about integrating them purposefully to achieve the goal of a particular writing project. Consideration of each influences our choices in language and tone.

That CSI clients are often stereotypically perceived as more involuntary or "undeserving" highlights the need for writing in CSI practice to come from a social justice perspective—using the language of social justice. Hawkins, Fook, and Ryan (2001), in a study of social workers' use of language, found that despite social workers' reported awareness of social environmental factors that influence individual client issues and challenges, the language they use is not consistent with social justice. They found that social justice terms are rarely used in clinical practice. Because the way we talk about our practice is related to the way we write about our practice, I would contend that a similar study that examined our writings would likely reflect a lack of social justice language therein as well. Imagine the impact we could afford our CSI clients were we to write in CSI practice using the language of social justice, demonstrating sensitivity to and empathy for the strengths and resiliencies of our clients.

My work with sex workers has taught me the importance and obligation of writing in ways that accurately reflect the individuals and life contexts about whom and about which I am writing, starting with strengths. I have learned to regularly examine and reexamine my own position and feelings about the issues my clients face. As you read this, I hope you will think about having someone else represent you, the power of giving over to another the right to represent who you are in written form. Consider carefully whether you will choose to promote stigma or status quo in writing for CSI, whether you will commit to a strengths-based model of social work in your writing, and whether you will shape the future of social work by using best practices in promoting social justice one client case note, one article about your practice at a time.

If we write as we practice, taking a strengths-based or generative perspective, then our work will memorialize strengths, suggesting a belief in the ability of the subject, person, group, or institution to achieve success based on his, her, or its own resources and abilities. As social work writers, we have a responsibility to elevate the concerns of our clients, of their individual and collective needs and concerns, both policy- and practice-related. If we are better prepared to write thoughtfully and generatively on behalf of CSI clients, without deficit, stigma, and oppressive language, we can create narratives that may carry forward positive meaning and impact.

References

Barker, R. L., & Branson, D. M. (2000). *Forensic social work: Legal aspects of professional practice* (2nd ed.). New York: Haworth Press.

Campagna, D., & Witte, S. S. (1987). *The sexual trafficking of children in North Carolina: A state report.* Raleigh: North Carolina Governor's Crime Commission.

El-Bassel, N., & Witte, S. S. (1998). Commentary: Designing effective HIV prevention strategies for street sex workers. *AIDS Patient Care and STDs, 12,* 599–603.

El-Bassel, N., Yoshioka, M., & Moultrie, C. (2001). Contemporary social problems. In R. A. Feldman and S. Kamerman (Eds.), *The Columbia University School of Social Work: A centennial celebration* (pp. 324–344). New York: Columbia University Press.

Hawkins, L., Fook, J., & Ryan, M. (2001). Social workers' use of the language of social justice. *British Journal of Social Work, 31,* 1–13.

Jolin, A. (1994). On the backs of working prostitutes: Feminist theory and prostitution policy. *Crime and Delinquency, 40,* 69–83.

Mackinnon, C. A. (1983). Feminism, Marxism, method, and the state: Toward feminist jurisprudence. *Signs, 8,* 635–658.

Moxley, J. (1992). *Publish, don't perish: The scholar's guide to academic publishing.* Westport, CT: Praeger.

New Zealand Occupational Safety and Health Service. (2004). *A guide to occupational health and safety in the New Zealand sex industry.* Wellington, New Zealand: Department of Labor. http://www.osh.dol.govt.nz/order/catalogue/pdf/sexindustry.pdf

Overall, C. (1992). What's wrong with prostitution? Evaluating sex work. Signs, 17, 705–724.

Schon, D. A. (1983). *The reflective practitioner.* New York: Basic Books.

Sloan, L., & Wahab, S. (2000). Feminist voices on sex work: Implications for social work. *Affilia,* 15, 457–479.

Swartz, S. (2006). The third voice: Writing case-notes. *Feminism and Psychology,* 16, 427–444.

Wahab, S. (2004). Tricks of the trade: What social workers can learn about female sex workers through dialogue. *Qualitative Social Work,* 3, 139–160.

Weiner, A. (1996). Understanding the social needs of streetwalking prostitutes. *Social Work,* 41(1), 97–105.

Witte, S. (1987, April 21). *The present state of exploited children. The missing link.* Durham, NC: Duke University Press.

Witte, S., El-Bassel, N., Wada, T., Gray, O., & Wallace, J. (1999). Acceptability of the female condom among women exchanging street sex in New York City. *International Journal of STDs and AIDS,* 10, 162–168.

14

WRITING IN THE FIELD OF AGING

Ann Burack-Weiss

Each life is an encyclopedia, a library, an inventory of objects, a series of styles, and everything can be constantly shuffled and reordered in every way conceivable.

ITALO CALVINO

Some time ago I had occasion to review century-old case records at a home for the aged in New York City. Exhumed from a basement where they had gathered dust for decades, they were in surprisingly good shape—hard cardboard covers protecting yellowing hand- or typewritten notes in files that rarely numbered more than a page or two. By today's standards the residents were relatively young—some not much over 50, few older than 75. They came because they were poor (the home was fully funded by philanthropy) or alone (without family to depend upon). As the home was then a residence and not a medical facility, health issues were reflected only in the workers' observations—"walks with a cane," "hard of hearing." Despite such elliptical comments, the older people live on in memory. Who can forget Miss P, who said on admission she had doubts about living with others as she had always "kept to herself." A four-word closing summary on her departure a week later noted that "she was not satisfied."

Fast-forward to the recording requirements of our day. "Record writing is essential for documenting and supporting diagnoses; meeting time frames; managing risk; meeting funding and audit mandates; and reflecting quality, coordinated care and client success" (Anderson, 2007). Because government oversight agencies and third-party payers hold the power to grant or deny care, today's recording focuses on the problem rather than the person.

In the field of aging, computerized check-off or fill-in-the-blank forms that might number a dozen or more pages are the norm.

Despite the reams of information that accompany the elders of today through the service system, it is possible to read most files without seeing the older person as a unique individual, different from all others who share his needs for care. (One can rarely get as clear a picture of the client as I received of Miss P or her experience of the home in one scant page.) In the files of today we rarely find anything about the older person's telling of the past or wishes for the future. Nor do we find the older person's strengths in mastering past adversities that can be marshaled to help her meet the challenges of today. What is missing is no less than the older person's "story."

What has remained the same are the reasons why most older adults approach or come to the attention of health and social service agencies—losses of significant others or of their own capacities and resources that render them dependent on "the kindness of strangers," often for the first time in their long lives. (Older adults who present to community or long-term care agencies today are typically over the age of 75; most are in their 80s, many in their 90s.)

A visionary of our profession, Carol H. Meyer (1993), in the dedication of one of her last books, wrote to "those social work practitioners who struggle to make sense of their client's stories, which are always scattered and resistant to external, structured attempts to organize them. The hope remains that thinking and informed judgment will never give way to the enticements of routinized, bureaucratic, or technical assessment instruments. We owe our clients a full and thoughtful hearing."

We also owe our clients a full and thoughtful writing. The one-page or paragraph-long narratives that today's social workers are asked to append to computerized forms have the potential of serving as crucial reminders of the individuality and humanity of the person who is named on the case record.

The following discussion illustrates the principles of story that are inherent in writing a client narrative, with examples drawn from recording requirements frequently encountered in settings that serve older adults and their families. It begins by introducing four individuals with whom I once worked and goes on to consider the responsibility of representation—ethical pitfalls inherent in writing about clients and ways they might be avoided. It continues with examples of how one might write about these four individuals in an intake and disposition, a referral, a chart note, and a psychosocial assessment. The discussion concludes with reflections on the enduring life of "story."

WHAT'S THE STORY?

The facts of an older person's life—of any life—don't speak for themselves. Whether identifying information (age, gender, race/ethnicity, medical diagnoses), one-time events (the birth of a grandchild, the loss of a loved one), or activities over time (work history, living arrangements), facts can be understood only in context. What meaning do the facts hold for the client? How do all the facts come together to affect how she lives her life day to day? What differentiates this older person from all others whose lives comprise similar facts?

Whenever the social worker writes about a client, she converts the facts of his life into a story. A story is a narrative told by someone, to someone, for a particular reason. The structure, length, and style of the story, where it begins and where it ends, what facts are emphasized and what are omitted, will all depend on the author's judgment of who will be reading it and for what purpose.

FOUR STORIES

When I met the clients described below, I was a beginning social worker in the field of aging, first in a community agency, later in a nursing home. I wrote about these clients many times while they were part of my caseload. Long after my work with them was done, I found myself needing to do what the cultural anthropologist Barbara Myerhoff (2007) termed "remembering"—bearing witness to the long, diverse, sometimes wondrous, sometimes tragic lives they had lived. I wanted to share the emotions that these individuals aroused in me in a way that would resonate with readers who had never met them. I wrote them up for a journal (Burack-Weiss, 1993).

She has just one question about the home: "Can you bring your own furniture?" She pulls a bound album from the shopping bag, colored Polaroid's. Her living room is what you would call a suite—a gold couch, matching tables, club chairs with antimacassars protecting the arms. The next pictures are close ups. The tables. The chairs. The couch. . . . The credenza is shot from two angles. . . . As she leans over to point out details, the concentration camp numbers on her arm shine faintly.

He is discussing his father's situation. He doesn't exactly need a home-maker. Nor a nurse. More of a friend, someone to talk to. He likes to talk. Is there such a person? He snaps open his oxblood briefcase and hands over a file. The name of his father is typed on the label. Inside are photocopies of everything. All the information anyone needs to know about the man is there.

Her grandmother was a slave. On her bureau sits a faded rag doll. She first saw it in Atlantic City when she was eleven. Her job was to look after the four year old girl in a family. They were out walking on the boardwalk and the father bought one for the girl. She saved every penny and when they returned the following year, was lucky to find they were still selling them. She bought herself this one, exactly the same.

At the end he spoke only of the plains. The way they stretched out all around as far as the eye could see. Wherever you turned there was the horizon—an unbroken line. You'd walk all day and hold that line fixed in your vision. Flat. "It wasn't dull?" "No. No." With an effort he pulls himself up on one arm to make his point. "In the plains was such . . . such . . ." He lies down again, exhausted, straight on his back in his bed.

To respect the privacy of the clients portrayed in my journal article, I did not include many other things I remembered about them. As my purpose in writing the article was to capture and share the impact the clients had on me in a way that would resonate with readers who had never met them, I included certain facts and arranged them in a way that I hoped would have the desired effect. I omitted other facts that would have compromised con-fidentiality, facts that would have been crucial elements of these stories had they been written contemporaneously for the case record or for interagency communication.

Before we look at how the stories might be converted to a case record, let us consider . . .

WHOSE STORY IS IT ANYWAY?

It is the client's life. Yet we social workers are entrusted with the right to write: to pick and choose among the facts we know about the older person, to tell a story that she may not recognize or may even reject. As Eakin (1999) noted, "The identity of the self who writes and signs as author includes and is included in the identity of the other whose story she presents. The signature on the title page, moreover, reflects the necessarily unequal distribution of power in situations of this kind. . . . An act of appropriation has occurred, and the self who signs may well be led to reflect on the ethical responsibilities involved" (p. 176).

The case stories written above were composed solely of facts. I wanted the reader to make her own inferences—to draw her into the process of questioning, which is the soul of assessment. What could it mean that the concentration camp survivor carries around pictures of her furniture? Why is she showing them to the social worker? What might the son's comments about his father and the file in his briefcase contribute to understanding the filial relationship? How could this information be used in helping to understand and resolve the conflict? What does the story of buying a doll for herself at the age of 11 say about the deprivations of a woman's life and the strengths with which she met them? What message might be drawn from a dying man's repeatedly speaking of the plains of his youth?

If I were writing for a case record, I would not be able to leave these questions open; I would be required to venture an opinion. In writing for a case record, facts and inferences must appear together and be clearly delineated. If fact does not precede inference (worse, if the two are commingled) the client's story is in danger of unwarranted judgments by the worker.

Any writing about clients is, in essence, an advocacy document. We write to persuade. We write for a reader whom we want to think and feel on behalf of our client. How does one keep faith with the facts of the older person's life by constructing a story that best serves him? Distinguishing between fact (information drawn from client or other sources) and assessment (the interpretation or meaning the writer ascribes to this information) is the critical first step.

> Mrs. L is a hoarder whose cluttered apartment is a fire hazard, posing a danger to herself and others.

This note may appear, at first glance, to be adequate. Yet a worker's "hoarding" might be a client's "collectibles." The specific factors that led to the conclusion that the apartment is a fire hazard are unknown, and the phrase "danger to herself and others" invites legal intervention. It could be that the client's housekeeping standards do not match those of the worker, but that is no reason to interfere in her life. The absence of evidence to back up the assessment is worrisome. The following entry is more clear, and the worker has provided evidence for her assessment.

> Mrs. L has stacks of newspapers blocking the windows and doors of her apartment. She often forgets where she has put down one cigarette and lights another. She claims she needs all the papers for "reference" and that the dangers of smoking have been "vastly overrated." The potential for a fire is strong, and since Mrs. L refuses to participate in any plan that may lessen the danger, a psychiatric evaluation leading to court intervention is indicated.

Perhaps you have noted that the recording above features the client's own words. This is a quick way to capture the essence of the individual client's personality. And speaking of words, our ethical responsibility alerts us to substituting such noxious terms as "manipulative" and "resistant" or innocuous terms such as "adaptive" with specific behaviors or actions that have led us to that conclusion.

> Mr. J is successful in involving many health care providers in his case.

This is a better note. It not only reframes "manipulation" as a strength, but it also leads us to further questions about Mr. J. What exactly does he say or do that is so effective? And so we ask and learn more about him, his life, his "story."

> Ms. L. refuses home care, saying "I am very particular about my food."

This note gives the reason for the "resistance" and opens the way to work on eliminating that obstacle.

> During the past month, Ms. V left the confines of her floor to attend home-wide activities—music appreciation, current events—and says they are her "window to the world."

This is a clear note. It not only describes "adaptive" but gives us insight into what Ms. V holds to be of value.

Differentiating between what the worker has observed and what she ascribes to that observation is particularly important when describing emotional states. If we write that an older woman is "anxious" about deteriorating health, a reader is perplexed. Did the client say that she was anxious? Or did the worker draw this conclusion on the basis of things the client said or did? A description of the behavior, in the following note, is more helpful.

> Ms. P was unable to focus on a description of the home aide's tasks and kept returning to a litany of her physical problems of the past year and fears that the aide will not know how to care for her.

Difficulty focusing, repetitive preoccupations, and fears explain "anxious" while identifying its specific manifestations in Mrs. P's life.

Cognitive and sensory deficits can be mild, moderate, or severe. Descriptions such as "legally blind" or "confused and disoriented" give little information. What is more important for the reader to know is how these conditions affect the functioning of the older person. The following notes fulfill that need.

> Ms. A has completed a course of vision rehabilitation as well as orientation and mobility training. She is now able to handle household tasks independently and find her way about the immediate neighborhood with the use of a cane. However, she requires the assistance of another person in unfamiliar settings.

> Mr. J refers to the nursing home as "this hotel" and may ask when dinner will be served minutes after he has finished eating it. However, he recognizes his children and grandchildren and is always happy during their visits.

TELLING THE STORY

Writing in the context of professional practice serves many purposes: fostering intra-agency and interagency communication about clients, justifying the use of funds to third-party payers, documenting the provision of services to oversight agencies. Consequently, the length, format, and vocabulary of any recording are influenced by the particular requirements of the agency for which it is written.

When beginning to write for an agency, it is always useful to ask for a "sample" or "model" of what is considered best writing in that setting. One agency may use a SOAP outline (subjective, objective, assessment, plan) to guide social workers in their quarterly chart notes about client status. Another agency may have a fill-in form that covers these specifics and encourages the worker to supply additional data. It may be helpful to practice writing about your client in the approved agency style, and seek feedback from your supervisor. In time, you will become adept at saying what needs to be said in the appropriate form.

The following section uses the four stories that introduced this chapter as case examples of the four types of writing about older adults that are most frequently encountered in agencies serving older adults: the intake, the referral, the chart note, and the assessment.

Relevant to all types of recording is that we will always know more about our clients than can be entered into the computerized form. A check in the box marked "Single" does not tell the whole story of an older man who is living in a committed relationship with another man, a relationship that is a marriage in all but legal terms. A check in the box marked "Social Security" does not tell the whole story of the couple whose adult children voluntarily supplement their parents' finances. Should we use the narrative section of the record to share such information?

It is especially important to uphold the privacy rights of older adults in a society that does not always accord them their due. If we are able to ask our clients what information they want shared about themselves, we must do so. However, it is often not possible, and we must decide on our own. Although agency records may be deemed "confidential," they are open to many people, and we cannot predict their reactions to what they read there. By volunteering only information that is relevant to the service to be provided, sharing additional information orally and selectively, and adding to the written record on an "as needed" basis, we can meet agency expectations while honoring the privacy rights of our clients.

THE INTAKE AND DISPOSITION

Agencies used to make a sharp distinction between intake and assessment. Intake (sometimes known as "screening") referred to a report of the initial interview and the worker's judgment as to the agency's ability to meet the client's needs. If the agency did not have the appropriate services, the client was referred elsewhere. If he had come to the right place, he was assigned to another worker, who would explore his situation at greater length. Assessment came later in the process, when the client was better known and understood. Many agencies retain this practice, but some—reflecting a compressed time frame—try to accomplish everything in one meeting.

The following example describes a traditional intake and disposition in the case of an older person whose needs could not be met by the agency to which she had been referred.

Let us imagine that the woman with the photo album had terminal cancer and was referred to me, an intake worker for a nursing home hospice program. After hearing her tell of her life, looking at the pictures, and seeing her reaction to my saying that residents were not allowed to bring in their own furniture, I came to the conclusion that home hospice would better serve her needs—a conclusion with which she strongly agreed. I would be aware that home hospice is generally limited to patients who have relatives or friends to oversee the care, and since this client was totally alone in the world, I would write a story that used the relevant facts to give an assessment that provided a rationale for my disposition. At the same time, I would be careful to differentiate between the client's understanding of the facts and my own.

The note might begin by describing facts that Miss B had shared with me. Not all the facts. There would not be sufficient space, and the points I wanted to make might be lost in a welter of irrelevancies. I would choose facts that (a) Miss B would recognize as true to her story (using, where possible, her words) and (b) were relevant to my charge. I would then use these facts to set forth my case summary and disposition.

Miss B, a 78-year-old never-married concentration camp survivor, has no living relatives. Her parents and all but one of her siblings perished in the Holocaust. She came to the US in 1950 under the sponsorship of an older sister who had emigrated from Hungary before the war. Ms. B and her sister worked together in various cafeteria kitchens, were "everything" to each other and shared great pride in furnishing and caring for their apartment. Since her sister's sudden death from a heart attack five years ago, Miss B "only goes out for shopping and doctors," finding comfort in the familiar surroundings in which she feels her sister's presence. Miss B cannot be separated from her furniture—bringing to the interview an album containing pictures of each of the items that mean so much to her. She spent the greater part of the interview telling where each was purchased, how much it cost, and how she kept it looking "like the day we bought it." She remarked that our hospice reminded her of the hospital where she had counted the days until she could go home.

Miss B. experienced a life of incalculable losses—her apartment and furnishings are all that remain to hold on to. The trauma of the concentration camp experience and separation from everything that she holds dear could easily be reawakened in an institutional setting where she feels powerless. Although more comprehensive care may be available in the nursing home, no benefit would compensate for the loss of all she holds dear. Miss B's wish to die at home among all that gives meaning to her life should be honored. Referral is made to the MNO Holocaust Survivor agency to act in place of family or friends in oversight of home hospice care.

THE REFERRAL

Older adults and their families sometimes have needs that require intervention from several agencies. For example, an agency might offer exemplary care to older people but lack services to families. Or there might be a need for psychiatric services or socialization opportunities that cannot be met. Therefore a referral is necessary.

What of the man who approached a home care agency seeking a volunteer to speak with his father? He was, at once, an easy and a difficult client to serve. The presenting problem was the father's need for a "friendly visitor." At the same time, the son appeared troubled over a fractured relationship with a parent with whom he could not communicate, even as he met this parent's concrete needs. In this case—after exploration revealed that my inference was correct—I might suggest he find some help for himself as well as for his father. If he agreed, I would be sure that appropriate release of information forms had been signed by both father and son before writing the referral to an agency that has both family support and a volunteer visitor program. The referral might read as follows:

Mr. R Jr. requests a volunteer for his 84 year old mentally alert, homebound father, Mr. R Sr., who receives full-time home care from our agency (Forms attached). Mr. R Sr. is satisfied with his aide but lonely since his next door neighbor died three months ago, and he has told our nurse that he needs "another man to talk to. . . ." He appears to be a good candidate for your friendly visiting program. Mr. R Jr. has had a strained relationship with his father over the years. He is open to the idea of counseling around improved communication. Father and son have been told of this referral and await a call from your intake department to schedule an appointment.

"Improved communication" suggests that things are not going well between father and son but does not describe the causes or the manifestations of the problem. Although I would briefly explore some of the strains in the relationship (the son's moving to the suburbs and visiting less often, the father's complaints of being forgotten), I would be careful not to begin a counseling relationship that was beyond the scope of the home care agency to continue. Rather, I would use what Mr. R. Jr. told me as examples of the kinds of situations typically handled by the agency he was being referred to.

THE CHART NOTE

Chart notes (also known as progress notes) will be required periodically throughout the tenure of an agency case. Quarterly or semiannual notes are the norm in most settings. Let us imagine that the man who spoke of the prairie was a nursing home resident in the end stages of Parkinson's disease. His condition had significantly worsened in the three months since the last chart note was due. The physical specifics were well documented by the MD and RN, but it remained to me to record changes in his psychosocial situation since the last recording. The note might read:

Mr. O is no longer interested in matters on the unit. He does not appear to differentiate among staff but speaks to all as if they were people from his past who understand the visions of early life that occupy him now. He speaks of the prairie where he was raised and struggles to convey its beauty to us. He smiles when someone sits down beside him, holds his hand, and listens. Plan: continue brief, frequent visits to his bedside.

THE ASSESSMENT

From the 1940s to the 1970s the "psychosocial" was the gold standard of agency recording in the field of aging. Psychosocials were written after the intake period (usually a few interviews) and updated as new information became available or the situation changed. Today the psychosocial is often abbreviated, the full form used most frequently in psychotherapy settings and in schools of social work. Nevertheless, the form is an invaluable tool to teach the novice social worker about disciplined thinking, and it serves as an alert to the experienced social worker not to make hasty or false assumptions.

A prominent feature of the psychosocial is its three distinct categories: the study, the assessment, and the plan. (Note: Sometimes the three categories are given different names, but the underlying principle remains constant.) There are two intractable rules governing its writing: every opinion in the assessment has to relate back to a fact in the study, and every recommendation in the plan has to relate back to an opinion in the assessment.

The psychosocial is an indispensable aid to thinking as well as to writing. It is impossible to make an inference or venture an opinion without asking ourselves: On what evidence is our thinking based? We cannot suggest an intervention or a case plan without asking ourselves: Have we accounted for the strengths and obstacles identified in the assessment?

Drawbacks of the practice—primarily the length and the time required to write and read a psychosocial—led to its eventual demise in most community and long-term care settings serving older people. Most commonly, we now see a brief narrative section following the facts on a computerized form. Nevertheless, there are still occasions (case conferences, staff trainings, academic and field student assignments) and practice settings that have been able to maintain the psychosocial's basic premises, adapting them to a changing landscape of aging needs and services.

In the course of consulting in the field of aging, I have been asked to provide an updated outline for the psychosocial. The outline encompasses three elements:

The Study: Nothing but the facts!
The Assessment: Inferences you have drawn from the facts.
The Plan: What you plan to do. How and when you will do it.

An annotated outline of the psychosocial—a complete description of each of the elements above—appears in the appendix to this chapter. My use of the outline, in the case of Ms. N, follows.

You will recall Ms. N as the woman with the rag doll she bought for herself in childhood. The challenge of integrating a long-term care facility would, thankfully, not have to be faced by an African American elder in the New York City of today. However, because the principles of the psychosocial remain constant, this masked "period piece" is presented as I might have written it then, following the outline below.

THE STUDY

Ms. N is a 95-year-old never-married African-American woman applying for admission to the Johnson Episcopalian Home for the Aged. She was referred to ABC Older Persons Service for help in gaining admission by Dr. L, her minister at St. B's church, who also serves as minister at the home. Ms. N has a home health attendant 4 hours a day, paid for by her former employer. She is cognitively intact but physically frail, suffering from the combined effects of osteoporosis, osteoarthritis, hypertension, and diabetes (medical history and list of medications attached). Although health problems have impaired Ms. N's ability to perform ADL, she notes her greatest loss to be her inability to participate daily in church services and activities. Moving to a home with on-site chapel is, for her, "a dream come true." That the minister of her church also serves the home is an added impetus. Ms. N lives alone in a small apartment she has occupied for the past 25 years, since retiring after 60 years of domestic service to three generations of a white, Episcopalian family in suburban Connecticut. She entered the household as a child of 10 with her mother, who was a laundress. She describes a lonely childhood in which she had to fend for herself. At the age of 11, she was sometimes charged with looking after children not much younger than herself. When asked about her adolescence or adult years, she changes the subject to church work, which seems to have occupied all her leisure time. Ms. N doesn't mention any relative other than her mother, with whom she shared a room until the mother's death at the age of 80. Ms. N, who was 60 at the time, wanted to retire but a new baby, "my buddy," had come into the family, and she was pressed to stay on another 10 years. "My buddy" is Mr. J, who is now a 35-year-old CEO of the family business, her only contact, and all her bills come to him. He is devoted to Ms. N, calls weekly and visits often. She proudly shows off pictures of his children. Mr. J. has tried, unsuccessfully, to introduce more comfort into Ms. N's life, but she refuses all but the bare essentials. He would gladly pay for 24/7 home care and for a car to take her to church whenever she wishes, but she has set her mind on admission and will not be dissuaded. When asked about her years with the family, Mr. J. claims that his grandfather was a "hard man" who "must have made it tough for her." His parents, who now have retired to Florida, were more "easygoing," and he remembers the first time he heard her singing hymns (she had a lovely voice) was in their home. The family always wondered at Ms. N's rejection of the black Baptist church in town and insistence on the Episcopal church, which had only a handful of black members, and where she sometimes met with veiled prejudice from white members. She never explained or complained. When asked how she might react to prejudiced comments or reactions from residents in the home, she asked if "the bosses" want her. When told that the administration and the board wanted her very much but were concerned that her needs and well-being not be sacrificed to the goal of integration, she replied, "I am an Episcopalian." We have made two visits to the home; each has increased her impatience to move. One time she was asked by a resident who I was, and she replied, with a wink at me, "That's my daughter." Ms. N will be sharing a room for the first time since her mother's death. Home administration requested delaying admission for one month, until the optimum roommate situation could be found. This happened within 10 days, and Ms. N is scheduled to be admitted on Thursday morning, Sept. 20, at 10:00 a.m.

THE ASSESSMENT

Ms. N, a 95-year-old never-married woman, will be admitted to the Johnson Episcopalian Home for the Aged on September 20. She will be the first African American resident in the history of the home. A former domestic worker who has devoted all her leisure time to the church, she is eager to move, minimizing the effect of any difficulties she might encounter. This appears to be a life-long pattern that has served her well through difficult times. She has no living relatives but two strong community supports: her former employer, Mr. J, and her minister, Dr. B, who will continue their involvement after her admission. Ms. N is physically frail but cognitively intact and can be expected to be an active participant in all religious activities in the home. Her strengths include a strong will, a quick wit, and deep religious conviction. In the past she has related more easily to people in authority than with peers, but this might change in her new environment. If she does encounter slights or prejudice from residents or staff, she will be unlikely to share with anyone unless directly asked. Independent and self reliant all her life, it is difficult for Ms. N to ask for help, but she can accept it if presented in her own terms.

THE PLAN

Our agency, with the help of Mr. J, will help Ms. N prepare for admission, including choosing what she will take with her, seeing her through admission day, and closing up the apartment. We will continue to consult on an as-needed basis with home staff—as well as visit periodically—as she makes the transition to her new living arrangement.

A COMPACT VERSION OF THE PSYCHOSOCIAL

In a computerized form, there will be boxes and spaces to capture key elements in the study, the assessment, and the plan. At the end there is usually a paragraph-length blank left for narrative—a place for the writer to share what she thinks is most important for the reader to know about the client. This is a valuable opportunity that should not be wasted by simple repetition of what can be found elsewhere on the form. The narrative can best be used to paint a word portrait of the person—a way of sharing what is individual about her and her story—to help the reader see beyond the form to the person it represents.

CONCLUSION

Social work with older adults is action-oriented, helping clients access and use the services that will aid them as they live their final years in comfort and dignity. Doing this work and writing about it in the case record are often seen as separate, unrelated responsibilities. In fact, case recording is not an add-on chore but an integral part of the work. Presenting our clients to the world, with all the strengths and deficits that constitute their humanity, is as important as anything else we do for them. As we select the phrase, the description, that brings them to life on a page, we motivate readers (other helping professionals or those who fund these efforts) to see and understand how this particular woman or man is different from any older adult they've encountered before. In so doing, we both engage others in the helping effort and honor the lives we serve.

EPILOGUE

Almost a year after the article containing my four stories was published, I received an envelope from Japan. It contained an explanatory letter (in English) from a social worker and my article (in Japanese). I read with amazement that these vignettes had been translated and inserted in a newsletter that was circulated to thousands of elderly residents of the district. They reportedly loved it, especially the story of the man and the plains! What did the stories evoke for them? How many people I will never know, in a country I will probably never visit, will recall these stories, perhaps share them with future generations? Not all client writing has such a broad reach. But every word we put to paper carries a life with it, and in doing so creates a potent and privileged trust.

References

Anderson, R. (2007) *Accurate record writing: Do it once, do it well* [Brochure]. Summary for NASW New York City Chapter Continuing Education Program Fall 2007 "Professional Development for Social Workers Today."

Burack-Weiss, A. (1993). Significant findings in *Notes from the Field. Social Work*, 38(6), 771–772.

Calvino, I. (1988). *Six memos for the next millennium*. Boston: Harvard University Press.

Eakin, P. J. (1999). *How our lives become stories: Making selves*. Ithaca, NY: Cornell University Press.

Meyer, C. H. (1993). *Assessment in social work practice*. New York: Columbia University Press.

Myerhoff, B. (2007). *Stories as equipment for living: Last talks and tales of Barbara Myerhoff*. Ann Arbor: University of Michigan Press.

APPENDIX

THE PSYCHO-SOCIAL SUMMARY OUTLINE

THE STUDY: NOTHING BUT THE FACTS!

- OVERVIEW: Face Sheet Data: Age, Gender, Living Arrangement, Marital Status, Race/Ethnicity, Religion

- PRESENTING PROBLEM: What is the problem? How did it come to your attention? (Client? Family member? Neighbor? Professional referral?) If not the client, what is his/her understanding of the problem?

- PRECIPITATING EVENT: Why is help being sought (or are you offering help) *now*?

- CURRENT SITUATION:
    A) *Physical Status:* illnesses, disabilities, medications
    B) *Mental Status:* cognitive abilities, emotional state, psychiatric diagnoses if any,medications
    C) *Functional Status:* capacity to handle ADL, any sensory, cognitive, or mobility deficits that get in the way of independent functioning. If home care is involved, who provides, from what source, with what frequency?
    D) *Family Relationships:* Family members and their relationship to the client
    E) Frequency and type of contact—If absence of contact, indicate reason(s)

F) *Other Informal Supports:* Friends, neighbors, church, club, etc.

G) Frequency and type of contact—If absence of contact, indicate reason(s)

H) *Formal Supports:* Other agencies who are involved and the nature of their involvement

I) *Financial Situation:* Income sources, difficulties, etc.

- RELEVANT BACKGROUND
    A) Loss of informal supports through death, distance, alienation, other
    B) Past occupation, skills, and recreational interests.
    C) Current activities
    D) Cultural, religious, and/or ethnic traditions that influence the client's development and viewpoint.

- STOP, LOOK. LISTEN: What is missing from this picture? Think about what needed information is missing from the study? Either get this information or say why you can't.

- THE ASSESSMENT: Inferences you have drawn from the facts

- A ONE-PARAGRAPH SUMMARY OF THE STUDY: Include all relevant facts about the client and his/her situation

- DSMI DIAGNOSIS (IF APPROPRIATE)

- STRENGTHS APPARENT IN THE CLENT AND SUPPORT SYSTEM: What does the client have going for him/her?

- DIFFICULTIES ANTICIPATED WITH CLIENT AND SUPPORT SYSTEM: What obstacles do you expect as you begin to work?

- THE PLAN: What you plan to do. How and when you will do it.

- SHORT-TERM GOALS

- LONG-TERM GOALS

- SOCIAL WORK TASKS

15

WRITING IN INTERNATIONAL WORK: POWER, KNOWLEDGE, AND SOCIAL INTERVENTIONS IN THE GLOBALIZED WORLD

Fred Ssewamala and Elizabeth Sperber

WRITING FOR AN INTERNATIONAL AUDIENCE in the fields of social work and social development encompasses different kinds of communication. One might, for instance, be presenting the results of work done in a developing country for a primarily Western-educated audience, in which case one set of cultural translations is required. In other instances, social science researchers are called upon to discuss the relevance of projects conducted in a Western industrialized context for an international audience, requiring a different kind of cultural translation. Further still, when social researchers attempt to procure funding for work in a developing country, they must frequently explain foreign contexts, sometimes including entire social welfare systems or the lack thereof, to Western grant-makers in a persuasive and succinct manner. Finally, perhaps the most culturally complex considerations are required when social researchers are hired by multinational organizations to consult on or evaluate programs operating in developing countries but run by staff from one or more third-party states. Here a mélange of cultural difference comes into play.

In each of these instances, the effective conveyance of ideas and observations depends on one's ability to approach issues from the perspective of multiple stakeholders and to assess the range of interpretations possible for the specific issues, strategies, and impacts brought up in the international work one does. Yet how do we know what is comprehensible and acceptable to various populations? What are the best ways to acknowledge the legitimacy of discrepant viewpoints in our communication about our work? If we accept that the goal of international social workers and researchers is to enhance access to basic social opportunity in the lives of individuals living in culturally and geographically diverse contexts, then we must ask, more specifically, how do we translate our ideas about social conditions, behaviors, and possibilities for social development across international and cultural divides? Finally, in a "shrinking" world, where disparate populations are increasingly linked by globalization and where dynamic, rather than static, sociocultural norms frequently frame international social research and writing, how do we communicate our findings in a way that is acceptable to a social work audience that is becoming ever more pluralistic? What are the pitfalls of such writing? What are strategies to ensure clear, inclusive communication?

This chapter reviews several key tenets that will help you communicate your ideas and results across boundaries. It opens with a brief discussion of the context for inclusive international social work writing, introducing the debate about global disparities in social opportunity and a capacity-based model of developmental social work. We then present several major theoretical and linguistic issues that arise in international social work writing. These include the concepts of capability-building and agency, possible gaps between local perceptions of events and social scientific notions of causality and correlation, and the hazard of normative inflection (writing that expresses or implies value judgment). Textual examples are deconstructed to illustrate these points. We also present strategies for successfully negotiating key issues in international social work writing, including article, report, and grant writing. Perhaps most importantly, we emphasize that the path to successful international writing often begins at the stage of project design. If you read widely and incorporate local stakeholders into the program's design, then your writing about the work is more likely to be accessible to audiences separated by national and cultural boundaries.

CONCEPTUAL UNDERPINNINGS OF SUCCESSFUL INTERNATIONAL WRITING

The first key to successful international social work writing is remembering to take the time to question assumptions that may be present in your work. Asking yourself what overarching premises undergird your thinking is the first step to inclusive social work writing in an international context. To this end, it is necessary for authors to consider the larger context of the diagnosis of social problems and the prescribed social remedies that follow them. This larger context centers on the way we understand how social resources and opportunities are allotted and developed at the global level. To understand the divergent meanings and connotations of various social, political, and historical events for people from different regions of the world, it is valuable to consider the lenses that people use to appraise global inequality and, therefore, how they think about possible solutions to problems arising from this inequality. Specifically, understanding a common pitfall in the conception of "globalization" is an important precondition for successful international social work writing.

In an excellent summary piece, Amartya Sen (2002) succinctly recounts the way in which globalization is frequently perceived as "global westernization" by both its proponents and its opponents. For many proponents, Sen notes,

> there is a nicely stylized history in which the great developments happened in Europe: First came the Renaissance, then the Enlightenment and the Industrial Revolution, and these led to a massive increase in living standards in the West. And now the great achievements of the West are spreading to the world. In this view, globalization is not only good, it is also a gift from the West to the world. (p. 2)

Critics of globalization, on the other hand, particularly people living in postcolonial states, frequently perceive globalization as an instance of highly exploitative Western dominance tantamount to Western imperialism: "In this view, contemporary capitalism, driven and led by greedy and grabby Western countries in Europe and North America, has established rules of trade and business relations that do not serve the interests of the poorer people in the world" (p. 2). Understanding these competing viewpoints is important to social work, and thus social work writing, because they frequently shape the way people in different regions of the world perceive social phenomena. In turn, such perceptions shape the way your diverse audiences will receive your writing about the phenomenon in question. Further, if your own perspective is blindly derived from one of these conceptions of globalization, you will be less likely to appreciate and represent the different understandings of social phenomena that are relevant for international social work writing. Such critical thinking should inform project design, as well as evaluation and dissemination of results.

Sen also suggests that globalization is not a recent phenomenon, nor need it be an exploitative one. Rather, for Sen, the crucial question about globalization is, How will we share the potential gains of globalization, both between and within nations? Sen writes:

> It is not adequate to ask whether international inequality is getting marginally larger or smaller. In order to rebel against the appalling poverty and the staggering inequalities that characterize the contemporary world—or to protest against the unfair sharing of benefits of global cooperation—it is not necessary to show that the massive inequality or distributional unfairness is also getting marginally larger. This is a separate issue altogether. . . . The real issue is the distribution of globalization's benefits. (p. 2)

For social science researchers writing for international audiences, these cautionary words remind us that the most important question in the globalization debate is that of empowerment. A crucial aspect of empowerment is social development.

The field of developmental social work espouses a belief in a "capabilities approach," which, like developmental models of social work, strives to empower individuals and communities by building on extant strengths and traditions as a culturally appropriate and sustainable strategy to increase access to socioeconomic resources and thereby enhance social development (Midgley, 1995; Payne, 2005; Sen, 2002). Adopting a perspective most prominently articulated by Sen, many social development practitioners in the international arena hold that development "can be seen . . . as a process of expanding the real freedoms that people enjoy" (Sen, 1999, p. 1). The goal of development is the "promotion and expansion of valuable capabilities," or those capabilities that relate to the amount of agency a person may exercise.

A similar approach has been adopted by the United Nations Development Programme (UNDP), which has emphasized the importance of "human capital" development, particularly over the last decade. In an introductory note to the Human Development Report of 2004, the UNDP wrote:

> People are the real wealth of nations. Indeed, the basic purpose of development is to enlarge human freedoms. The process of development can expand human capabilities by expanding the choices that people have to live full and creative lives. And people are both the beneficiaries of such development and the agents of the progress and change that bring it about. This process must benefit all individuals equitably and build on the participation

of each of them. This approach to development—human development—has been advocated by every *Human Development Report* since the first in 1990. (p. 127)

Alongside a capabilities approach to development, what this paragraph alludes to is *agency*, or the human ability to make conscious, meaningful choices. Agency indicates the degree to which an actor is able to "envisage and purposively choose options" (Alsop & Norton, 2004, p. 4). In seeking to "expand the choices that people have to live full and creative lives," the UNDP implicitly acknowledges the importance of agency to international social development. It is important to keep the question of agency and the tenets of the capabilities-based approach in mind when writing for an international social work audience.

EXAMPLE: HIV PREVENTION IN SOUTH AFRICA

A prime example of successful international social work writing that demonstrates sensitivity to power sharing and agency, and that works from a developmental social work model to enhance capabilities as a means toward social development, is available in writing about the CHAMP Family Program. CHAMP is a community-collaborative HIV prevention and mental health promotion program originally implemented in Chicago, Illinois. It was then adapted and operationalized in Kwa Zulu Natal, South Africa. The authors of the following passage do a good job of using clinical language from a developmental social work model to help explain the goals and processes associated with the program. The passage is excerpted from an article by Petersen and colleagues (2006), which appeared in the *Journal of Health Psychology*. It reads as follows:

> The original CHAMP was developed in the USA as an urban community based family intervention targeting preadolescents with a specific focus on improving parent-child relationships as a protective factor against HIV infection in adolescents (Madison, McKay, Paikoff, & Bell, 2000) [S1]. Evidence suggests that the complex interplay between individual and family variables can promote healthy behaviour and inhibit early sexual activity in children approaching adolescence in a high-risk context (Paikoff, 1995) [S2]. A key aspect of the CHAMP model is community involvement at all stages of

implementation. Key concepts in the CHAMP model are the re-institution of the adult protective shield and the rebuilding of the village [S3].

The writing in this passage—like the program itself—is clearly shaped by a developmentally informed conception of social work. First, the language is direct and nearly bereft of adjectives or adverbs that are not clinical or professional in nature. For instance, consider each of the adjectives used in the first two sentences: *urban, protective, complex, individual, family, healthy, early, sexual, high-risk*. Many of these terms are subjective—they reflect the assessment of the authors. In each instance, however, the descriptive term is supported with a citation for further reference. Thus, if you questioned the notion of what determined "healthy" behavior, as it is alluded to in sentence 2 [S2], you are advised to refer to Paikoff (1995). While the use of clinical language and related citations does not eliminate the element of subjectivity in writing, or in social work, it does help to clarify more precisely what the authors mean.

Second, consider the emphasis in the content of this passage on restoration and enhancement of capabilities and community involvement. In sentence 1, "protective factor" denotes a behavior endorsed by parents and family units that has been empirically related to decreased risk of HIV infection. In other words, these are the things that parents and families do to protect themselves and their children socially. Sentence 3 emphasizes the role that community members play at "all stages of implementation"—a claim that is expanded upon later in the article, as well as in the articles referenced therein. Finally, in sentence 3, the use of the prefix *re-* in the verbs *re-institution* and *rebuilding* functions to emphasize the fact that the capabilities being developed through this program were once present and, in the context of this program, were culturally acceptable; the current program seeks to redevelop and enhance those capabilities, which were damaged by apartheid and the HIV epidemic in South Africa.

These aspects of the writing underscore for the reader the fact that the participants in the program being described bear within themselves, historically, the types of behavior and community functioning that the program seeks to enhance. This form of prose relates to the issues of agency, capabilities enhancement, and power sharing discussed above insofar as it leaves no room for the reader to infer that the international social work being described is teaching normatively correct behavior to people who, without the intervention of these experts, would not know how to function. Instead, the description relies strictly on clinically supported and descriptive terms, coupled with an emphasis on community involvement and capability. This communicates to the reader that the social work being described is focused on the program participants' (re-)empowering themselves, which has been necessitated by the history of apartheid and the HIV epidemic (as is explained elsewhere in the text). Again, the success of this writing is related to project design. A good project design does not guarantee more accessible writing about that work, but a project design that is culturally sensitive and well informed often is correlated with a project report that reflects those same characteristics.

NORMATIVE INFLECTION

In the example above, the international social work writing succeeds, in part, because it avoids normative inflection, or writing that implies or expresses value judgment, or judgment that holds one perception up to a perceived universal standard. Perhaps the most dangerous pitfall for international social work writing is the kind of uncritical description that we too frequently find, particularly concerning sub-Saharan Africa. This writing often uses emotionally resonant descriptive diction—especially adjectives and adverbs—to portray its subjects in value-laden terms. Recognizing this problem, Kenyan author Binyavanga Wainaina (2006) satirically advised anyone writing about Africa as follows:

> Throughout the book, adopt a *sotto* voice, in conspiracy with the reader, and a sad *I-expected-so-much* tone. ... Africa is to be pitied, worshipped or dominated. Whichever angle you take, be sure to leave the strong impression that without your intervention and your important book, Africa is doomed.

In this passage Wainaina succinctly encapsulates something that is familiar to anyone who has studied Africa, regardless of discipline: Writing on Africa all too often collapses distinctions between regions, countries, and ethnicities, and adopts the perspective that, as Wainaina puts it, Africa is to be pitied (frequently by liberals), worshipped (frequently by radical leftists), or dominated (frequently by conservatives), but rarely is "Africa" treated in terms of equal engagement or acknowledged for the very real potential of many African peoples to collaborate, if provided the opportunity. In the example offered above, we have highlighted the ways in which the authors refrained from including value-laden language and buttressed subjective descriptors with references that could clarify their meaning. In the next several passages, we examine similar strategies and pitfalls in the context of violence against women (VAW), a complex and potentially controversial topic.

EXAMPLE: VIOLENCE AGAINST WOMEN IN EAST AFRICA

The following text illustrates the integration of multiple perspectives, the use of neutral language and framing (as opposed to normative inflection), the acknowledgment of possible gaps between local perceptions of events and social scientific notions of causality and correlation, and a cautious approach to controversial issues in the field of international development, such as gender rights, violence in the home, and sex work. Specifically, this paragraph is excerpted from the executive summary of an Oxfam GB research report (Ssewamala, Ismayilova, Nyambura, & Kalungu-Banda, 2007), conducted with men and women living in different communities in three East African countries. The focus of the report was to investigate local perceptions of and attitudes toward gender and, specifically, violence against women.

> Nearly all of the study participants cited pervasive poverty as the predominant cause of violence against women [S1]. Although economic hardship significantly contributes to stressful environment in the family, the participants were able to identify many impoverished families that have harmonious relationships [S2]. This confirms that sometimes abusive practices occur irrespective of income [S3]. In addition, the participants shared that violence against women has been exacerbated by shifting cultural norms regarding women's role and status in the family and society [S4].

In deconstructing the strategies employed here to achieve clear, inclusive, and empowering communication, let us think first about what the text is saying, and how. The first three sentences [S1–S3] describe a fissure between what the participants in the study believe and what the social scientists conducting the study believe, in terms of causality. The first sentence [S1], for instance, explains that a majority of study participants believed that poverty was the "predominant cause of violence against women." Yet the second sentence [S2] complicates this finding by stating that there are "many" families that live in poverty and do not experience VAW. The second sentence [S2] also tells us that study participants affirmed this fact. The next sentence [S3], which is brief and declarative, offers the reader a conclusion about the relationship between poverty—income poverty, in particular—and VAW, in which the authors reject the causal relationship between income poverty and VAW described in the first sentence. Instead, in this sentence [S3], the authors imply that the causes of VAW, in their opinion, may include but *are not limited or reducible to* poverty. The fourth sentence [S4] suggests that culture, and in particular, sociocultural changes that are under way, may relate to incidences of VAW.

Now that we have established *what* the paragraph is saying, let us consider *how* it communicates these ideas: The way this information is conveyed—its order, tone, and explanation—demonstrates that the report's authors are not blaming participants for the existence of violence against women, nor are they using their newfound knowledge about the way that participants perceive the problem to present the participants as less knowledgeable or wrong, according to a presumed universal standard, which would be—in that case—what the social scientists believe to be true. Rather, in the first few sentences of the paragraph above, the reader is cued to sense that the authors' goal is to identify objective truth about what's going on with violence against women in this village, but only within the context of respect for the experience and perceptions of local people. The use of the word *cited* instead of *believed* or *suggested* conveys this tone, as it is a firm, value-neutral term that does not connote hyper-certainty or doubt, as other possible word choices, such as *believed* or *suggested*, might imply.

The authors also structure the paragraph around knowledge and perceptions enumerated *by the participants*, thereby including them in the development of the knowledge presented in the paragraph. Additionally, the repeated use of active phrases to describe the information presented by the participants to the social work researchers (e.g., "participants cited," "participants shared that") emphasizes this inclusion of participants in the process of making meaning within the paragraph—as well as the study. These structural and linguistic details reflect the emphasis on community-level collaboration and a strengths-based approach described earlier.

To understand the impact of these techniques more viscerally, imagine that the paragraph had been written in a different way. Imagine, for instance, how the same paragraph might sound if it were not concerned with including the perspectives of the participants in a value-neutral way. It might read something like this:

> Virtually all of the participants believed that poverty causes violence against women. When asked if all poor families experience violence against women, however, most participants backtracked and, contradicting themselves, stated that cultural factors also play a role in rates of VAW.

The difference in tone is stark. In both passages, word choice imbues the ideas presented with tone, but whereas in the first passage *cited* imparts neutrality and alerts the reader to the fact that the author is not judging the participants' responses normatively, the use of *believe* in the second passage functions in the opposite way, lending participants' statements a sense of personal gravity that the author is presumably judging. This sense is reinforced in the second passage through the use of *backtracked* and *contradicted*, words that bear a negative connotation. Such terms are called value-laden, because they connote a normative judgment about the subject at hand and, as such, are not value-neutral. The effect of these choices is to underscore the difference in positions between the authors and the participants, and in so doing, to reinscribe the power difference between the researchers and the participants. This kind of writing should be avoided.

EXAMPLE: NEUTRALITY AND DISPUTED TOPICS

The Oxfam report continues, confronting a series of delicate sociocultural topics, including the ways in which contemporary socioeconomic shifts have affected women's work and related social relations:

> These contemporary shifts have placed women in both the formal and informal/shadow economy [S1]. Some women have entered the workplace in legitimate jobs or used micro-finance loans to start their own businesses [S2]. Other women have more barriers to working in a formal economy and start making money by brewing alcohol or getting involved in sex for money [S3]. Sex work—specifically—increases a woman's susceptibility to violence and HIV/AIDS [S4]. Some young women and girls are forced into servitude for lack of viable alternatives, which puts them at risk of violence or sexual coercion [S5].

In this paragraph, women's increasing employment and household respon-sibility are described alongside social changes that the authors presume may be related. Note the use of short, precise sentences that generally avoid value-laden descriptive adjectives. This style helps to convey information in a direct and relatively neutral way. However, this paragraph does include one pitfall. Consider the use of the word *legitimate* in sentence 2: Given the context of the paragraph and the report, the reader can deduce that *legitimate* is intended to denote formal-sector or legal employment here. It would have been best to replace the term *legitimate* with *formal-sector,* so that the author would not run the risk of someone interpreting the use of the word *legitimate* as a value judgment on the kinds of work being discussed. The lesson to take from this sentence is that being extremely specific often helps us avoid familiar terms, such as *legitimate,* which may in fact connote unconscious value judgments or may simply evoke a sense of judgment for people from other cultures or backgrounds even when that's not what we want to imply.   Another aspect of this paragraph to consider is its handling of sex work as a risk factor for women. Sentences 3 through 5 explain why sex work puts women at risk without condemning, or directly advocating sympathy or support for, the women who engage in it. The issue of sex work is complicated. Some scholars and activists have argued that sex work can be empowering. Others argue that regardless of how one feels about sex work, it should be legalized in order to protect public health and increase safety. The criminalization of sex work, some suggest, constitutes a burden on the poor who are forced to earn a living this way—or, as others argue, the women who choose to earn a living this way. Speaking about sex work as an implicitly shameful act further marginalizes these people.

In the context of the Oxfam report being cited here, which focuses spe-cifically on women's safety with an aim of increasing women's access to health and social opportunity, there is no space for a full discussion of the debates about sex work. Rather, sex work is relevant here only insofar as it is associated with specific risk factors, namely the heightened risk of HIV or STIs, violent attack, and/or sexual coercion. By enumerating these risks as specifically and plainly as possible—in other words, by describing them in plain language without including descriptive words that might connote a personal judgment of individuals engaged in sex work—the authors attempt to enumerate the objectively real risks to sex workers without condemning the women who engage in such work.

Now imagine how this paragraph might have been written differently, including more value-laden adjectives and different syntax that did not strive for objectivity and neutrality. What might that paragraph look like and what would we learn from it?

> Even at this late date, East African women are sometimes forbidden from entering the proper economy [S1]. These women are frequently reduced to selling their bodies for money [S2]. Sometimes girls and young women are taken into forced servitude by a man or another family [S3]. These women become vulnerable to disease and violence and urgently require assistance to help them become independent [S4].

Note how the different language conveys a different tone and, with it, a different concept of power and capability. First, the opening phrase, "even at this late date" [S1], implies that East African society, in general, is behind the times—implicitly premodern or primitive—because "women are sometimes forbidden from entering the proper economy." The trope that Africa is somehow "catching up" to modernity has existed for a long time. Although the first humans originated in Africa, and although many of the earliest philosophical notions that were later canonized in Egyptian and ancient Greek philosophy took their root in the beliefs, ideas, and traditions of African peoples (Bernal, 1987; Fagan, 2004; Taiwo, 1998), ahistorical and racist notions that Africans are like "children" or that Africa is "primitive" compared to the rest of the world have long been used to put Africa down (Fabian, 1991, 2002). The phrase "even at this late date" is therefore value-laden in that it conjures the idea that Africa is somehow belated in the context of the world; such wording sets the wrong tone for any social science writing. Instead, writing that is sensitive to this history—including the myriad debates surrounding the intellectual history of "modernity" as a temporal concept—will avoid using phrases that place Africa in any temporal relation to other parts of the world.

Other aspects of this second example are also value-laden. It is generally accepted that social research and writing—including international research and writing —should strive for objectivity and neutrality. Words such as *forbidden* [S1], *proper* [S1], and *reduced* [S3] denote specific meanings that are not supported by data or evidence in the paragraph. For instance, the use of the word *forbidden* leads readers to infer that men are actively telling women they cannot participate in the formal, wage-labor economy. While that *may* be the case, no evidence is provided here to justify such an inference. Also, although overt exclusion of women from certain types of labor does sometimes occur, it is generally accepted that subjugated groups, such as women or racial, ethnic, or religious minorities, are often excluded from participation in certain sectors of the economy through unspoken mechanisms of power, as opposed to overt "forbidding." Rather, sociocultural norms often combine with ecological factors such as food scarcity, disease, imperial occupation, or war to shape the availability of opportunity to different strata of societies *indirectly* (see Alsop & Norton, 2004 and Spivak, 1988 for further reading). For instance, if poor maternal health is a prominent issue in a society, women may not have equal access to education and therefore to social mobility, but it is not because men overtly forbid them to work in the formal economy. With this in mind, we can see that the choice of the word *forbidden* in the paragraph above is a mistake. The phrasing in the first example is more desirable because it is plain and specific, leaving little to inference.

Second, the use of the word *proper* would suggest that the informal economy is somehow improper, though there is little proper or improper about an economy unless one is passing moral judgment on the type of work being done. No moral argument is made in this paragraph to support such a claim. Thus this value-laden word is out of place. Finally, the use of the word *reduced* to describe a woman's turn to prostitution as a means to earn a living implies a normative judgment of prostitution. Regardless of one's personal opinion, there is no place for such normative language in a brief social science paper that is not primarily concerned with the merits and demerits of prostitution.

OTHER SENSITIVE TOPICS IN INTERNATIONAL WRITING

Although none of the examples we have discussed here consider rape in marriage, genital mutilation, and bride price, it is worth noting that, like sex work, the concept of rape in marriage, the practice of female genital mutilation, and the tradition of paying a bride price are issues that arise in international social work writing that considers disparate cultures. As someone interested in writing about international social work, or writing about social work for an international audience, you should note that many cultures around the world do not conceptualize women's rights the way that Americans and Europeans do. For instance, in America, one partner is entitled to withhold sex from another by law; the simple act of refusing sex does not give a spouse the right to force it. In the Oxfam report quoted above, for instance, a male focus group participant commented: "The woman may refuse sex, this may force either of them [the husband or wife] to get sex outside [of the marriage] or rape within the marriage. . . . People don't believe there can be rape in marriage, but you find force will [be] used to get sex from the woman" (Ssewamala et al., 2007, p. 15). This is but one of many issues that challenge those of us working across national and cultural boundaries. As suggested above, the respectful inclusion of diverse local opinions and perspectives, and a commitment to teasing out the meaning of various acts and traditions for different people, will help you to approach such delicate issues with sensitivity and to write about them in an accessible way. Again, here the key to good writing is only partly the writing; the study design that underlies the writing will determine the degree to which you can successfully include such perspectives.

Female genital mutilation is another such issue: A long-standing tradition in some cultures, it has been the topic of fierce debate for decades. Although many indigenous women have spoken out against the practice, some have associated criticism of the practice with a kind of feminist imperialism or "first wave" feminism, in which predominantly white Western women positioned themselves as liberated saviors in opposition to their darker-skinned, poorer sisters around the world. This intersection of race, class, and gender power dynamics has caused many of the debates about female genital mutilation to become extremely complex. If you write about this practice you will be well advised to be sensitive to this history and to do much further reading. Reading local newspapers (often available online) and anthropological work on the areas you are studying is a must for anyone involved in international social work.

Finally, the practice of paying a "bride price" or "dowry" when a man marries a woman is commonplace in many parts of the world, although it would be deemed offensive to many Westerners. The tradition is frequently rooted in local economic history and cultural evolution, which is not to say that it does or does not have adverse consequences—again, debates about the merits of the practice from different points of view are available for further reading—but you should not assume that everyone in the world has the same instinctual reaction as some in the West do to the idea of an exchange of money for marriage. Alternatively, if you are writing a grant or article about a society where any of these practices are considered more familiar or accepted than they are in the West, it would behoove you to provide some neutral sociocultural context so that readers from other cultures are not distracted by the starkness of the difference. Again, background reading and a willingness to attempt to understand local practices from multiple perspectives are essential.

GRANT WRITING

Thus far, the examples included in this chapter have come from a peer-reviewed journal article and a professional consultancy report for a major international NGO. Yet social workers and researchers working in the field of international social development also frequently encounter another kind of writing: grant writing. Specifically, international social work writers may face the challenging task of reducing complex contexts in developing nations to simple, compelling descriptions for Western grant-makers in order to procure funding for programs. In these situations it is very important to translate details about social welfare systems clearly (for example, differences in the structure of the local educational system). You should not assume that western grant-makers are knowledgeable about the specific details of the region in which you propose to work, even if they have funded projects there before. Instead, you should always aim to clearly articulate the basic social welfare structure in the country before proposing a project or intervention.

Even individuals born and raised in a developing nation often find themselves challenged by the necessity of translating their school system, for instance, into the American terms of grant-makers. For instance, instead of discussing "primary school," investigators must choose among American terms like "middle school" or "junior high." Such seemingly minute details are, in fact, very important to the success of international grant proposals. They are also important in program descriptions for international audiences more generally. Asking a colleague who is familiar with the cultures at hand to edit your text, and remaining open to constructive criticism, is the best strategy for avoiding problems in this area. Such consultations are most valuable if they begin at the stage of project design, however. Working hard to better understand local contexts before you begin your work is, again, a key foundation for successful international writing.

CONCLUSION

This chapter has highlighted fundamental elements of the conceptual landscape that partially contextualizes international social science research and writing, and it has examined several strategies and pitfalls to be mindful of while writing about social work and social research across national and cultural boundaries. In the examples deconstructed above, the importance of an empowerment or capabilities approach to social development work and writing is evident. What one is left to conclude, at the end of this brief foray into a critical consideration of issues in international social work writing, is that communication about controversial issues across cultural and regional boundaries can be either an opportunity to build empowering understanding or a trap in which our own cultural difference and lack of cultural experience become apparent through the use of value-laden language and a limited (and limiting) perspective. We have also urged you to consider these issues early in the process of project or study design, if possible. The material introduced in this chapter amounts to only a small step toward a more broad understanding of the challenges that social science researchers and development workers face when they attempt to communicate across significant differences. Yet it is our hope that the ideas and strategies enumerated here can provide a foundation upon which you might build a more culturally aware approach to international social and development work through sensitivity to the written communication surrounding it.

References

Alsop, R., & Norton, N. (2004). Power, rights, and poverty reduction. In R. Alsop (Ed.), *Power, rights, and poverty: Concepts and connections* (pp. 3–14). Report on the working meeting sponsored by DFID and the World Bank, March 23–24, 2004.

Bernal, M. (1987). *Black Athena: The Afroasiatic roots of classical civilization*. Vol. 1, *The fabrication of ancient Greece, 1785–1985*. London: Free Association Books; New Brunswick, NJ: Rutgers University Press.

Fabian, J. (1991). *Time and the work of anthropology: Critical essays, 1971–1991*. Chur, Switzerland: Harwood Academic Publishers.

———. (2002). *Time and the other: How anthropology makes its object* (2nd ed.). New York: Columbia University Press.

Fagan, J. C. (2004). The Black Athena debate: An annotated bibliography. *Behavioral & Social Sciences Librarian, 23*(1): 11–48.

Midgley, J. (1995). *Social development: The developmental perspective in social welfare.* London: Sage.

Payne, M. (2005). *Modern social work theory.* Houndmills, England: Palgrave Macmillan.

Petersen, I., Mason, A., Bhana, A., Bell, C. C., & McKay, M. (2006). Mediating social representations using a cartoon narrative in the context of HIV/AIDS: The Ama-Qhawe family project in South Africa. *Journal of Health Psychology, 11*(2), 197–208. Accessed June 1, 2008, at http://hpq.sagepub.com/cgi/content/abstract/11/2/197

Sen, A. (1999). *Development as freedom.* New York: Knopf.

——. (2002). How to judge globalism. *American Prospect, 13*(1), A2–A6.

Spivak, G. C. (1988). Can the subaltern speak? In C. Nelson & L. Grossberg (Eds.), *Marxism and the interpretation of culture* (pp. 271–313). Urbana: University of Illinois Press.

Ssewamala, F. M., Ismayilova, L., Nyambura, C., and Kalungu-Banda, A. (2007). *Violence against women: Field baseline assessment—Kenya, Uganda, and Tanzania.* Field report. London: Oxfam International.

Taiwo, O. (1998). Exorcising Hegel's ghost: Africa's challenge to philosophy. *African Studies Quarterly, 1*(4). Accessed May 2008 at http://www.clas.ufl.edu/africa/asq/legal.htm

United Nations Development Programme. (2004). *Human development report 2004: Cultural liberty in today's diverse world.* Available at http://78.136.31.142/en/reports/global/hdr2004/

Wainaina, B. (2006). How to write about Africa. *Granta 92: The view from Africa.* www.granta.com/extracts/2615

NOTES

Chapter 4. Inscribing Knowledge

1. Attempts to use the Toulmin model as a software-based cognitive aid in decision making (Cheikes, Lehner, Taylor, & Adelman, 2004) and a rubric for
   practical and pedagogical purposes (Fulkerson, 1996) have met with mixed
   success. Adelman, Lehner, Cheikes, and Taylor (2007) suggest that more empirical evidence is needed to support use of the model.

2. Adoption and Foster Care Analysis and Reporting System (AFCARS), 2006.
   http://www.ndacan.cornell.edu/ndacan/Datasets/Abstracts/DatasetAbstract_
   AFCARS_General.html

3. Tumposky (2004) draws our attention here to the power of language to clarify
   and obscure, noting how persistently this dialogue has been framed as a "debate" or a "war." Kuhn later conceded that his definition of a paradigm, which
   rapidly gained currency in the culture, had been confusing in the first edition
   of this volume. In the second edition (1970) he notes: "My original text leaves
   no more obscure and important question" (p. 181). The postscript focused on
   two definitions, the more fitting one here being "the entire constellation of
   beliefs, values, techniques, and so on shared by the members of a community"
   (p. 175).

4. See Denzin and Lincoln (2000) for a thorough treatment of these and other
   innovative qualitative methodologies.

5. Anthropologist Clifford Geertz (1973) introduced the term "thick description"
   to refer to the dependence of meaning in human actions and interactions on
   the richness of context. See Ponterotto, 2006.

6. Following on Geertz's notion of "thick description," Denzin (1989, p. 83) introduced the term "thick interpretation" to mean that the analysis of qualitative
   data must extend beyond mere description.

7. Proctor (2005) offers a thoughtful, compelling agenda for social work research in five questions: (1) What are the practices in social work practice? (2) How does social work practice vary? (3) What is the value of social work practice? (4) What practices should social workers use? (5) How can social work practice be improved? The specifics of Proctor's agenda are beyond the scope of this chapter, but writing on the substance of these questions will certainly help to clarify and advance the field.

Chapter 6. Writing For and About Clinical Practice

1. NASW Ethical Standard 1.05. See http://www.socialworkers.org/pubs/code/code.asp
2. NASW Ethical Standard 1.12. See http://www.socialworkers.org/pubs/code/code.asp

Chapter 11. Writing in Family and Child Welfare

1. For a full discussion of case exploration, psychosocial assessment, and service planning, see C. H. Meyer, *Assessment in social work practice* (New York: Columbia University Press, 1993), Chapter 2.

CONTRIBUTORS

ALIDA BOURIS, PhD, MSW, Assistant Professor, University of Chicago School of Social Service Administration

DENISE BURNETTE, PhD, MSSW, Professor, Columbia University School of Social Work

KATHRYN CONROY, DSW, MSW, Executive Director and CEO, Hedge Funds Care, Preventing and Treating Child Abuse; Former Assistant Dean and Director of Field Education, Columbia University School of Social Work

RONALD A. FELDMAN, PhD, MSW, Ruth Harris Ottman Centennial Professor for the Advancement of Social Work Education; Dean Emeritus, Columbia University School of Social Work

SHIRLEY GATENIO GABEL, PhD, MPh, MS, Associate Professor, Graduate School of Social Service, Fordham University

WARREN GREEN, Writing Center Director, Columbia University School of Social Work

VINCENT GUILAMO-RAMOS, PhD, LCSW, Professor, Silver School of Social Work, New York University

LINDA HOFFMAN, MSW, LMSW, ACSW, President and Chief Executive Officer, New York Foundation for Senior Citizens

SHEILA B. KAMERMAN, DSW, MSW, Compton Foundation Centennial Professor, Columbia University School of Social Work; Co-Director, Institute for Child and Family Policy at Columbia University; Co-Director, Cross-National Studies Research Program and Clearinghouse on International Developments in Child and Family Policies

VICKI LENS, PhD, JD, MSW, Associate Professor, Columbia University School of Social Work

SUE MATORIN, MS, ACSW, Adjunct Associate Professor, Columbia University School of Social Work; Treatment Coordinator/Affective Disorder Team, Payne Whitney Clinic, New York Presbyterian Hospital; Faculty, Department of Psychiatry, Weill Cornell Medical College

BRENDA MCGOWAN, DSW, MSW, James R. Dumpson Chair of Child Welfare Studies, Fordham University Graduate School of Social Service; Former Ruth Harris Ottman Chair of Family and Children's Services, Columbia University School of Social Work

MARION RIEDEL, PhD, LCSW, Associate Professor of Professional Practice, Columbia University School of Social Work.

BARBARA SIMON, PhD, MSS, Associate Professor, Columbia University School of Social Work

MARY SORMANTI, PhD, MSW, Associate Professor of Professional Practice, Columbia University School of Social Work

ELIZABETH SPERBER, PhD Candidate, Department of Political Science, Columbia University

FRED M. SSEWAMALA, PhD, MSW, Associate Professor of Social Work and International Affairs, Columbia University School of Social Work

JEANETTE TAKAMURA, PhD, MSW, Dean, Columbia University School of Social Work

ELAINE WALSH, PhD, MSW, LCSW, Associate Professor and Director of Public Service Scholar Program, Hunter College, Department of Urban Affairs and Planning; Former Adjunct Professor, Columbia University School of Social Work

ANN BURACK-WEISS, DSW, Faculty, MS program in Narrative Medicine, Columbia University; Partner, SBW Partners (Silverstone & Burack-Weiss, LCSW, PLLC)

SUSAN S. WITTE, PhD, LCSW, Associate Professor, Columbia University School of Social Work

INDEX

CPSIA information can be obtained
at www.ICGtesting.com
Printed in the USA
LVOW03s0507050817
543828LV00004B/13/P